Heterosexual Africa?

D1559395

NEW AFRICAN HISTORIES SERIES

Series editors: Jean Allman and Allen Isaacman

David William Cohen and E. S. Atieno Odhiambo, *The Risks of Knowledge: Investigations into the Death of the Hon. Minister John Robert Ouko in Kenya, 1990*

Belinda Bozzoli, *Theatres of Struggle and the End of Apartheid*

Gary Kynoch, *We Are Fighting the World: A History of Marashea Gangs in South Africa, 1947–1999*

Stephanie Newell, *The Forger's Tale: The Search for Odeziaku*

Jacob A. Tropp, *Natures of Colonial Change: Environmental Relations in the Making of the Transkei*

Jan Bender Shetler, *Imagining Serengeti: A History of Landscape Memory in Tanzania from Earliest Times to the Present*

Cheikh Anta Babou, *Fighting the Greater Jihad: Amadu Bamba and the Founding of the Muridiyya in Senegal, 1853–1913*

Marc Epprecht, *Heterosexual Africa? The History of an Idea from the Age of Exploration to the Age of AIDS*

Heterosexual Africa?

The History of an Idea from the Age of
Exploration to the Age of AIDS

Marc Epprecht

OHIO UNIVERSITY PRESS
ATHENS

UNIVERSITY OF KWAZULU-NATAL PRESS

Ohio University Press, Athens, Ohio 45701
www.ohioswallow.com
© 2008 by Ohio University Press
All rights reserved

Published in 2008 in South Africa by
University of KwaZulu-Natal Press
Private Bag X01, Scottsville, 3209
South Africa
Email: books@ukzn.ac.za
www.uknpress.co.za

University of KwaZulu-Natal Press ISBN 978-1-86914-157-8

Printed in the United States of America
Ohio University Press books are printed on acid-free paper ⊚ ™

15 14 13 12 11 10 09 08   5 4 3 2 1

Library of Congress Cataloging-in-Publication Data

Epprecht, Marc.
  Heterosexual Africa? : the history of an idea from the age of exploration to the age
of AIDS / Marc Epprecht.
    p. cm. — (New African histories series)
  Includes bibliographical references and index.
  ISBN-13: 978-0-8214-1798-0 (hc : alk. paper)
  ISBN-13: 978-0-8214-1799-7 (pb : alk. paper)
    1. Homosexuality—Africa—History. 2. Gays—Africa—History. 3. Africa—Social
life and customs. 4. Africa—Politics and government. 5. AIDS (Disease)—Africa.
6. HIV infections—Africa. I. Title.
  HQ76.3.A356E64 2008
  306.76'60967—dc22

                                                              2008009908

To my friends and colleagues

Contents

Preface

For this book I owe deep gratitude to a broad range of colleagues and activists going back over many years in the struggle for sexual rights in Africa, Europe, and North America. I have already acknowledged the many who facilitated the original field and archival work for my previous book on this topic, *Hungochani*, research that continues to inform the present study. But I want to reiterate my appreciation to those in particular who got me thinking and acting on the project: Keith Goddard, Bev Clark, Brenda Burrell, Patricia McFadden, Wolfram Gleichmar-Hartmann, Jeff Piker, and Cary Alan Johnson. I also want acknowledge in general terms the guidance and inspiration I received from colleagues, activists, and sex workers at the AIDS in Context and the Sex and Secrecy conferences at the University of Witwatersrand (April 2001 and 2003, respectively), the PhD workshop on sexualities held at Roskilde University (May 2006) and the inaugural International Resource Network workshop in Dakar (February 2007). Any mistakes and misinterpretations that follow are of course entirely my own.

Financial and in-kind support came from Queen's University, Kingston, Ontario. This included a modest research grant from the Advisory Research Council plus, more significantly, time off for research leave in South Africa. The latter was supported by the International Development and Research Centre (Ottawa) and my host institution, the University of KwaZulu-Natal, facilitated by Rob Fincham and Trevor Hill. My participation at the Dakar workshop was facilitated by Deborah P. Amory and Sybille Ngo Nyeck and was partially subsidized by the Ford Foundation.

Andrew P. Lyons first encouraged me to develop my scattered insights on the ethnography into a coherent article, toward which I greatly benefited from the suggestions of the anonymous reviewers, editor Winnie Lem, and Stephen O. Murray. Chapter 2 is a revised version of my article "'Bisexuality' and the Politics of Normal in African Ethnography" (*Anthropologica* 48 [November 2006]: 187–201; used with permission). For chapter 3, Tiffany Jones assisted by sharing insights and sources from her doctoral research into the history of psychiatric care for blacks in South Africa. Antony Manion facilitated my search for documents pursuant to Louis Freed at the William Cullen Library and the Gay and Lesbian Archives, Johannesburg. Bodil Folke Frederiksen kindly shared her research on an important personal connection between psychiatry and Africanist ethnography.

Chapter 4, on HIV/AIDS, ventures into an especially sensitive area and as such I wanted to expose the ideas to as wide an audience as possible to garner reactions and suggestions. In chronological order, I received pointed feedback from Elaine Salo, Jane Bennett, Deborah Posel, Lisa Ann Richler, Signe Arnfred, Philippe Denis, Mai Palmberg, Taiwo Oloruntoba-Oju, and Charles Gueboguo. Open-ended public discussions were very helpful at the Center for African Studies at Rutgers University, the African Gender Institute at the University of Cape Town, the Department of History seminar series at the University of Zimbabwe, and Eleanor Preston-White's graduate seminar in ethnography at the University of KwaZulu-Natal. Commentary at most of these venues tended to be relatively gentle. A lively audience at the Lesbian, Gay, Bisexual and Transgender Community Center in New York in November 2006, enabled by support from the International Gay and Lesbian Human Rights Commission, thus provided me a salutary baptism of fire. I also owe a big debt to students and tutorial assistants in my upper-year course at Queen's—AIDS, Power, and Poverty—over the past few years, especially those from nursing and various other health science–oriented departments. Their essays and other contributions to the class pushed me toward a better and fairer understanding of the science of HIV/AIDS.

I did conduct a small number of key informant interviews. Special thanks go to Dr. Julie Dyer, formerly medical officer of health for Msunduzi Municipality, South Africa, who gave unsparingly of her recollections in an extended interview. Keith Goddard, Edwin Cameron, and Zackie Achmat shared their personal recollections of tensions within the gay rights and Treatment Action movements. Barbara Brakarsh and Margo Bedingfield shared insights on the production of their antihomophobia education kit, *Auntie Stella*. Edward Hooper and Wilson Carswell shared their recollections of life on the frontlines of the epidemic as it broke in Uganda in the mid-1980s.

I am grateful to Charles Gueboguo, Chris Dunton, and Erik Falk for their astute critical commentary on chapter 5 and suggestions about pertinent novels, while Robert Morrell and Andrea Cornwall offered very helpful suggestions on a thematically related publication, "The Marquis de Sade's Zimbabwe Adventure: A Contribution to the Critique of African AIDS" (*Sexualities* 10.2 [2007]: 241–58, special issue on southern Africa). Neville Hoad generously shared from his (then) forthcoming book on very closely related themes and analysis arising from cultural studies.

Bringing it all together in a coherent package has been a surprisingly complicated struggle. T. Dunbar Moodie provided both a trenchant critique and heartfelt encouragement in the first round of revisions, as he has done on several other occasions in the past. Gillian Berchowitz, Jean Allman, Allen Isaacman, and a further anonymous reviewer for Ohio University Press deserve much praise for helping me discipline thoughts and keep the focus on African history. In cases of discrepancies between this book and previous publications, their input gives me confidence that this one corrects any earlier overstatements or overlooked scholarship. Where errors, omissions, and overstatements have nonetheless survived the revision process, they remain my responsibility. Jennifer Epprecht and Jessica Cammaert assisted with preparation of the works cited and index, while Bob Furnish did an exemplary job of copyediting. The cover photograph was taken by Millcent Tanhira, and is of friends at Gays and Lesbians of Zimbabwe.

Finally, Allison Goebel provided moral support throughout the process and worked tirelessly to facilitate the penultimate stages of the research in South Africa. None of this would have been possible without her patience, love, and faith in the value of this effort to the scholarship and to our lives together.

Abbreviations

ALP   AIDS Law Project

ANC   African National Congress

GALZ   Gays and Lesbians of Zimbabwe

IGLHRC   International Gay and Lesbian Human Rights Commission

LEGABIBO   Lesbians, Gays, and Bisexuals of Botswana

lgbti   lesbian, gay, bisexual, transgender, and intersex

msm   men who have sex with men but do not necessarily identify as
             gay, homosexual, or bisexual

TAC   Treatment Action Campaign

UDF   United Democratic Front

UNAIDS   Joint United Nations Programme on HIV/AIDS

USAID   United States Agency for International Development

wsw   women who have sex with women but do not necessarily
             identify as lesbian, homosexual, or bisexual

1 ❦ A Puzzling Blindspot, a Troubling Silence, a Strange Consensus

Reflections on the Heterosexual Norm in "African AIDS"

THE RESEARCH QUESTION

HIV/AIDS WAS IDENTIFIED IN AFRICA south of the Sahara in the mid-1980s.[1] At that time its rapid, atypical progress in populations focused considerable attention on / so-called African sexuality./ Scientists, theologians, pundits, gender activists, and other researchers were all struggling to explain both the unprecedented rates of HIV infection and the fact that men and women appeared to be equally affected. This suggested a different epidemiology than in the West, where HIV infections occurred mostly in gay and bisexual men. Efforts to solve the mystery were complicated by the relative paucity of African epidemiologists and other researchers in the search for answers. Indeed, the vast majority of those who published their findings in the early years of the epidemic were European or North American. Only about one in twelve of the participants in the very first AIDS in Africa conference in 1985 actually came from Africa (Putzel 2004, 21), while the most widely cited publication to synthesize their findings with the ethnographic record was authored by three Australian demographers (Caldwell, Caldwell, and Quiggin 1989).

Not knowing Africa or African languages all that well, and under intense pressure of time and the looming health calamity, foreign researchers relied heavily on received wisdom and rational logic to fill in the many critical gaps in knowledge about the disease in its African manifestation. Their work in turn contributed to a new problem that in many ways continues to frustrate research, prevention, and education initiatives. The problem resides in the notion that a singular African sexuality exists and that it exacerbates the risks of HIV transmission particularly for women. This hypothetical singular African sexuality includes, above all, the supposed nonexistence of homosexuality or bisexuality, along with Africans' purported tendencies toward heterosexual promiscuity, gender violence, and lack of the kind of internalized moral restraints that supposedly inhibit the spread of HIV in other cultures. Another common thread is a tendency toward age discrepancy in sexual relationships (mostly older men with young women, girls, or even female infants), and, compared to the West, a relative absence of romantic affection and a predominance of transactional relationships (sex in exchange for money or gifts). Further examples of such "otherizing" or pathologizing of African sexuality in the popular media are legion, and many will be discussed in the chapters to follow. But a sobering example in the peer-reviewed academic press is worth pointing out here. Rushton (1997, esp. 178–83) claims a relationship between Africans' penis size and sexual behavior that can account for the high rates of HIV/AIDS among women in Africa and in the African diaspora.

African opinion makers often responded defensively to Western claims about an African sexuality. Yet ironically, they often at the same time buttressed one key aspect of it. Hence, on the one hand, African critics pointed to the colonialist (or even older) provenance of received wisdom about African sexuality. They have suggested that the long shelf life of negative stereotypes in contemporary discourses was evidence of whites' pervasive unthinking racism against Africans. As late as 2004, for example, South African president Thabo Mbeki angrily rejected questions about the high rates of rape and HIV infection in that country by accusing whites of clinging to apartheid-era demonizations of black men.[2] Yet on the other hand, many African leaders accepted or even amplified the accompanying stereotype that homosexuality was exotic in Africa. In some cases they baldly asserted that male-male sexual transmission was so rare that it should and would not be discussed, even as a theoretical possibility. Both African and foreign scholars proved surprisingly receptive to this unscientific assertion. Important scholarly texts aimed at health care professionals sometimes went so far as to say that there are only three modes of HIV transmission in Africa (that is, heterosexual intercourse, intravenous injection, and mother-to-child transmission; hence, there is no transmission through homosexual intercourse and it is therefore not worth mentioning on the precautionary principle, let alone as a substantive issue).[3] This understanding of African sexuality is now typically so much taken for granted that it does not even warrant a footnote to substantiate or qualify it.

To be fair, the phrases *African sexuality* and *heterosexual African AIDS* made a lot of sense to many people at the time of the onset of the disease. The phrases not only appeared to account for the high rates of heterosexual transmission (men infecting women and vice versa), they accorded with the consensus of expert opinion dating back a century or more. These expressions accorded as well with what African informants themselves often claimed in strong terms, and with the evident absence of anything remotely approaching a "gay scene" outside select (white-dominated) urban centers in South Africa and Zimbabwe. The fact that the dominant clade, or genetic variation, of HIV-1 was different in Africa from the clade that was infecting gay men in the West added to the accumulating logic of difference. Moreover, the appearance of heterosexual African AIDS was timely and convenient for political struggles in the West, notably the struggle against homophobia. Heterosexual African AIDS allowed gay rights advocates in the West to deflect prevalent blame for HIV/AIDS away from the "homosexual lifestyle," a huge political achievement.[4] An essentialized, singular African sexuality also suggested a problem that could be fixed with education, aid dollars, and Western advice drawn from painful experiences fighting AIDS in the early 1980s.

It was a winning combination, or a perfect storm, depending on one's perspective. This book takes the latter view. Indeed, I maintain that the idea of an African sexuality and, stemming from it, an exclusively heterosexual African AIDS, are both wrong and decidedly harmful to struggles for sexual health and sexual rights in Africa and globally.

Comprehensive scholarly critiques of crude forms of the African sexuality and heterosexual African AIDS arguments in fact followed closely upon their assertion. In particular, the Rushton penis theory and the promiscuity thesis of the Caldwells and Quiggin drew withering criticism and have by now been refuted with a wealth of empirical data.[5] We know that some Africans do engage in sex with multiple partners and other high-risk behaviors, just as elsewhere in the world. Many do not. Careful studies have shown that sexual initiation for African youth actually tends to come later than in the West and that high rates of multiple partners are associated with the specific circumstances of migrancy rather than with African culture per se (e.g., Dyson 1992 or Crush et al. 2005). High rates of sexual and gender violence that contribute to the risk of infection (where they in fact exist, which is not everywhere) have also been shown to be historically contingent. Far from being essential to Africanness, gender-based violence is often remarkably responsive even to such simple interventions as providing microfinance (Pronyk et al. 2006).

In light of this growing evidence about diverse and historically changing African sexualities, a strong consensus has emerged that HIV/AIDS needs to be understood not as singular in its epidemiology but as distinct, overlapping pandemics in different parts of the continent. This view has entailed a marked move away from morally judgmental language (like *promiscuous*) and sweeping generalizations (like *African sexuality*). Rather than looking for single explanatory factors, researchers have now also increasingly concentrated their efforts on unraveling the many factors that seem to overdetermine so much of Africa's vulnerability to HIV. Much of that research points to nonsexual and even non-African factors, such as malaria and the yawning inequities of the global economic system.[6]

A similar discrepancy between the sweeping claims of "African sexuality" and the empirical evidence has also been established with regard to the claim or assumption of no homosexuality. True, few Africans south of the Sahara even today would identify as homosexual, bisexual, lesbian, gay, queer, or any of the other terms coined in the West to signify a more or less innate individual sexual orientation. We now know, however, that many people who do not so identify nonetheless sometimes, and sometimes even predominantly, have sex with people of the same sex. It was known even in the mid-1980s that such people existed in Africa south of the Sahara and that consequently there were not merely three potential modes of transmission of HIV among black Africans. Admittedly, references to such people were sometimes buried in easily missed footnotes or subordinate clauses following assertions of the predominantly heterosexual nature of transmission. They were nonetheless in the public record. The famously prickly director of one of Africa's first AIDS Control Programs, for example, responded to a direct question from a journalist about homosexuality in Uganda in 1986. Dr. Samuel Ikwaras Okware reportedly first asserted that it was rare, but then voluntarily conceded that "the situation might be different in the prisons" (Hooper 1990, 250).

The resolute silence that followed this admission can also be put in context with another contemporary account by an African journalist. Mark Mathabane's memoir of growing up in the black township of Alexandria, near Johannesburg, in the 1960s is ultimately a celebration of black middle-class dignity, triumph over racism, and the affirmation of African heterosexual and other signifiers of normalcy. But it also includes a description of the young Mathabane's visit to a male-only mine hostel where he witnessed high-risk male-male sexual encounters. Not only does this account vividly juxtapose with the by then already solid scientific consensus about the nonexistence of male-male anal intercourse among Africans. That the book was published by a major press in the United States, was widely reviewed, and was easily available to interested researchers makes the lingering invisibility of the issues it raises all the more remarkable. As Mathabane put it,

Before I fully realised what was happening, the boys, now completely naked, had begun lining up along the three bunks. They then bent over and touched their toes, their black anuses high up in the air. One of the naked men brought out a large bottle of Vaseline and began smearing, lavishly, the boys' anuses, and then his long, swollen penis. My eyes darted to the other men; they too had begun smearing their penises with Vaseline. . . . I looked at the men, and one of them said to me, as he continued rubbing his long, veined penis with Vaseline: "This is a game we and the boys play all the time." He grinned; I tensed [. . .]

"Don't be afraid, boy," said one of the men softly, dreamily. "It's only a game we play, and nobody gets hurt." (1986, 72)

The gap between such accounts and the silences in mainstream HIV/AIDS discourse is dramatic, and it is tempting to suspect that homophobia lies behind the determined refusal to admit the existence of homosexualities in Africa. Without denying that possibility, however, almost nothing in the published scholarly material indicates homophobia as a direct cause, at least in the sense of an active aversion or opposition to conducting research on same-sex sexuality. On the contrary, the first cohort of HIV/AIDS researchers clearly adhered to a professional code of ethics and the antidiscrimination (including antihomophobia) praxis of the World Health Organization. Moreover, the homophobic rhetoric that certain African leaders became notorious for did not start until well after the scientific orthodoxy was firmly established— more than ten years after in the highly publicized case of Zimbabwean president Robert Mugabe. Unlike in the United States, therefore, HIV/AIDS researchers in Africa did not encounter significant overt, political homophobia or a swell of popular reaction against "the homosexual lifestyle" when they conducted their initial research. Such a lifestyle scarcely existed in Africa, and where it did, was visible primarily as an elite, white, exotic phenomenon of no interest to the vast majority of Africans potentially at risk for HIV.

Something other than homophobia, in other words, was going on to engender this particularly stubborn element of the African sexuality stereotype. That element has not been given the attention it merits, although, I will argue, the notion of no homosexuality is at least as wrongheaded and harmful as the stereotype of African promiscuity. How the idea came into being, and came to be so strongly believed across such a wide spectrum of identities and politics, will be the focus of this book. Specifically, I aim to trace how "the invisible presence of homosexuality" (Phillips 2004) was concocted, conjured, confirmed, and contested over time through various professional and scientific discourses in and about Africa south of the Sahara. I aim to explore exactly how the stereotype of an exclusively heterosexual African sexuality was established and maintained over the years in the face of suspiciously weak or directly contradictory evidence.

The presumption throughout is that an understanding of how a falsely constrained notion of African sexuality was constructed in intellectual terms can help us deconstruct it. From there, we may be better able to reformulate some of the most basic—and evidently ineffective—tenets of HIV/AIDS and other health and human rights interventions in Africa today. The history of an idea thus might have applications for a reconfiguration or invigoration of activist struggle, language, and politics, including the politics of alliance among civil society groups and across insider-outsider or academic-activist divides. In short, understanding the history of flimsiness in the base on which a significant body of contemporary HIV/AIDS research and activism stands might improve our ability to make stronger interventions in the future.

SAME-SEX SEXUALITY IN AFRICA: ISSUES, CONCEPTS, OBJECTIVES

Let us begin with two basic facts. First, African men sometimes have sex with other men or boys, today as in the past. They do so in a variety of ways, including anally, between the thighs, and by mouth or hand. They do it for money, for love, or when drunk. They identify as gay, straight, he, she, or some other persona . They do it by rape, out of curiosity, out of shyness or fear of women, and for many other reasons. They do it in their bedrooms, in hotels, prisons, dormitories, nightclubs, cars, in the bushes, and elsewhere. Sometimes they feel ashamed or embarrassed by such behavior, and sometimes they feel just fine. As one married Mosotho informant told me, "I mostly like to fuck, anal or between the thighs. This is called 'in the passage' here. Interestingly, sometimes I like to be fucked by these manly men I have talked about before." As to why he and other often-married men like to do this: "Why? Because it is fascinating" (Epprecht 2002, 384, 382).

Second, African women also sometimes have sex with other women or girls, today as in the past. They did not, and still for the most part do not, identify this as lesbian behavior or even as sex. That reluctance points to an interesting question or two about definitions. To quote from one important study from Lesotho, "I learned of fairly common instances of tribadism or rubbing, fondling, and cunnilingus between Basotho women, with or without digital penetration" (Kendall 1998, 233). Deep kissing, mutual manipulation of labia majora, dildo play, and female-female marriage were also all noted both by Kendall and in earlier anthropological studies. Such relationships clearly did not detract from the traditionally high value placed on heterosexual marriage and reproduction. On the contrary, in the context of severe economic strain, and high levels of male absence and male sexual irresponsibility, the lesbianlike relationships that Kendall's informants describe probably strengthened traditional heterosexual marriage forms by allowing women to avoid entanglements with men outside marriage.

The Sesotho culture is unique, and Lesotho is a small country that experienced relatively extreme demographic and social stress under colonial rule and racial capitalism. It absolutely cannot be taken as representative of the whole of Africa or even southern Africa. The Basotho people nevertheless share much in common with other African peoples, including their views on this issue. Indeed, while forms of heterosexual marriage with a gendered hierarchy of power are widely held up as ideals in Lesotho, as throughout Africa south of the Sahara, same-sex sexuality is also alluded to fairly widely. It is substantively documented in scores of scholarly books, articles, and dissertations in a wide range of academic disciplines, in unpublished archival documents such as court records and commissions of enquiry, in art, literature, and film, and in oral history from all over the continent. These will be discussed in depth in the chapters to come. For now, let me just mention Henri Alexandre Junod (1962 [1916]), Evans-Pritchard (1971), Gay (1985), Moodie (1988), Dunton (1989), Harries (1990, 1994), Jeay (1991), Krouse (1993), Achmat (1993), Gevisser and Cameron (1994), GALZ (1995), Bleys (1995), and Murray and Roscoe (1998) as groundbreaking or "canonical" studies in laying the theoretical and empirical foundations for what is sometimes termed queer scholarship in Africa. My own earlier work has drawn attention to a rich history of struggle over, and changing meanings of, sexuality and sexual identities in southern Africa (Epprecht 2004; see also GALZ 2008). Morgan and Wieringa (2005) offset the prevailing concern with male sexuality in many of the above studies with close anthropological studies of lesbianlike relationships in southern and eastern Africa, while Niang et al. (2002, 2003), Gueboguo (2006a, 2006c) and Eboussi Boulaga (2007) have begun to challenge received wisdom in francophone Africa. Current events, reports on legal status and government policies, international links, and other up-to-date information and debates concerning gay rights from all over the African continent can be easily accessed through the Web site Behind the Mask (www.mask.org.za). Same-sex issues in the struggles for human rights and HIV/AIDS awareness around the continent are closely documented, with strong policy recommendations, in Johnson (2007). A growing number of studies from around the continent have meanwhile begun to trickle in that establish credible baseline statistics on and testimony from women who have sex with women who experience heterosexual assaults (Reid and Dirsuweit 2001; Potgeiter 2005; Swarr forthcoming), and of men engaging in high-risk same-sex sexual activity. Jewkes et al. (2006) is a particularly powerful intervention in that respect, on account of the size and quality of the survey it was based on. It demonstrates that male-male sexuality is more widespread *in a rural setting* (nearly 3.6 percent of informants admitted to it) and has a higher correlation with HIV infection than ever before imagined. Niang et al. (2002) is also significant in that its survey of 250 Senegalese men revealed high levels of violence in male-male relationships. No less than 13 percent of those informants had experienced rape by ostensibly heterosexual police.

The language by which same-sex relationships are described in many of these sources is often Eurocentric—the word *homosexuality*, notably, suggests a clarity arising from a specific history of scientific enquiry, social relations, and political struggle that did not historically exist in Africa and still does not very accurately describe the majority of men who have sex with men or women who have sex with women in Africa. The language Africans have used to describe such relationships is in fact commonly euphemistic or coy almost to the point of incomprehensibility beyond those in the know. Africans are by no means unique in this, of course, as cross-cultural studies and as students of secret gay dialects have well documented (esp. Prieur 1998; Cage 2003; Leap and Boellstorff 2004; and Reid 2006, notably). Yet in recent years this subtlety has begun to change quite dramatically. The result is that depictions of same-sex sexuality are now becoming increasingly explicit and frank, even from places with a strong reputation for conservatism on this issue. Nigerian author Temilola Abioye, to give but one of many examples, frames a short story around five female friends who complain to each other about men's irresponsibility. The one out lesbian character among them wraps up the discussion by asking cheerily, "Why don't we all take a shower and go down on each other. It wouldn't be copulating, it would be a lot of petting, smooching, and caring" (in Azuah 2005, 136).[7]

To be sure, this kind of writing is not broadly available in Africa and many Africans would probably be surprised by it. Even among the small out gay communities and sexual rights associations, until very recently there has been little awareness of the historical and ethnographic evidence about same-sex sexuality. A further limiting aspect of the existing material is that many of the cutting edge studies on "how homosexuality became un-African" (Aarmo 1999) are narrowly focused by theme or geography. For instance, and very problematically, South Africa as a place has overwhelmingly predominated in the production of such knowledge. This allows determined naysayers elsewhere to rationalize their disinterest in the topic even when the most carefully researched material about lesbian, gay, bisexual, transgender, and intersex people (lgbti) in Africa is presented to them. This can be frustrating, if not disorienting in an Alice in Wonderland way. I have found, for example, that evidence from South Africa or even rural Zimbabwe and Namibia is often given little credence among people who regard those countries as not "real Africa" on account of having had so many white settlers.

Yet by now, it all starts to add up: while most African societies historically did and still do tend to place a very high priority on heterosexual marriage and reproduction, many allowed or even celebrated "pseudohomosexualities" and "sex games," providing they occurred within the bounds of specific rituals, sacred or secret spaces, and designated social roles.[8] They also generally had ways and means to explain why some people did not always and easily fit those heterosexual marital ideals and norms. Whether that was because they refused to marry, or they were unable to consummate their marriage, or they were caught engaging in same-sex or other disapproved sexual practices, such people existed and were known to exist. No doubt some experienced cruelties and humiliations for failure to conform to gender and sexual ideals and norms. And no doubt different societies differed in degrees of tolerance toward individual exceptions and eccentricities, and some may well have approached implacable in their intolerance or violence of reaction against difference. But on the whole, the ways and means to explain and accommodate sexual differ-ence appear to have been relatively humane and respectful of the dignity of the persons involved. This was provided, crucially, that he or she did not put the integrity of the family and community at risk by his or her behavior. That latter provision was not as hard to meet as proponents of African sexuality might think. It could be met in a wide variety of ways, including not naming the nonnormative behavior, not identifying it as an individual sexual choice, and covering it up from public awareness. The keeping of secrets was of para-mount importance and could include, as Kendall's and Abioye's women sug-gest, hiding meanings from even that intimate "public" of one: the individual's own self-consciousness.[9]

These discretions, as well as the ways, places, and frequencies that same-sex sexuality could be expressed, changed over time in response to many factors. The growth of cities and industries, migrant labor, prisons and boarding schools, new cultural influences from outside of Africa, and changing material relations between men and women are just a few examples. Others include the international gay rights movement and all the vocabulary and political boldness that its participants have generated. Changing relations between ethnic groups within postcolonies have also been a factor in giving rise to new attitudes and state policies toward homosexuality, as Namibian lesbian activists

Madeleine Isaaks and Elizabeth Khaxas reveal. By their account, ethnic domination by the strongly evangelized Ovambo over the more traditional Damara partially explains the rise of explicit homophobia in Namibia in the postindependence era (Morgan and Wieringa 2005, 79–80, 92, 125). A similar link has been argued in the case of new forms of intolerance or active homophobia against the Hausa 'yan daudu, who are taken by some Nigerians as a lightning rod for gathering resentment against corrupt Northern domination of the federal government and economic malaise in the 1980s (Aken'ova 2002).

What appears or is asserted as timeless African tradition today, in other words, is often historically quite recent and contested. Same-sex sexuality and attitudes toward it thus clearly have a history in Africa, just as they do elsewhere in the world.[10]

A great many gaps in this history remain. Islamic jurists wrote judgments and advice on civil cases throughout a huge swathe of Africa, creating in the process a documentary archive that extends back for a thousand years or more. This almost certainly contains decisions and learned reflection on same-sex issues (as it does elsewhere in the Islamic world where close research has been carried out).[11] Portuguese documents, also extending back hundreds of years, might similarly shed light on changing ways that male-male sexuality in particular was understood and regulated over time (see Sweet 1996 and 2003, for preliminary investigations). Anthropological and sociological studies specifically focused on uncovering histories of female-female sexuality have only barely begun, while indigenous African-language novels, television shows, advertisements, and other mass media remain almost entirely unexplored for their allusions to and treatment of same-sex sexuality. One remarkable study of prison graffiti, for example, hints both at men's attitudes toward same-sex relationships and at a censorious role by African research assistants who appear to have erased evidence (Koopman 1997, 81). Newell's biography of the Nigerian trader John Stuart-Young (Newell 2006) also suggests another potentially rich source: oral histories and private diaries of public personalities who did not quite fit the mold in terms of marriage, children, and sexual preferences. The fields of demography and "colonial gynaecology" that flourished in French colonial Africa, meanwhile, tended to explain low levels of fertility among African women in ways that were useful to the colonial state. As Nancy Hunt (1999) and Charles Becker and René Collingnon (1999) discuss, this analysis maintained that female infertility was a result of heterosexual immorality leading to uncontrolled heterosexually transmitted infections. Unpublished observations by the researchers or confidential correspondence might reveal more complex local histories about African sexualities under stress in the colonial era.

As Adam Ashforth eloquently described in the case of his research into somewhat analogous secrets around witchcraft in contemporary Soweto, all of the above would need to explore the "latticework of local knowledge that supports such silence, the tracery of suppositions . . . the skeins of gossip and idle speculation—oft-repeated, half-remembered—that are the living history of the community" (Ashforth 2005, 11). Exploring these gaps and querying these secrets suggest formidable methodological challenges.

Yet even acknowledging the limitations of the research thus far, the evidence presented in existing studies is strong enough to beg the question, why would anyone doing research or activism about gender and sexuality ignore the evidence? And yet they do. Indeed, many of the examples to follow suggest a powerful will not to know that flies in the face of recommended best practices to address HIV and AIDS. For example, study after study of this devastating disease insists on the "urgent" or "immediate" need for research into real as opposed to aspired sexuality if progress is going to be made in the fight against it (e.g., Williams 1992; Parker and Aggleton 1999; Caldwell 2004; Lwabaayi 2004; Allman et al. 2007). Why then issue a report on addressing HIV in prisons in Zambia (the country with the steepest drop in life expectancy attributable to HIV/AIDS) that does not even mention the possibility (rather, the well-known fact, even in Zambia [Simooya et al. 2001]) of male-male transmission in prisons? Why conduct a huge, very expensive survey of sexual practices and attitudes among youth in Botswana (the country with the highest seroprevalence in the world) that does not venture a single question about homosexuality or bisexuality? Why publish a "definitive text" on the pandemic in a country with a well-established and vocal lgbti community that does not make one single mention of same-sex sexuality in African communities? Why, in short, tacitly condone or even encourage ignorance, denial, and stigma regarding actually existing sexualities when such ignorance, denial, and stigma expose young people in particular to unsafe sexual practices?[12]

Homophobia and cultural sensitivities undoubtedly account for some of this fatal discrepancy and the reluctance to raise controversial topics. Crude, threatening expressions of homophobia by African leaders in recent years have in fact been a tempting and easy target for human rights activists (e.g., Long, Brown, and Cooper 2003), sometimes addressed in provocative or sarcastic language (Anele 2006; Gueboguo 2006b). But neither homophobia nor culture as such can explain the durability of silences, stereotypes, and stigma against same-sex sexuality in Africa among professional scholars or gender and human rights activists. On the contrary, many of the authors and activists at the forefront of struggle against HIV/AIDS were obviously striving for nonjudgmental research on scientific lines, were aware of and respectful of gay rights and the diversity of human sexuality, were not afraid of controversy, and were even, in some noteworthy cases, proudly out homosexuals themselves. Edwin Cameron, for example, South Africa's first openly gay Supreme Court judge, cannot be accused of homophobia. But even in his otherwise hard-hitting memoir (2005, 83), he makes but a single passing reference to the possibility that male-male HIV transmission may be understated in the dominant discourse.

Further complicating the picture is a gap between state- or church-sponsored homophobia on the one hand, and grassroots disinterest or de facto tolerance of discreet sexual difference on the other, a gap I will explore through an analysis of African literature and film in chapter 5. Not to underestimate the pain of "real homophobia," my sense is that much of the reported violence against suspected gays and lesbians in Africa is displaced misogyny or anger at economic or other marginalization among young men, not always neatly distinguishable from regular criminal violence or sexism against professional women. The latter might explain, for example, the glaring difference between the treatment Ugandan sociologist Sylvia Tamale describes receiving for her public support of gay rights (stunning vitriol), and the nonchalance or even national pride that greeted Monica Arac de Nyeko for her prize-winning story of a lesbian affair between two Uganda girls just a few years later.[13]

In short, something far subtler than homophobia appears to be at play. Trying to get to it — that is, to unlock subtleties and secrets from the dominant discourse — requires specialized methods to interrogate the data. I begin by clarifying the key concepts, terms, and analytic tools that I (and many of the colleagues who laid the groundwork for this study) have employed toward that end. First and foremost is the concept of queer theory.

Queer became a term of abuse in post–World War II America, roughly on par in its meanness with *faggot* or *homo*. The word was then co-opted as a marker of pride by activists in the gay liberation movement of the late 1960s and '70s. North American gay and lesbian intellectuals subsequently adopted it to describe their efforts to stretch feminism, Marxism, subaltern, and other radical critical theories in order both to facilitate enquiry into issues regarding same-sex sexuality that are hidden within the dominant discourse and to deploy the enquiry toward healing or dismantling coercive ideologies of gender, sexuality, and national or other sexualized identity. While Michel Foucault and Judith Butler were the highly Westocentric guiding lights to queer theory in the 1980s and '90s, queer theory has since expanded its horizons to include critical race theory and global political economy.[14] Partly as a consequence, it has gained some currency among non-Western and African diaspora scholars,[15] and has now proponents among African lgbti. As one anonymous contributor to the Web site Behind the Mask put it in answering his or her own rhetorical question, "Why queer?"

> Well, yes, "gay" is great. It has its place. But when a lot of lesbians and gay men wake up in the morning we feel angry and disgusted, not gay. So we've chosen to call ourselves queer. Using "queer" is a way of reminding us of how we are perceived by the rest of the world. It's a way of telling ourselves we don't have to be witty and charming people who keep our lives discreet and marginalized in the straight world. We use queer as gay men loving lesbians and lesbians loving being queer. Queer, unlike gay, doesn't mean male. And when spoken to other gays and lesbians it's a way of suggesting we close ranks, and forget (temporarily) our individual differences because we face a more insidious common enemy. Yeah, queer can be a rough word but is also a sly and ironic weapon we can steal from the homophobe's hands and use against him.[16]

It was in that spirit that I began the present research, queer serving as convenient shorthand to describe an antiessentialist approach to researching gender and sexuality that is open to the whole range of human sexual diversity; that underscores sexuality as a critical component in the construction of class, race, national, ethnic, and other identities; that analyses language and silences in relation to material conditions and struggles; and that engages with current debates about global economic and other inequalities coming out of African feminist, subaltern, and critical masculinity studies, both as those debates play out in academe and in the broader political sphere. Important markers in those debates — challenging naturalistic fallacies and Eurocentric assumptions about the relationship between physical sex and social gender identities and roles, interpreting Foucault and Gramsci to reconstruct histories of prostitution, marriage, class, and ethnicity formation in Africa, destabilizing the conflation of women and gender found in much of the early feminist scholarship, and more — include Amadiume (1987), White (1990), Oyéwùmí (1997), Mbembe (2001), Arnfred (2004a), Morrell (1998, 2001), Lindsay and Miescher (2003), Nnaemeka (2005), and Jeater (1993, 2007). Glen Elder (2003) is also important for introducing the term heteropatriarchy — a reminder against the marginalization of nonnormative sexuality that sometimes happens in feminist critiques of male domination. Arnfred (2004a) provides an astute analysis of the muted nature of discussion of sexuality in general in African feminist writings that queer theory, hypothetically, could usefully challenge, while Newell (2006) uses queer theory to effect in uncovering sexual secrets in middle-colonial Nigeria.

These debates, however, now suggest to me that queer theory is not necessarily very helpful anymore. Indeed, three potential problems that were evident in the late 1990s have since become more clearly manifest. The appropriateness and value of the word *queer* in scholarship and struggles for sexual rights in Africa has to be reassessed in light of those problems.

The first issue is that Africans and Africanists who do gender and sexuality research remain extremely reluctant to embrace the term *queer* even when they make use of insights from the queer canon.[17] This is understandable given the long history of Western theories, fads, and prescriptions imposed inappropriately and uncritically on Africa. Because the term derives from a specific North American context of political struggle rather than emerging organically from African intellectuals and activists, it carries for many the strong whiff of North American "gay imperialism" (Blackwood and Wieringa 1999, 3) and of trying to shoehorn African evidence and perspectives into ill-fitting North American formulations. On the continent, many would add South African hegemony through "unreflexive" and "homogenizing" interventions that purport to be sympathetic to black gays and lesbians elsewhere in the region but are nonetheless inattentive to specificities and subtleties of culture, history, and struggle outside South Africa (for a succinct critique of that tendency in the South African magazine *Chimurenga*, see Shaw 2004, 197). As Morgan and Wieringa remind us in explaining their choice to eschew the term *queer* (2005, 310), there was nothing queer at all about many of the African women living with women that they encountered in their research in places like Uganda, Tanzania, and rural Namibia. The women there expressed their sexuality in line with existing gender categories and as such were perfectly normal in the cultural context.

Second, notwithstanding recent efforts to globalize queer theory, it remains heavily dependent on Western empirical evidence and referenced by Western theoretical frameworks. African material and African intellectuals tend to be overlooked, seemingly token, or relegated to the margins in ostensibly global queer literature. A further concern is that Western queer researchers in Africa do not always write or publish with African audiences in mind and that their publications are not easily available or accessible in Africa. A number of the studies noted above—and I acknowledge that this could include some of my own interventions—are written in a peculiarly dense, jargon-laden prose that is hard to make sense of outside a narrow circle of North American researchers immersed in North American cultural referencing. This begs the questions, who exactly is queer theory trying to talk to, and how effective or sustainable is it in acknowledging discrete audiences by continuing to use quotes around the word *queer?*

Third, in methodological terms, far from representing a radical break from colonizing traditions of Western scholarship, queer theory in practice can be strikingly old-fashioned. Through the 1980s and '90s this conservatism appeared mainly in the form of cherry-picking obscure references in select ethnographies by sometimes dubious Western adventurers, racists, and amateurs in Africa under the umbrella of homosexual (see Dynes 1983, for example, and others to be discussed in chapter 2). Note also the casual androcentrism in the defense of queer from *Behind the Mask* cited above (which assumes all homophobes are male). But this conservatism also persists in the form of the conceit that strong opinions about African societies can be expressed without reference to African authors or even visiting the places pronounced upon. William J. Spurlin (2006) provides a sobering example of this in a monograph by a major queer studies publishing house, metaphorically returning to the mission porch to announce what he terms "insurgent" (no definition provided) sexuality in southern Africa. It has been at least five decades since anthropologists rejected root and branch the idea that Western scholars could reasonably comment on African societies without living in Africa, learning the languages, and working in close collaboration with African partners, especially when venturing close to topics as sensitive and secretive as sexuality can be. Spurlin, by contrast, ventures an extended critique of Judith Gay's pathbreaking ethnographic study of lesbianlike relationships among Basotho girls and young women without going to Lesotho to reconnoiter local knowledge. The result is a mishmash of speculation and cross-cultural analogies, empty rhetorical questions, and outright absurdities. The latter include the assertion that mummy-baby relationships are "a feminist practice" and "a potential site of decolonization" (Spurlin 2006, 76), when not one single Mosotho feminist, let alone the women and girls that Gay interviewed three decades ago, has ever made such an analytic leap.

Justification for this aspect of the methodology further undercuts the credibility of queer theory in Africa when it feeds into heart-of-darkness stereotypes about Africa in North America. To pick on Spurlin again, he suggests that Zimbabwe was too "dangerous" to do research into same-sex sexuality when he visited briefly in 1996, hence the need to rely for his information on unnamed (why?) "underground" writers and activists from afar (2006, 5). In fact, there were numerous researchers in Zimbabwe at that time openly doing their research, publishing in the local papers, and unabashedly supporting the objectives of Gays and Lesbians of Zimbabwe (GALZ). This included foreigners, like me, then employed by the Zimbabwean state, as well as local

Zimbabweans. Except for mine, however, Spurlin does not refer to any of the work produced by these obviously brave individuals (Antonio, Chigweshe, Phillips, Sibanda, Goddard, Machida, Aarmo, and numerous contributors to GALZ publications, for example, including in its monthly news magazine, the GALZette). This disinterest in African researchers cannot be explained by difficulty of access, since many of the publications were readily available, even from outside Zimbabwe.

Homophobia is a real issue in Zimbabwe, as it is in Wyoming and many other places. But who exactly gains by inflating its pervasiveness and danger? Zimbabweans, including lgbti activists who have publicly supported their homophobic president against Western imperialism, will not, particularly when the Western authors who overstate the dangers of talking or reading about same-sex sexuality in Africa at the same time blithely overlook the work of African and Africa-based researchers. This gap between queer theory as stated and queer research as practiced, in short, deeply compromises the project. Until unambiguous interventions from African intellectuals and activists persuade me otherwise, I have to conclude that it is important to acknowledge but not to promote queer theory as a research strategy in Africa.

For the purposes of the present study, therefore, queer theory's most important and original contribution is simply to make explicit what is commonly implicit in, for example, critical men's studies and other antiessentialist research. Primarily it alerts us to ask about the often extremely subtle ways by which same-sex sexuality is rendered invisible or is stigmatized in hegemonic culture. What, in precise instances, are the discursive tools and tactics by which the ideology of exclusively heterosexual Africanness was asserted and is maintained in the face of accumulating contradictory evidence? What can we see in Africanist discourses when applying a sharp eye for allusions to sexual difference, ambiguities, and change over time?

The most obvious rhetorical techniques in this regard are those clumsy forms of homophobia noted earlier that have become a staple among certain political and religious leaders. These include conflating homosexuality with rape, child abuse, bestiality, or prostitution. Such rhetorical homophobia extends to direct threats against lesbian, gay, bisexual, transgender, and intersexual people themselves and against those researchers and sympathizers who work to reduce the invisibility and stigma against African lgbti people. Homophobia on this scale is frequently amplified with barely veiled innuendo of racism or imperialism against Africans. The government of Uganda offered a disturbingly forceful case of denial in November 2004 when it threatened to bar international donors from the country if they provided safer-sex education to homosexuals. The government of Nigeria is meanwhile seeking to expand its current criminalization of homosexuality to include people who so much as "witness, celebrate with or *support* couples involved in homosexual relationship [*sic*]," coded language presumably directed mainly against foreign donors and activists.[18]

A more subtle form of homophobia is the apparently reasonable argument that lgbti people are an insignificant minority and gay rights a sideshow to the larger challenges African governments are facing. Maina Kahindo of the Ministry of Health in Kenya, for example, explained why he opposed new research into same-sex sexuality: "taking into account other modes of transmission of HIV/AIDS, homosexuality is negligible, and should not take up our resources and time." He continues, "We have other, far more pressing areas which affect the majority of our people and therefore need urgent attention" (Panos Institute 2005). That argument ignores the fact that out lgbti are but the tiny, visible portion of a web of profound cultural attitudes and sexual practices that includes men who sometimes have sex with men but do not consider themselves homosexual or bisexual (msm) and women who sometimes have sex with women but do not consider themselves lesbian or bisexual (wsw). Characterizing lgbti people as an insignificant minority also underplays the significance of homophobia in shoring up other prejudices in society, notably, when it serves a vicarious attack on women's empowerment against sexism, or when used as a smear tactic and scapegoat by xenophobes, tribalists, and racists.[19]

At the level of scholarly analysis, dogmatic opposition to allowing discussion of same-sex sexuality is not very widespread. Denial, stereotyping, and stigma generally occur in much more subtle and often unconscious ways. Rather than homophobia, such blindness and presumption are known as heterosexism. In simple terms heterosexism means naively assuming that the social ideals and norms of heterosexual reproduction, marriage, sexual attraction, and so on are *not* predominantly or even significantly social. Rather, the heterosexual form is conceived as a predominantly natural phenomenon, intrinsic to the human race and consequently not historical. Exceptions to that form are assumed to be a basically freakish minority of genetic dead ends. A heterosexist mindset involves *not* thinking about exceptions to the presumed normal majority, *not* asking questions that challenge presumptions of normality, and *not* wondering if attitudes toward presumed normality might be implicated in wider issues of development, health, and governance.

Once attuned to the concept of heterosexism, it is not hard for a critical reader to spot when it occurs. Silence is the most obvious expression, which can be achieved by not looking or asking in the first place, or by self-censorship of evidence that complicates the heterosexist narrative. Some of the starkest illustrations of such silencing appear in educational material on HIV and AIDS in Africa. As alluded to above, one authoritative volume aimed primarily to educate health care providers (Essex et al. 2002) does not even include homosexual contact among its list of modes of transmission (see esp. the chapters by Piot and Bartos, and Kristensen). Issues of specific concern to women who have sex with women but do not identify as lesbian, or women who may be infected with HIV by men who have sex with men but do not consider themselves gay, are meanwhile almost totally absent in mainstream AIDS discourse. A quick search of the UNAIDS Web site for sub-Saharan Africa in late 2005, for example, turned up precisely zero documents for each of the keywords *homosexuality, lesbian, msm, wsw, bisexuality, homophobia* and *anal sex*—the only part of the world to be so systematically uninformed.[20] Abdool Karim and Abdool Karim (2005) manage only two passing references to homosexuality in hundreds of pages of text surveying the history and epidemiology of HIV/AIDS in Africa, both of which refer to the initial years of epidemic among gay white men in South Africa.

Another common manifestation of heterosexism appears in studies that purport to be about sexuality in general but in fact are specifically if not exclusively about heterosexuality. Controversial AIDS researcher John C. Caldwell sets the tone with his magisterial overviews of "social context" that somehow manage to avoid reference to the discussions of same-sex issues (and even masturbation) that occur in some of the very ethnography that he relies on to make his argument (Caldwell, Caldwell, and Quiggin 1989; Caldwell 2000). Jock McCulloch's study of "sexual crime" (2000), to give another example, draws on archival documents that include hundreds of cases of male-male sexual crime. Yet he systematically ignores those cases in what amounts to an analysis of so-called Black Peril crimes only (sexual relations between black men and white women). Innumerable other studies on gender and sexuality in Africa (and even of "perversion"—Jeater 1993) overlook the possibility of same-sex sexualities or "explain" them in passing as anomalous or insignificant, or both.

Obviously one can only do so much in a monograph. But when titles do not accurately reflect content, or do not use qualifying adjectives to avoid overgeneralization, they serve to normalize the ostensible nonexistence of same-sex sexuality. In other cases, the frustration arises when scholars do recognize the importance of queer theory, point to the need for research into African homosexualities, and in some cases even announce their intention to seek new evidence or perspectives on same-sex sexuality. For whatever reason, however, they commonly do not follow through in any substantive manner. Nigerian physician A. Olufemi Williams, for instance, was an early voice to note that "the silent or the undiscovered bisexual/homosexual African may be a very important host for the dissemination of HIV" and that "all efforts" needed to be made to identify and reach out to such a person (1992, 74). Yet elsewhere in the same book he categorically denies their existence based on speculative, xenophobic logic and isolated, uninformed studies (65). William Rushing (1995) also speculates on secretive "bisexuality" as a possible vector of HIV from men to women. Yet he too does not provide much more than the barest references to empirical evidence that might justify the speculation. Arnfred (2004b), meanwhile, correctly points out the urgency of rethinking colonial-era and racist conceptualizations of African sexualities, including by tackling the stereotype of pure African heterosexuality. But only one of the contributors to the volume she edited even briefly takes up her challenge (Mumbi Machera, reflecting on her difficulties with raising the topic of homosexuality in her lectures on gender at the University of Nairobi).

The major scholarship in French adheres to the same striking pattern. Beginning in the early 1990s, Bibeau (1991), Dozon (1991), and Dozon and Vidal (1995) offered powerful critiques of medical scientists' disregard for social science in their approach to HIV/AIDS in Africa, and of Western scholarship in general for naïve and uncritical reiteration of colonial-era stereotypes and slanders. Homosexuals remained invisible, however, to the extent that they, msm, wsw, inmates, and street children are absent even from the list of absent groups in the review of social science literature in Dozon ("les groups absents" refers only to intravenous drug users and recipients of blood transfusions [1995, 43]). Becker et al.'s (1999) groundbreaking collection also sharply criticized Western neocolonialism in the knowledge production process. It noted as well the existence of two linguistic solitudes, with the anglophone scholarship significantly dominating the francophone in quantity and in the quality of its theorization of sexuality. Yet while calling for greater interdisciplinarity, collaboration with African researchers across language barriers, and attentiveness to historical, cultural, political, and other social context, and while at least one contributor mentions in passing that "homosexuality is widespread" (in the Sudan, north and south; El-Battahani 1999, 312), Becker et al. never significantly question the heterosexuality narrative. Indeed, in some cases contributors seem almost deliberately to shore up that narrative by failing to state the obvious. In a survey of Nigerian university students' perceptions of HIV/AIDS, notably, Edlyne Anugwom found that they regarded the disease as a white, Western phenomenon with no mention of its association with homosexuality. The chapter thus erases what was in fact common knowledge throughout Africa at the time (Anugwom 1999, 501). A subsequent overview of the history of HIV/AIDS (Denis and Becker 2006), while sensitive to the colonizing tendencies of Western scholarship, continues that same strand of erasure by simply ignoring the proliferation of studies and Web sites that have appeared in the intervening years. It makes no mention of same-sex issues in black communities notwithstanding that at least two studies are cited in the bibliography that focus primarily on situational male-male sexuality among black men (Harries 1990 and Niehaus 2002).

This juxtaposition of theoretical awareness and de facto silence or denial within a single volume also occurs in a weighty collection of erudite articles entitled *HIV and AIDS in Africa: Beyond Epidemiology* (Kalipeni et al. 2004). That book was one of the specific motivations for this one, and for that reason I will belabor the critique for another paragraph. *HIV and AIDS in Africa* is impressive for its breadth, its passion, and its critical perspective on the theoretical and methodological flaws of earlier research. Among other points, coeditor Susan Craddock introduces the notion that same-sex sexuality and attitudes toward it may be underinvestigated in Africa. Oliver Phillips follows up with an incisive chapter on how the topic of homosexuality is avoided in mainstream AIDS discourse. He traces that avoidance back to silences generated in part by the colonial legal systems and customary discretions in African languages. The two of these come together in one striking anecdote that Phillips relates: during the trial of former Zimbabwean president Canaan Banana for sodomy and indecent assault, a female court interpreter had to be dismissed because she was unable or unwilling to translate the Shona word for penis (Phillips 2004, 166n8). Yet none of the other twenty-three contributors to the volume either engages Phillips's argument or evidence or pursues the lead that Craddock offers. Anal sex (which is often wrongly assumed to be only a male-male issue) is not discussed in nearly four hundred pages of dense text. Oral sex is not discussed. Homophobia is discussed only briefly in one chapter, and that with an incorrect citation (Akeroyd 2004, 98–99). Bisexuality is not discussed except to be dismissed in mocking terms. Indeed, in that chapter, two of the contributing editors reiterate an argument they had made several years earlier that harshly reviewed the book by William Rushing mentioned above (Oppong and Kalipeni 1996, 2004).

Rushing was undoubtedly careless to transpose a concept like bisexuality from North America to Africa without conducting local research or even consulting much existing scholarship. But Oppong and Kalipeni are flatly wrong when they claim that there is "not a shred evidence" to support what they call "the myth of the bisexual African homosexual" and "the mythical African homosexual, Rushing's creation" (Oppong and Kalipeni 2004, 52–53). They are also inflammatory to invoke the specter of white racism ("bias") against Africans in order to discredit this one aspect of Rushing's book.

To be sure, big books, Web sites, and official documents do not tell the whole story, and in fairness it must be stressed that much more is going on on the ground than academic tomes and cyberspace might suggest.[21] Nonetheless, the tentative or hostile attitude toward same-sex sexualities in mainstream HIV/AIDS and Africanist discourse is apparent enough to vindicate at least some of Cindy Patton's powerful polemic on the topic, "Inventing African AIDS" (1999). There appears to be a prior, unspoken commitment to promoting a uniquely heterosexual Africanness that overrides open-minded scholarship on this issue. As Phillips (2004) puts it, homosexuality is an invisible presence in AIDS and presumably other social science research in Africa. That presence skews questions, findings, and logic. We need, therefore, to contest that invisible presence and those who would defend and perpetuate it.

Toward that end, this book aims to support those African intellectuals, including health care professionals at the frontline of HIV/AIDS struggles, who have begun to recognize the harm that the invisibility causes. An important if understated remark by Adamson Muula, head of the Department of Community Health at the University of Malawi made this point in the *Lancet Infectious Diseases*. "When teaching about virus transmission, we need to go beyond politically correct thinking. Anal sex between a male and a heterosexual female certainly happens in Africa but it is rarely spoken of; this must change." So too: "homosexuality happens"—deal with it.[22]

I do not want to underplay the potential risks in engaging with this debate. It is a fact, for example, that homophobic white supremacist groups in America are beginning to use evidence about homosexuality, bisexuality, and anal sex in Africa to promote their iniquitous agendas.[23] There is also the danger, already evident in Nigeria and other parts of the continent, that Christian, Islamic, or other fundamentalist groups might exploit evidence of African homosexualities to promote reactionary visions of moral order that further disempower women and sexual minorities. Among witchcraft believers there is the potential to inflame links in popular culture between sexual transgressions, disease, and what Adam Ashforth (2005) has described as an almost debilitating "spiritual insecurity" and accompanying violence. There is the potential, seen in analogous debates about life "on the down low" by African American men, that exaggerated claims about secretive, insatiable bisexuality could cause panic and despair among African women, who are otherwise the major focus of empowerment initiatives (King 2004; Boykin 2005). There is also the danger that raising the profile of people, activities, and idioms that for the most part still fall under the public radar could invite homophobic or xenophobic reaction against them. The risk of reaction is especially high when it is non-Africans who are doing the research (as has tended to be the case in queer scholarship in Africa so far, myself included). How to guard against non-African queer researchers and activists eliding into what Obioma Nnaemeka (2005) scathingly refers to as "insurgents" whose overzealous interventions might actually demean African agency and dignity or place them at heightened risk? A dramatic illustration of exactly this kind of tension arising from Western appropriations or interventions occurred following the World Social Forum in January 2007. This culminated in a harshly worded denunciation of the "blatant disrespect" and "neo-colonialism" of pioneering UK lgbti activist Peter Tatchell by leading African lgbti activists.[24]

I am acutely aware that I am running the same risks by tackling the topic on a grand scale, and that I am exposing myself to charges of overgeneralization from scant or "negative" evidence according to a Western, gay rights logic. Several strategies can allay these risks. First is to bear in mind a point that I try to make in all my interventions on this topic. Winning human rights for lgbti people equal to the rights theoretically guaranteed to all citizens is not simply my personal "white," let alone queer, priority. As the quickest of glances at gay rights Web site Behind the Mask makes clear, African activists and intellectuals, including religious leaders and broad civil-society movements like the Treatment Action Campaign, have begun to make this argument forcefully and articulately. Many African governments have also made the same commitment. In the case of South Africa, this has been done explicitly through its constitution, which since 1996 has prohibited discrimination against anyone on the basis of sexual orientation. Ten years later, in Banjul, Gambia, the African Union's Commission on Human and Peoples' Rights also explicitly endorsed the principle of extending nondiscrimination and equal protection for lesbian and gay people across the continent.[25]

In other cases, the commitment to lgbti rights is implicit in treaty obligations such as, above all, the African Union's Charter on Human and Peoples' Rights. That document, presently ratified by all fifty-three member states, recalls a founding principle of the Organization of African Unity: "freedom, equality, justice, and dignity are essential objectives for the achievement of the legitimate aspirations of the African peoples." It accepts the validity of the United Nations Universal Declaration of Human Rights. It calls for the elimination of "all forms of discrimination." And it commits to guarantee the protection of those rights "without distinction of any kind such as race, ethnic group, color, sex, language group, religion, political or any other opinion, national and social origin, fortune, birth or other status."[26] The African Youth Charter (2006) further specifies young people's right to freedom of expression, access to information, education, and the acquisition of life skills including on HIV/AIDS, reproductive health, and cultural practices that are harmful to women and girls.[27]

The African Union's protocol on the rights of women (July 2003) makes an even stronger commitment to that end. Article 2, so far signed by forty-three African states and ratified by twenty-one, declares:

> States Parties shall commit themselves to modify the social and cultural patterns of conduct of women and men through public education, information, education and communication strategies, with a view to achieving the elimination of harmful cultural and traditional practices and all other practices which are based on the idea of the inferiority or the superiority of either of the sexes, *or on stereotyped roles for women and men.*[28]

It is true that not many African governments would concede that the above commitment is logically connected to lgbti rights. Indeed, they would likely argue that the African Union's obligation to promote family and "positive morals" supersedes any implicit commitment to the rights of lgbti individuals. I believe that that argument cannot survive in the long run, however, particularly as African lgbti people demonstrate their own practical commitments to family and moral living (which they often do in both very creative and sometimes surprisingly conservative ways). And what else is homophobia if not a practice that both polices and gives rise to stereotyped roles for women and men?

The danger of fueling suspicions of Western academic imperialism can also be allayed in part by turning to African lgbti groups for vocabularies. This is not always practical for trying to make broad observations or comparisons given that there are hundreds of languages in Africa. Almost all of them likely have vernacular terms and culturally specific idioms to indicate shades of meaning about gender identity and sexuality. While some of those terms are known cross-culturally over large areas—*skesana, matanyola, istabane, ngochani* across much of southern Africa, for example; *woubi, oubi, ibbi* across francophone West Africa; *kuchu* across much of east Africa—they often suggest varying degrees of social disapproval or even insult. They have also sometimes drastically changed meaning over time—not unlike the word *queer* has. African activists are addressing the clutter and mutability of African terms in part by judiciously borrowing from the West to develop a common language. But the results here can also be remarkably unstable. A term specifically invented to avoid identity politics, notably, is now commonly used in precisely that way (to wit, "Is he gay or bi?" "No, he's msm"). Even some francophones have embraced the new acronym without explaining why they choose to identify in English as opposed to French.[29] Attempts to become visible also sometimes come up against the power of the market to marginalize poor, black, female, and even "normal gay" experiences vis-à-vis high consuming white male drag queens.[30]

My own way to minimize the problems inherent in the terminology is, first, to use local and historical terms when referring to local and historical instances of same-sex sexuality. Second, when making more general arguments, I use the terminology now generally preferred by African lgbti associations in their activism.[31] This includes queer but also, still more commonly, msm, wsw, and lgbti (which recognizes diversity within a common political rubric). Following Van Zyl and Steyn (2005), I have used the lowercase rather than the reifying uppercase as a gesture to their mutability and contested meanings, making exceptions only for proper nouns and those identities derived from geographic places (Africans, Arabs, Europeans, Western, for example). More general descriptors and analytic categories (*identity, modern, traditional, black, white,* and so on) are similarly open to debate, dispute, and dissimulation. I employ them bearing in mind the cautions and qualifications pointedly discussed by Mudimbe-Boyi (2002a) or Setel (1999). Frederick Cooper's (2005) reflections on historical method and Western epistemologies in African studies are also apposite to my approach. This analysis recognizes the limitations of language for capturing the protean, historical natures of identities. Indeed, the dissonance between words that describe people's sense of identity (or projection of identities onto others) and people's actual behavior is a major focus of the enquiry that ensues.

Problems in deciphering local meanings are enormously compounded when the scope of the analysis is extended to the whole of Africa south of the Sahara. There are powerful arguments against even attempting such a vast project. I respect those arguments, and I acknowledge the risks that painting on so broad a canvas necessarily entails. On the other hand, the many evident parallels in the empirical data from around the continent, including north of the Sahara (e.g., Cobham 1993; Hayes 2000; Mudimbe-Boyi 2002b; Ahmed and Kheir 2002; Jacob 2005; Inhorn 2005), are compelling. I am also persuaded by critical pan-Africanist theory to take the risk. Some African intellectuals have pointedly castigated petty nationalisms and postmodern dithering in certain streams of Africanist research that narrowly and artificially frame research questions (esp. Zeleza 2005, 2006–7; Mkandawire 2005). They call for sensitivity to the local within the broad framework of a continental liberation struggle. As Joseph Ki-Zerbo expresses it, "The strategic goal of African intellectuals should, therefore, be to forge a new nationalism wherein pan-Africanism will be an integral part, serving as a driving force and giving it meaning." Paraphrasing Kwame Nkrumah, he makes a convincing argument that "nationalism without pan-Africanism is meaningless and pan-Africanism without a liberation dimension is also an absurdity" (2005, 90; see also Mkandawire 2005, 2). Since the struggle for lgbti rights and gender transformation has moved to the continental scale, and since resistance to sexual rights often shares the same logic and vocabulary across the continent, a continentwide assessment of the scholarship on sexuality is warranted. This can serve as goad, and perhaps a guide, to the kind of close local investigations that are ultimately needed. It may offer insights into similar struggles against other invisibilities on a continental or even global scale such as, notably, the struggle for disability rights or for men's empowerment understood through a pro-feminist lens.[32]

Finally, two concepts introduced by anthropologist Michael Herzfeld have proven very helpful for teasing a sense of history from the silences and innuendo concerning nonnormative sexuality. "Cultural intimacy," first, refers to "those aspects of a cultural identity that are considered a source of external embarrassment but that nevertheless provide insiders with their assurance of common sociality." Herzfeld gives examples of "those alleged national traits — American folksiness, British 'muddling through,' Greek mercantile craftiness and sexual predation, or Israeli bluntness, to name just a few — that offer citizens a sense of defiant pride in the face of a more formal or official morality and, sometimes, of official disapproval too" (1997, 4). People, from common folk to intellectuals to bureaucrats and politicians, express or play with these "self-stereotypes" in complex, often ironic ways as part of their engagement with (or avoidance of) power, including resisting, sidling up to, and exercising power. J. Lorand Matory applies this analysis with effect in unraveling the construction of secrets around same-sex sexuality within trans-Atlantic (African and Afro-Brazilian) religion. Particularly fascinating and directly pertinent to the present study is Matory's demonstration of how homophobic portrayals of *candomblé* were deployed over the decades to promote feminist politics in North America, Brazilian nationalism, and antiracist performance among United States–based African scholars. Remarkably, as weak as the empirical evidence behind the various claims ever were, they took on a life of their own among Brazilian gays and lesbians (Matory 2005).

Herzfeld terms this process of self-stereotyping and linguistic play "social poetics" or "the analysis of essentialism in everyday life" (31). Where Herzfeld helpfully differentiates social poetics from Benedict Anderson's similar and widely used concept of "imagined community" is first, by applying it to different scales than the nation-state (in my application, Africa, African, and Africanist), and second, by emphasizing the dialectic between top-down and grassroots or between insider and outsider in promoting or subverting certain self-stereotypes. In other words, no one party has the power to impose self-stereotyping, but it emerges over time through alliances, marriages of convenience, expedience, and strategic silences. The concepts of African sexuality and heterosexual African AIDS appear to fit this model.

SOURCES, METHODS, AND LIMITATIONS

Charting the history of an idea that is often unspoken and unrecorded is inherently more difficult than uncovering evidence of human activity. I acknowledge that my principal sources leave significant gaps that often require extrapolation from scanty and geographically uneven evidence. One of the goals of the book is thus to appeal for further research that can start to fill the gaps with more empirically grounded data and analysis.

My main sources are published books and articles, principally in English but also some in French. These sources include descriptive accounts and original ethnographic or other research ranging from 1352 to 2007. Several hundred such accounts over five and a half centuries of writing about African gender and sexuality make some mention or allusion to same-sex sexuality, albeit often in as little as a fragment of a single sentence in an entire book. Published sources include memoirs and biographies of some of the authors of those accounts, plus secondary studies that draw on unpublished documents and oral interviews. I have not included in the reference list many hundreds of other scholarly publications and probably thousands of newspaper or other popular media articles that make no mention of same-sex sexuality, although this negative evidence is an important part of the research.

I have cast the search as widely as possible over the whole of Africa south of the Sahara, although, for historical reasons that will be discussed, the pertinent scholarship is far denser in southern Africa. My own closer familiarity with obscure and unpublished material in southern Africa acquired over several years of close archival research in Zimbabwe, South Africa, Lesotho, and Malawi may reinforce the impression of a bias toward that region, and an unwarranted extrapolation from it to the whole. I have tried to offset that bias in the historical material by drawing, where possible, on current debates elsewhere in Africa on Internet sources—above all, Behind the Mask—and through my personal electronic networks. Much of this material has been culled from the popular press or sociological research in different African countries. This in turn may at times create a presentist feel—little of the material from Nigeria predates the late 1990s, for example. Nonetheless, there are sufficient implicit histories in the contemporary material to warrant carefully qualified comparisons and analogies with southern Africa.

This is not to impose southern African experiences or models elsewhere but to suggest avenues for productive future research in the different subregions.

Far more problematic for an exercise in African history than this regional imbalance is that so few Africans contributed to the published record before the very recent past. African voices overwhelmingly appeared in the scholarship through the muffle of European, North American, and latterly white South African or Zimbabwean translators and interpreters. Men like Alfred Nzula, Jomo Kenyatta, and T. Adeoye Lambo did eventually acquire training in European scholarly methods and established profiles in their respective fields. For reasons to be discussed, however, African professionals' main contributions on this specific issue were commonly silence, derivative reiterations of received wisdom, romanticized portraits of so-called tribal heterosexuality, or active attempts to still research and speculation that might challenge the consensus. Virtually all the substantive, explicit, and original contributions to the research on same-sex sexuality thus continued to be done by cultural outsiders well into the 1990s, and in many cases remain so. The history of the idea that there is no homosexuality in Africa thus tends at times to read like an extended, albeit minor, footnote in European intellectual history.

To offset that enormous imbalance, and to pry out more direct African input into the discussion, I had to turn to sources that are not normally given much credence in the scientific or even historical scholarship—African fiction, plays, and videos. These sources provide a powerful countervailing African voice to the silence and denial that predominate in empiricist-minded scholarship. They cannot be taken as realistic in an empirical or objective sense. However, the ambiguities, nuances, and compromises that they often portray almost certainly convey, in a figurative or subjective sense, more realistic representations of society than dogmatic or ideological silence. African artists are inventive and manipulative, to be sure, but on this topic they may also be a more reliable guide than African scientists trained and immersed in homophobic or heterosexist European intellectual traditions. They also shed new light on the ways that European ideas about sexuality were refracted through African eyes.

To do this history properly requires much more. Oral testimony from African informants would go far to offset Eurocentric tendencies and assumptions in the published material, but I have not gathered such evidence in any remotely comprehensive manner. I have done some, however, in the form of face-to-face and e-mail interviews with key informants, conversations with academic colleagues and activists, and participant observation (for example, of annual general meetings and other gay rights activism). Reflection on my years as a teacher in boarding schools in Zimbabwe and Lesotho might be considered another form of participant observation. Still, I acknowledge that this aspect of the research is underdeveloped. An appropriately systematic level of oral history remains another project, which could involve, for example, interviewing specific authors and research assistants who wrote msm and wsw out of their publications or who translated research instruments and interviews in contentious ways. It could involve interviewing community and church leaders to explore specifically how and when those leaders established their knowledge and certainties about homosexuality. It could involve interviewing gay rights activists on specific strategic choices they made in their struggles or in downplaying their presence in public discourse (especially in the early days of HIV/AIDS).

Another pronounced bias in the sources is toward male-male sexuality. African women are largely invisible in much of the Africanist scholarship before the 1960s (and in some disciplines remain so even now). Disinterest in women and female sexuality is particularly evident and inexcusable in colonial-era ethnopsychology. But while women and gender have become staples of much Africanist scholarship and development-oriented literature since then, female sexuality continues to be decidedly underinvestigated or encrusted with assumption and moral judgment.[33] I have tried to balance the bias toward men in the published sources by highlighting the relatively sparse research or discussions of female-female sexuality. The androcentrism, however, is not always blameworthy. With respect to the chapter on HIV, notably, I accept the worldwide consensus that female-female sexuality does not represent a significant mode of transmission. There are huge issues of specific concern to wsw about HIV, and transmission of the virus can occur through some kinds of lesbianlike encounters. But the risk appears to be so much lower than male-male or male-female sexual intercourse that the disinterest by researchers and activists through the 1980s (the focus of my study) can probably be forgiven.

Finally, the HIV/AIDS crisis has created a fertile field for wild conspiracy theories and over-heated if not slanderous accusations. That makes it important to clarify in explicit terms what I am *not* going to do. I will not be suggesting that Africans as a group have a unique problem with keeping sexual secrets. On the contrary, I will be drawing attention to the myriad ways within the dominant discourse that different African cultures kept, winked at, or flaunted sexual secrets not unlike people elsewhere. I am also not going to dispute that the demographic most vulnerable to HIV in Africa south of the Sahara is young women who are infected by men through heterosexual intercourse. Hence, I do not propose that homosexuals, bisexuals, msm, or wsw constitute major vectors of HIV. All I will be saying is that the numbers of msm and wsw are bigger than commonly assumed and asserted, and that there are further indirect costs to denying their existence. In a context where many millions of people are infected, a revision of even only a percent or two upward translates from the assumed negligible into hundreds of thousands of citizens.

Leaving these people out of the picture is to seriously undermine the holistic or cross-sectoral approaches to HIV/AIDS that most people now agree are essential to tackling the disease. My goal here is not to position histories of individual lgbti, msm, wsw, or specific subcultures of nonnormative sexualities in the center of the picture. Rather, it is to focus on how and why they were left out of the picture in the first place, and so often continue to be. It aims at strengthening the argument in favor of a truly holistic and cross-sectoral approach to HIV and AIDS and other sexual health and human rights discussions.

～

The present volume follows influential ideas, silences, and presumptions about same-sex sexuality in Africa as they developed over time. Specifically, it asks how various forms of prejudice and presumption concerning sexuality infuse science and acquire a misleading authoritativeness that spread throughout other academic disciplines and "common sense." The book posits that there are parallels or synergies in research between more densely researched southern and anglophone Africa and the rest of Africa south of the Sahara that suggest possibly fruitful future research. It shows that compromising links can be demonstrated between colonial-era representations of African sexuality and early HIV/AIDS research. From those links, is it possible to draw lessons from history that might help us imagine more effective, less ideologically burdened interventions in the future?

Reflecting on my earlier work on the history of same-sex practices and subcultures mostly in Zimbabwe and South Africa, I have identified four bodies of scholarship and art that were especially influential in establishing, and then beginning to destabilize, the consensus about the supposed nonexistence or irrelevance of same-sex sexuality in Africa south of the Sahara. I then query each of these overlapping discourses in roughly chronological order of their appearance. I trace intellectual connections and, in some cases, personal relationships between authors promoting these ideas. I link their analyses of African sexuality to broader debates and trends in contemporary international scholarship and to the political economy of the times and places in which each discourse emerged as influential. I will not, however, claim a comprehensive expertise in each of these fields, nor do I intend to imply moral superiority over the work I critique. Each of the disciplines has grappled with and, I believe, has surmounted or is theoretically capable of surmounting the problems I point out. I nonetheless contend that it is salutary to be reminded of just how extreme, casual, and not very far away in time the racism, androcentrism, and homophobia could often be in even the most respectable scholarship on which we depend to address current pressing problems in health and social justice.

The new discipline of anthropology was established in the nineteenth century and developed in relationship to colonial exigencies and anticolonial critiques through the mid-twentieth. Early representations or intimations of same-sex sexuality in Africa got lost or suppressed as the field matured. Here I focus on vicissitudes in the appearance and disappearance of *homosexualism, uranism, Oscar Wilde-ism, unnatural vice,* and the many other terms inappropriately deployed in that field of enquiry. Most professional anthropologists came from Europe and North America and their findings (often little more than speculations) were heavily influenced by debates taking place in their home countries. A small number of African intellectuals added an affirming voice to these debates, but I argue that the majority, by their very silence, provided an important confirmation of the dominant colonial narrative.

Pursuing a similar analysis of ethnopsychiatry and other mental health sciences, one finds efforts in the 1930s and '40s to use Freudian methods in order to render an understanding of "the African mind," a term then commonly used as shorthand for Africans' decision-making processes about sexuality. Much of this "science" drew on the extant ethnography and direct advice from approving Christian missionaries and colonial officials. African initiatives were further coached by European psychiatrists for whom new evidence from Africa helped to strengthen their claims about the universality and intellectual respectability of the discipline back in Europe. The scholarship that emerged thus often served to consolidate deeply heterosexist understandings of sexuality. These in turn promoted racial, gender, and class identities that were expedient for the dominant colonial political and economic interests in both Africa and Europe at the time (white versus black, African versus Arab, savage versus civilized, gentleman versus working man, man versus woman, etc.).

As well as being often transparently self-serving, much of this discourse was arcane and jargonistic. Yet in at least one case—colonial psychology—it resonated into popular culture in a significant way. This was through a pseudo-Freudian interpretation of the early-nineteenth-century Zulu leader Shaka. A thread runs through the historiography of southern Africa from the

1920s that uses the notion of disturbed sexuality to "explain" Shaka's violent and ultimately self-destructive behavior. This psychohistory has in turn been used to justify various political claims both for and against apartheid and neo-colonialism elsewhere on the continent. In one of the many ironies I expose in this history, that same fundamentally homophobic and arguably racist thread has in recent years been picked up and co-opted by black gay males in Africa and North America. In that twist, Shaka emerges as emblematic of primordial, heroic black homosexuality.

The earliest epidemiological and other scientific studies of HIV/AIDS (or slim disease, as it was first known in Central Africa), tentatively raised, but very quickly dismissed, the possibility of male-male sexual transmission of HIV. Men who have sex with men but do not identify as gay or bisexual were hastily written out of the investigation, and science served once again to confirm the old ethnographic stereotypes as unchallengeable truths. Here I closely analyze the methods, unspoken assumptions, and language of the major research contributions at the onset of the epidemic in the leading English-medium scientific journals. The focus is on a short but critical moment in time, from 1982, when the first alert about the new disease was specifically directed to medical practitioners in Africa, up to 1988. In that year Ugandan and South African medical professionals with the backing of their respective governments adopted comprehensive—*except for msm*— strategies to contain HIV/AIDS. Today nonheterosexist research is being achieved under daunting circumstances, offering potential lessons for HIV/AIDS campaigns. It is beyond the scope of this study to consider the findings in depth, but I do include some discussion of the new research to underscore the point that it can be done. Africans will admit to and talk about same-sex sexualities when approached in sympathetic ways.

Throughout this entire period of an emerging hegemonic African sexuality, alternative evidence and representations were available but largely overlooked or dismissed. Subtle references to same-sex sexuality in African fiction often belied public claims of homophobic intolerance in African societies and in some cases even offered pointed critiques of Western stereotyping of African heterosexuality. African authors and filmmakers themselves began to destabilize the stereotypes—mainly from the 1970s but in increasingly explicit and gay-friendly terms since the early 1990s. The varied masculinities and femininities they describe underscore the irony of Western intellectual investment in maintaining the old stereotype. The irony is deepened by the fact that today in debates about sexual rights it is often African intellectuals citing Western sources who authenticate African customs and supposed family values that were absolutely and essentially intolerant of homosexualities.

These sources include, above all, Christian theologians who pepper their attempts to justify discrimination with a small number of verses from the Bible, with quotes from ancient European saints, and with selections from colonial ethnographies.

The irony that African theologians have taken up the cudgels against gay rights using carefully chosen Western sources has a bitter edge to it, and sometimes deeply dispiriting consequences. The resurgent rate of HIV infection in Uganda, for example, has been linked to an alliance of Christian fundamentalists in North America and Uganda pressing an abstinence campaign that has curtailed the supply of condoms in the country and that has propagated harmful stereotypes and silences concerning sexuality (H. Epstein 2005; Cohen and Tate 2005). The International Gay and Lesbian Human Rights Commission even alleges that American taxpayers through USAID have directly funded faith-based groups in that country which incite hatred against gays and lesbians.[34] But a positive side to the irony exists as well that I hope to steer the conclusion toward—notably, where the righteous wrath of some African Christian leaders condones or even demands family ostracism of gay and lesbian children, the Gays and Lesbians of Zimbabwe (GALZ) today places the highest priority in its counseling service on healing family rifts. Oral testimony from out lgbti in the African diaspora suggests that loyalty to family honor is one of the most compelling values they share.[35]

Finally, this history holds implications that extend far beyond the exegesis of dusty old texts or the politics of small solidarity groups. The history exposes an unsavory side to scholarship that presented itself as rigorously scientific. It shows that a seemingly small element in an ideological construct of identity can have big, long-term, insidious effects on culture and health. It also suggests potential constructive outcomes if awareness of history is incorporated into, for example, HIV/AIDS prevention and education campaigns or strategies to empower women and youth. If an African sexuality that denied Africans' full humanity, and still denies their rights to sexual knowledge and sexual health, can be made in the first place, then it can also be unmade.

This lesson is not intended simply to apply to activist struggles, but is aimed as well at colleague African and Africanist scholars across a range of disciplines. Social history, the history of women and gender, health and science studies, political history, cultural studies, and no doubt many other fields of enquiry could surely be enriched by careful attention to the subtleties of sexual meaning and tension hidden within the dominant discourses of African studies. Moreover, disinterring subaltern African perspectives on these issues can potentially enrich queer and other sexuality studies in the West, where ethnocentrism or tokenism toward African evidence remain evident. The hope is that researchers and activists working to end the stigmas and stereotypes that so clearly exacerbate HIV/AIDS worldwide might consider this little piece of the puzzle of the disease in Africa as they frame their research questions in the future.

2 ⤳ The Ethnography of African Straightness

ANTHROPOLOGISTS PLAYED A CENTRAL ROLE in documenting the diversity of human sexuality as it is understood and expressed in different cultures around the world. Scholars in many other disciplines, including my own of history, are often heavily dependent on their research. However, as Lyons and Lyons (2004), among others, have persuasively demonstrated, anthropologists at times "conscripted" select evidence and even fabricated "facts" about the people they studied in order to advance ideals and preferences concerning gender and sexuality in their own societies. By conjuring idealized or exoticized Natives, Primitives, and other Others, they helped to create an understanding of "normal" and "modern" by way of contrast and edification. In the process they created a body of purportedly empirical or scientific data that in retrospect we can see as deeply flawed and morally normative. In some cases the scholarship was complicit, indeed enthusiastically so, in the construction and maintenance of oppressive colonial structures. Among those structures were reified "tribes" with borders and chiefs, and policed male migrant labor systems that tore African families apart. Forms of indirect rule and native law or *indigenat* to police these systems froze patriarchal interpretations of custom into institutionalized law convenient to white settlers and capital. To one African critic, the ethnography of African cultures generated by European and North American anthropologists to establish the baseline of so-called traditional was so corrupted by its proximity to colonial power and consequently so "useless" in empirical terms that its only real value is for the light it sheds on how colonial structures were built and could function for so long (Owusu 1978). Villia Jefremovas (2002) goes even further by linking the ethnography of Rwanda to the consolidation of oppressive gender, ethnic, and class relations that ultimately led to genocide in that country.[1]

Owusu was much too harsh in his sweeping judgment, and even in the case of Rwanda there is much to respect in the work of anthropologists who pioneered in often extremely demanding circumstances. On the topic of sexuality, however, the critique is warranted to a significant degree. Most of the blame falls on lazy and exaggerated descriptions of exotic heterosexual rituals and attitudes (as pointed out by Bibeau 1991 and Fassin 1999, for example). In this chapter, however, I want to focus on the heterosexism of the ethnography. Specifically, the commonplace assumption or assertion as an unqualified fact that Africans south of the Sahara did not practice same-sex sexuality derived at least as much from a set of normative beliefs as from the cool scientific observation that many anthropologists claimed. From the vast generalizations of late-eighteenth- and nineteenth-century travelers to current studies of sexually transmitted diseases, sexuality, prisons, street children, masculinities, and more, the great weight of the ethnography expresses an opinion of what African sexuality should be like, rather than what it really is. It creates the impression that Africans are virtually unique in the world in the absence of, ignorance about, or intolerance toward exceptions to the heterosexual norm. It provides a scientific-sounding canon that gives authority to contemporary claims about the narrowness of what is traditional, authentic, and indigenous on the one hand, and what is deviant, nonexistent, modern, or exotic on the other. Because so many other disciplines rely on anthropology for their research starting point, this canon then gets amplified into all kinds of unexpected places and policy or research prescriptions. A reference to one or two scattered anthropological studies from around the continent is often all that is needed to justify noninterest or outright hostility to research on same-sex sexualities in Africa.[2]

But how trustworthy is that canon? Dynes (1983) first flagged homosexuality—and Aina (1991), bisexuality—in Africa as potentially important research questions hidden within the tacit consensus about African sexuality.[3] Murray and Roscoe (1998) then provided the first substantive corrective to the dominant view. They demonstrated key discrepancies in the documentary record dating as far back as the eighteenth century and right up to the present-day testimony of African gays and women who have sex with women. Their evidence did not propose a timeless, archetypal gay or lesbian in opposition to the older stereotype. Rather, the men and women who had same-sex sexual relations most often also continued to marry, have children, and to engage in heterosexual relationships as well. Whether they should properly be termed bisexual or queer or lgbti remains a matter of debate. But, following the publication of Murray and Roscoe's collection, and indeed several other important studies that appeared soon after, it could no longer reasonably be disputed that men who sometimes have sex with men but do not identify as gay or bisexual (msm), and women who sometimes have sex with women but do not identify as lesbian or bisexual (wsw) needed to be considered in studies or interventions around African sexualities, past and present. That msm and wsw are still regularly ignored in the literature on sexuality and sexual health thus becomes significant beyond the simple fact of their existence.

What remains to be done is to show specifically how and why the silences that helped define an essentially heterosexual Africanness were first achieved, changed over time, and were defended or contested. Those changes and contests offer insight into the complex relationship between professional scholars, colonial rulers, and subjects. They can also help us understand why some people today, including Africans who are otherwise sharply critical of colonialism, racism, and sexism, remain attracted to and defensive of colonial-era notions of unwavering African heterosexuality.

EARLY ACCOUNTS OF GENDER AND SEXUALITY

The first accounts of gender and sexuality in Africa by European travelers came from West Africa—Ibn Battuta's shocked description of female nakedness and the familiarity of Muslim women with their male friends in fourteenth-century Mali, for example, and various pronouncements by the Portuguese authorities on the relations between Portuguese seamen and their African hosts. In the sixteenth century, the Portuguese also produced a wealth of material on southern and eastern Africa, including Zimbabwe and Ethiopia. By the late nineteenth century they had been joined by travelers and traders from many different European countries who had created a substantial body of literature detailing many intimate aspects of life. While this mostly focused on societies along the coast, in some cases their accounts extended well into the African interior.[4]

These accounts tended to stress what they perceived as African women's subservience and easy sexual availability to men, Africans' lack of sexual modesty and guilt, the practice of polygyny, and the emphasis on fertility in African cultures. In retrospect it is clear that these accounts were frequently exaggerated, sensationalized, judgmental, and imbued with error stemming from naïveté or linguistic misunderstanding. As Beach (1980) points out, for example, early Portuguese descriptions of the advisors of the Mwene Mutapa (king; lit., master conqueror) as "women" reflected a literal translation of a word that the Karanga people used metaphorically. These early accounts nonetheless on the whole captured a basic truth: African societies tended to place an extremely high and prodigiously overdetermined value on heterosexual marriage and reproduction. Individual sexual desire was largely subsumed to the broad interests of the extended family or lineage. Those interests included reputation, political alliance, material production, spiritual health, and ritual protection of the natural environment. Yet people being people, individuals could and did sometimes veer from the preferred path through adolescence to fecund and loyal marriage. Whether this arose from individual sexual desire or curiosity, some physical disability, or metaphysical defect, it could generally be accommodated in ways that did not endanger the broad interests of kin. Hence, for example, the highly valued chastity of unmarried girls in many African societies could be preserved while at the same time allowing a limited outlet for adolescent sexual curiosity and desire through the custom of nonpenetrative (between-the-thighs) sex play. Hence also a wide range of fictive kinship relationships that assured family and lineage stability while allowing for idiosyncrasies and shortcomings of individual sexual behavior such as adultery, impotence, and celibacy.[5]

Same-sex exceptions to heterosexual norms and ideals were also noted in descriptive accounts of African societies from as early as the sixteenth century. These were usually couched in vague but strongly disparaging language. Sir Richard Burton's grand overview of world sexuality, for example, refers to a Portuguese document from 1558 that observed "unnatural damnation" (a euphemism for male-male sex) to be esteemed among the Kongo (1885, 246–47). Andrew Battell, who lived among the Imbangala (in modern-day Angola) in the 1590s, was similarly disapproving: "They are beastly in their living, for they have men in women's apparel, whom they keepe among their wives" (in Purchas 1905 [1613], 376). Jean Baptiste Labat, cribbing from an Italian explorer in the same region of Angola, also described a caste of crossdressing male diviners known as *chibados* or *quimbandas*. Their leader was "a shameless, impudent, lewd man . . . deceitful to the last, without honor. He dresses ordinarily as a woman and makes an honor of being called the Grandmother" (1998 [1732], 163).[6] Images of African polymorphous perversity and flexible gender systems along these lines then found their way into European middlebrow culture in the eighteenth century, notably in the ostensibly realistic novels by Castilhon (1993 [1769]) and Sade (1990 [1795]).

We need to be extremely cautious about taking these early accounts at face value. Moreover, little was said in them about the erotic content of same-sex relationships. Jumping ahead in time, however, research that specifically asked about this issue has established that the early passing condemnatory references contained a fundamental truth. Notwithstanding the many powerful forces conditioning people to heterosexual marriage, same-sex relationships existed in African societies with a wide variety of motives, practices, and emotions involved, including affection and fertility control. We have also learned that there was often a ritual or symbolic significance to, for example, anal penetration by one man of another. Like with incest, breaking a normally strong taboo could bring the taboo breaker into direct contact with powerful ancestral or other spirits. To perform anal intercourse with a male under proper conditions could thus bring good crops or hunting, protection from evil spirits, and greater virility in marriage. According to Günter Tessman (1998 [1921], 156), adult, married Pangwe men in the German colony of Kameroon understood mutual acts of sodomy not as an act of pleasure but as "wealth medicine." From elsewhere in Africa also come hints of African men who expressed same-sex practices in the idioms of traditional medicine or magic: chiefs who fortified their authority against political rivals, warriors who prepared for battle, boxers who steeled for their matches, and mine workers who sought protection from rockfalls or achieved a promotion and pay raise. The power of the medicine stemmed in part, and indeed was amplified by, the degree of the secrecy of the act. New research by lesbian anthropologists suggests that there were also unspoken erotic relationships between African women within the rubric of spirit mediumship or divination. All this was in addition to the kinds of same-sex sexual play, experimentation, "accidents," "relaxation," and love affairs between Africans that turn up periodically in documents throughout the colonial and apartheid eras.[7]

Between the early, obscure, and scandalized allusions, on the one hand, and contemporary queer scholarship, on the other, something happened. With rare exceptions, a more or less collective silence descended on the topic. That silence creates an impression of radical discontinuity between the present and near past, an apparent discontinuity that in turn is sometimes cited as proof that same-sex sexuality did not exist in Africa until introduced by whites in the colonial or even more recent periods. A close examination of the silence as it is affirmed in key texts, however, suggests that the major discontinuity was not in Africa at all, but in Europe and North America, whence came the authors of those texts. As a first step toward understanding the yawning gap in African ethnography on this issue, therefore, we need to consider factors in Europe and North America that may have affected the way that anthropologists and other social scientists saw, interpreted, and wrote up their African evidence.

Michel Foucault (1978) provides the starting point. He argues that the industrial and scientific revolutions of the late eighteenth and nineteenth centuries brought about a profound transformation in ideas about the nature of sexuality and the propriety of certain gender roles and identities. This change occurred as a result both of new scientific knowledge and of changing class structures. As many scholars have since richly detailed with specific reference to Europeans' and Americans' relations with non-Western societies in this period, the rising class of bourgeoisie in the industrializing countries promoted ideas in a language of scientific certitude that served their material interests. One of these ideas was the notion that broad types of people were by their very nature not only different but less suited to govern and to enjoy the economic and social privileges that the bourgeoisie were claiming for themselves. These racial and sexual Others also provided negative standards against which new social norms and ideals among the bourgeoisie could be affirmed—notably, respectable bourgeois against foppish aristocrat, black or native as opposed and inferior to white, and female or feminine as opposed and inferior to male and masculine.

One critical element in the emerging ideology was that unwavering heterosexual desire and self-control over all other sexual feeling or expression indicated a strength of moral character that was transferable to all other activities. Same-sex sexual relations had of course long been taboo—indeed, punishable by death in many cases—in Western European society. In the preindustrial era, however, such relations were understood as discrete acts of sin that could be atoned for or purged through prayer or mortification. In the emerging ideology, by contrast, sin gave way to the notion of homosexual character in which the discrete act implied a whole range of deep personality flaws. An array of scientific-sounding argument consolidated that character into a figure to be despised, shunned, and repressed (ideally, self-repressed) out of existence. Scientific homophobia in turn helped to consolidate a sex/gender system that emphasized virile masculinity and domestic femininity, both inextricably linked to physical anatomy. A reified dichotomy of gender roles and identities was then harnessed to the causes of the formation of a bourgeois class, more efficient exploitation of a disciplined industrial labor force, and nation or empire building. Sexual self-discipline extending to a rigorous prohibition against masturbation became a marker of the right to hold and exercise power.[8]

This emerging consensus about sexuality acknowledged that a small proportion of the population consisted of "real" or "inborn" homosexuals, probably consistent across time and cultures. Homosexuality was nonetheless anomalous to nature. It existed, and even flourished, only under certain unnatural—that is, human-influenced—conditions. Above all, the more decadent or lax the civilization in policing sexual discipline, the more widespread was the character and cultural flaw. Proponents of this view often cited the late stages of ancient

Rome and the Arab or Turkish empires both as a proof and as a harsh lesson: decadence leads to widespread homosexuality, which leads to effeminacy and pacifism among men. The latter ineluctably leads to military defeat and humiliation by more virile societies. This understanding of history implied that homosexuality could (indeed, should) be contained or eliminated through rigorous moral instruction, strict parenting, and state intervention when necessary to combat unnatural tendencies.

Africans figured significantly in the debates in Europe about nature versus civilization, and virile versus decadent. The prevailing prejudice was that Africans were uncivilized and close to nature. For a long time many Europeans actually considered Africans a distinct species, somewhere between animals and humans on the hierarchy of moral and mental fitness (Lyons and Lyons 2004). By definition this meant that they could neither be decadent nor exhibit social traits and behaviors that were assumed to come with a sophisticated level of culture. The emerging consensus on homosexuality thus required that Africans conform to the expectation of a supposedly natural heterosexuality and lack of sexual diversity (or even the "higher" emotions like love). This was precisely the view (or rather, the wishful thinking) of Edward Gibbon, the first to put this idea forth in print. Gibbon made the point in a passing footnote to his explanation of how "the primitive Romans were infected" with homosexuality by the more civilized Etruscans and Greeks (1909 [1896, 1781], 535, 537).

Gibbon had never been to Africa and knew virtually nothing about it, apparently not even extant accounts from Angola. But soon after him, someone who had actually traveled there brought the first authoritative seal of personal observation to the theory. The English explorer William Browne spent several years wandering about the Middle East and North Africa in the 1790s. In his account of those travels he noted simply that "paederasty" was rare in ostensibly primitive Sudan as compared to decadent western Asia (Browne 1806 [1799], 293).

The idea that Africans did not engage in same-sex sexual practices gained currency as the frontiers of European rule expanded into the interior. Christian missionaries and colonial officials at the forefront of that expansion contributed significantly through writings that portrayed a common, continentwide "savagery" or Rousseauesque primitiveness. These emphasized an African sexuality that was at once a formidable obstacle to their mission yet also conceivably mutable to the ideals of bourgeois European culture. The main obstacle to the mission in this view was Africans' barbarous lack of control over heterosexual instincts—an excess of natural virility. Indeed, the missionaries had their hands full challenging the array of what they regarded

as heterosexual immoralities in African societies, including polygyny, child be-
trothals, marriage by cattle, female genital cutting, widow inheritance, widow
cleansing, notions of female pollution, and so on. More secretive and presumably rare homosexual practices fell low on the list of priorities for railing
and reasoning against or even for making too close an enquiry. A comprehensive search through private correspondence or internal mission documents
may one day reveal private concerns, and it is possible that some missionaries purposefully self-censored out of concern for the sensitivities of their supporters in Europe.[9] The dominant tendency of complete silence on the topic,
however, suggests that old, powerful force of wishful thinking. The absence
of overt homosexual relationships may in fact have been missionaries' and administrators' one straw of hope for reshaping African sexuality toward their
ideal of the civilized. Harry H. Johnston offered a rare acknowledgment of
this when he claimed that the "vicious propensities" of the king of Buganda
"disgusted even his negro people," who rationally calculated that his example
might lead to "the disappearance in time of the Uganda race" (1904, 2:685).
Likewise, Sir Frederick Jackson, a colonial official reflecting on the first
decade of British rule over Kenya and Uganda, noted "the good sense of the
natives and their disgust" toward the bestial vices practiced by "Orientals"
(1930, 326). This, according to the prevailing scientific homophobia, was
one of the few unambiguously positive things to be said about African morals
and character.

Missionaries and early colonial officials consolidated their first impressions
when they compiled the first generation of African-language dictionaries.
There are hundreds of such dictionaries from the nineteenth century, and a
random survey will easily confirm this point. For the most part they simply
did not provide translations for words they considered obscene, while in some
cases they imposed crude and judgmental translations of words that erased
nuance in the indigenous usage. The first English translation of the Swahili
word *hanithi*, for instance (in 1882), renders it as "catamite" (from Latin, usually meaning a passive, boy homosexual partner), when in fact modern
studies suggest *hanithi* appears to derive from an Arabic word that connotes
cross-dressing, male prostitution, or "male homosexuality" in a more general
sense (Amory 1998, 74; Kuria 2005, 108). Driberg's translation of the Langa
word *Jo Apele* as "impotents" is another example where the men so described
appear by his own account to be something quite different, perhaps what
we would now call transwomen (Driberg 1923, 210). Also commonly used to
translate African words for ritual same-sex practices or gender-inverted roles
was the term "sodomite," even though the meaning of sodomy was then generally understood to include bestiality as well as male-male anal penetration

or even heterosexual debauchery. Another linguistic convention from the era that had a similar erasing or blurring effect was to switch to Latin or Greek when describing the intimate aspects of the lives of African subjects. While most public school–educated Britons and middle- to upper-class Europeans would still have understood the language in the late nineteenth century, over time the offending passage would have been passed over as meaningless to an increasing majority of readers. This clearly suited the interests of some of the authors. As Johnston put it in his ethnography of the peoples of modern-day Malawi, African behavior was sometimes simply too depraved "even to be expressed in obscure Latin" (1897, 409n1), a reference to their "vicious" tendencies, itself a euphemism for masturbation among boys. His informant was a European missionary.[10]

Efforts by colonial regimes to codify African customary law around gender and sexuality similarly showed scant interest in querying exceptions to Africans' heterosexual norms and ideals. Far from complicating the rhetoric of the civilizing mission and possibly involving themselves in all kinds of embarrassing and difficult disputes, officials typically prompted African informants to confirm the prevailing African-as-savage (close to nature, heterosexual) interpretation. Again, the case of Basutoland is instructive. Soon after it became a protectorate of the Cape Colony, a commission of enquiry was set up to find out what Sesotho custom said. Interviewing elderly Basotho men through an interpreter, the commissioners raised the issue of "unnatural crime" with two witnesses only. These two senior chiefs calmly assured the commissioners that such crime did not exist and hence had no punishment, which was duly accepted as incontrovertible fact (Cape Colony 1873, 40). In other cases where even that much direct testimony was not available or solicited, colonial magistrates simply applied their own logic and presumptions to fill in the gap. Why, for example, would African men and boys turn to each other for sexual release when African women and girls were so easily available for their enjoyment, including by thigh sex? By this reasoning, since there was no apparent need for same-sex sexuality in African societies, it should not have existed and therefore there was no need to upset sensitivities by even asking about it.[11]

Exceptions to this emerging consensus arose from those rare cases where male-male sexual behavior among Africans was so overt that it could not be blithely rationalized out of existence. In those cases, it tended to be construed as a consequence of Africans' contact with decadent outsiders, Arabs above all, whose sordid reputation in Orientalist discourse was already firmly entrenched (e.g., Burton 1885; Haberlandt 1998 [1899]). The most infamous instance in this regard was that of Mwanga, the *kabaka* (king) of the Baganda people

from 1884 to 1899. Missionary propaganda hinted that Mwanga had been corrupted toward bisexuality by his Muslim advisors at court, a moral danger that
culminated in the sexual abuse and martyrdom of numerous young Christian converts (Ashe 1970 [1889], 218; Johnston 1904, 2:685; Faupel 1965, 82).
Cureau (1915, 166), meanwhile, accounted for more mundane occurrences of
"homosexuality" in French territories by pointing to "Semites" coming
from the east and disreputable Europeans from the west. Ibrahim Fawzi, an
Egyptian soldier and administrator under British generals Gordon and
Kitchener in the Sudan, portrayed the sodomy he observed in the Sudan as
symbolic of the moral decay of Egypt's Turco-Circassian rulers. The Mahdist
revolt emerges from this trope as a legitimate, purifying, African response to
foreign immorality (Jacob 2005, 159). The unpublished commissions of enquiry
into "unnatural vice" among mine workers in the Johannesburg area in
1906 and 1907 added Chinese and Portuguese to the list of potential corrupting elements (Epprecht 2004; Harris 2004), while Frederick Jackson
(1930) lamented the behavior of Indians imported to construct the railway
in East Africa.

This is not to say that claims of exotic influences on African societies were
unalloyed Orientalist fabrications. On the contrary, the fact that Arabic- or
Persian-derived words for homoerotic relationships are widespread in Islamic
parts of Africa suggests at least a modicum of truth in the claim of cultural transmission on this issue.[12] That the theory of an exotic origin of same-sex sexuality became generalized to the whole of Africa, however, was definitely not the
result of careful research by missionaries or anyone else. The most authoritative statement of that theory in fact came from an unabashedly racist man with
only limited experience in Freetown, Dahomey, and on the Swahili coast—Sir
Richard Burton (1885).[13] His terminal essay to the *Arabian Nights* is a grand mus-
tering of prevailing conceits and snippets of evidence into a global theory of
sexual "perversion." It does not specifically refer to Africa at all, beyond declaring
that the so-called Negro parts of the continent lay on the outside of what Burton
called the Sotadic zone of the world (Swahilis and Somalis were, in this definition, not Negro). By this fantastical climatic/cultural zone Burton meant
those places where same-sex sexuality was supposedly tolerated if not widely
practiced or celebrated. Being outside the Sotadic zone meant that most
Africans shared with northern Europeans—also deemed outside the zone—an
ignorance or strong disapproval of same-sex sexuality. Unlike northern Europe,
however, Africa's assumed low level of cultural sophistication placed its in-
habitants at heightened risk of contagion by Sotadic zone enthusiasts.

Absurd as it may seem today, Burton's thesis proved popular and enduring. In retrospect this popularity was clearly not due so much to its empirical

accuracy but to how its subtext played to the conceits of his main audience: imperial-minded, bourgeois, and self-consciously virile Englishmen. The notion that sexually innocent, non-Sotadic Africans stood to be corrupted by decadent Portuguese and Arabs almost directly served the paternalistic vision of colonial and missionary interventions to protect Africa from those outsiders. Henri Alexandre Junod, the preeminent missionary voice on the issue from that era, came closest to making the connection explicit. Junod blamed the industrial and migrant-labor system in general, rather than naming specific foreigners, for giving rise to homosexual immorality among the Shangaan in the early twentieth century. However, his appeal to the British and South African governments to protect the morality of people who lived under Portuguese authority essentially confirmed the Burton argument (Junod 1962 [1916]). So obvious and commonsensical had that threat to Africans from morally corrupt outsiders become by the 1930s that government officials in some cases expressed amazement and disbelief when confronted with evidence to the contrary.[14]

Yet even as this narrative of primitive, natural, but vulnerable African heterosexuality was being constructed, a small number of anthropologists and other researchers who looked closely were finding evidence to contradict it. In their wanderings in Africa in the late nineteenth and early twentieth centuries, men such as J. Weeks, Ferdinand Karsch-Haack, Kurt Falk, Günter Tessman, Louis Tauxier, Adolphe Cureau, R. P. G. Hulstaert, and Melville Herskovits all reported forms of same-sex sexuality among Africans in rural settings, including, as noted above, male-male anal penetration for "wealth medicine" and female-female sexuality. It may be that some of these reports were made by men who were wrestling with confusion about their own personal sexuality, and the reports may have consequently been exaggerated for self-interested or self-justifying reasons. Bleys cites several German sources to suggest that Tessman, for example, was "attracted to men, more particularly African men whom he encountered during his ethnographic expedition in Cameroon" (Bleys 1995, 219). In most cases, however, the authors cast themselves unequivocally as seekers of scientific truth. The bold presentation of discomfiting facts allowed them to distance themselves from missionary bromides and noble-savage condescension. They painted African societies in more complex terms than before in order to stake a claim for the intellectual rigor of their new, secular, and still suspect discipline.

African evidence was particularly useful to those who wished to do battle against moralistic and xenophobic models of homosexual corruption in European society. Ferdinand Karsch-Haack, notably, drew on his findings among hunter-gatherers in Angola and Namibia to argue that they proved homoeroticism was not a condition of decadent civilization but a phenomenon innate to all humankind: "We should finally give up the fiction that Sodom and Gomorrah are only in Europe and that everywhere else holy customs reign. . . . The most unnatural vices, which we regard as the most recent ways of stimulation of an over civilized culture are practised there in the light of day, in the open, as common practice."[15] Tessman also used his evidence from Cameroun to suggest lessons for contemporary European audiences: "Punishment through temporal justice exists among no tribe, since no one feels harmed by homosexual relations" (Tessman 1998 [1921]; cited in Murray and Roscoe 1998, 156). At a time of an emerging cult of militarist and extremely homophobic masculinity in his home of Germany, this was a bold political point to make.

Karsch-Haack's seeming proof of inborn, universal homosexuality, and Tessman's and others' of unexpected sophistication in supposedly primitive societies, did not attract much attention among Africanists at the time. On the contrary, they were mostly overlooked, even by those who otherwise took a relatively positive or respectful view of African sexuality. The aforementioned references to same-sex phenomena or transvestism were thus generally not noted, let alone debated, even by authors who found analogous occurrences in their own studies. Isaac Schapera (1963 [1930]) offers a rare exception in this regard when he refers in passing to Falk (1925–26) in lieu of conducting his own enquiry into same-sex practices among the Khoisan in modern-day Botswana. But a subsequent collection that he edited (Schapera 1956 [1937]) is more typical for the discipline in this period. In that volume the contributors were keen to show their empathy as well as expertise for the various peoples they reported on, and to acknowledge indebtedness to the intellectual pioneers of the field. Out of respect for the latter, they cited the missionary-ethnographer Henri Alexandre Junod more times than any other scholar. But not one of the contributors mentioned Junod's findings on male-male sexual relations on the mines despite their direct pertinence to a central concern of the book (urbanization).

Another illuminating example of this marginalizing, trivializing, or containing discourse comes in an article by Percival Kirby entitled "A Secret Musical Instrument" (1942). Behind its anodyne title, a mystery of Africa's strange ways is unfolded and solved for the reader. A percussion instrument, not been seen by a European since 1694, turns up at an exhibition in Windhoek. The intrepid anthropologist goes far into the bush in search of its meaning. The "tribesmen" there are surprised and amazed to see the instrument but refuse to say more until the white women in the visiting party are withdrawn. A player is sent for but vigorous debate ensues. Who, really, could join in the song? Was it for men, women, or "hermaphrodites" (Kirby does not provide the source of this translation)? Kirby pursues the investigation by consulting his two main informants, both European. Finally, on the penultimate page of the article, he reveals the answer to the mystery: doctor and "sodomite" can play the *ekola*. Together they use the instrument and accompanying song to assist men so inclined to come out from their masculine gender role to a feminine one, apparently a permanent but only mildly stigmatizing condition. Conclusion: "It would appear that in the *ekola* we have an example of a ritual musical instrument of considerable antiquity, the true nature of which has hitherto remained unexplained, and the use of which has, in spite of the march of civilization, lingered on to the present time" (Kirby 1942, 350). In this backhanded way, Kirby suggests that Burton was wrong about savage sexuality but nevertheless right about the need for European colonialism, all without the least acknowledgment of the other pertinent studies from the region (viz., Karsch-Haack 1911, Falk 1998 [1923 and 1925–26], and perhaps Schapera 1963 [1930]).

Perhaps surprisingly, even the dubious genre of "sexology" that emerged in the middle colonial period also notably understated or denied the possibility of same-sex sexuality in Africa. Authors such as Bryk (1964 [1925]), X (1937), and Rachewiltz (1964), do not deserve respect for their methodology (mostly gossip and hearsay), apparent intention (to cater to a voyeuristic readership who preferred their pornography in a reputable disguise), or tone (often frankly racist, sexist, and homophobic). Nonetheless, they did catalogue a range of sexual behaviors (and indigenous African terms for them) that took place within the rubric of normal village life. By not including plausible evidence about same-sex sexuality in that catalogue, however, they contributed to erasing the issue from the realm of discussion. Rachewiltz (1964, 280), for instance, in a single chapter devoted to "sexual deviations" gives a single example of homosexuality that is not lifted from Bryk and X. This refers to an oasis in Libya. Bryk was even more definitive when he pronounced simply, "The abnormal in sexual life is despised in Africa" (1964 [1925], 230).

One reason for this lack of interest or acknowledgment may be that, according to the prevailing taxonomy of perversion, no "real" or "inborn" homosexuality was involved. On the contrary, the same-sex practices occasionally noted clearly did not impinge on highly valued marriage, reproduction, and gender roles or identities. The men and women who took partners of the same sex in fact were often adolescents or young adults self-consciously practicing for marital roles. In other cases they were properly married and reproductive adults who nonetheless took same-sex lovers for various reasons, including ritual protection of men's masculine dignity against "pollution" by women. Far from effeminizing the men, as the decadence paradigm would predict, male-male sex seemed to have had the opposite effect. Tauxier (1912, 569–70), for example, described how particularly beautiful young boys were groomed as *soronés* (pages) for the Mossi chiefs and other court dignitaries. Dressed as girls, they played the role of passive sex object on Fridays only, when elites were proscribed from touching the female flesh that they enjoyed for the rest of the week. Martin (1913) and Seligman and Seligman (1932) also mentioned age-differentiated homosexual relations among warriors in the powerful military state of Azande. Those warriors were often simultaneously the heads of large polygynous households. S. F. Nadel, writing about southern Sudan, even noted a bisexual polygamous marriage among the Nuba (a male husband with both a female wife and a male wife) and other "perverts." Not only did they not exhibit the traits of "real homosexuality" but they eventually graduated without social stigma to normal marriage (1947, 109, 285).

For the majority of anthropologists in the early decades of the 1900s, this evident lack of "real homosexuality" somehow proved that there was no need to investigate any further. In this view, Tessman, Falk, Nadel, Kirby, and others had simply recorded what amounted to a colorful but basically rather embarrassing and irrelevant native foible. Indeed, the one man who did substantively investigate it during his fieldwork in the 1930s did not see fit to publish his findings for nearly four decades (Evans-Pritchard 1970, 1971—see below). As for the relatively widely observed practice of woman-woman marriage, only a single speculative exception from Dahomey allowed for the possibility of an erotic element (Herskovits 1967 [1938], 340). Elsewhere, structural-functionalist explanations of the practice prevailed. These emphasized the role of woman-woman marriage in strengthening heterosexual kinship ties (that is, it provided heirs for widows by allowing them to have sexual intercourse without marriage, securing the lineage against potential claims by biological fathers). When girls obsessively helped each other stretch their labia majora, that too was interpreted as a functional service to future husbands (Chevrier n.d.).

A final tendency of note among the first generation of ethnographers was to lump various diverse forms of "perversion" or "aberration" together in a single sentence and then to make the most extreme claims about punishment, gathered, in most cases, from elderly male informants. A towering figure in the field from the 1930s put it this way in his summary of law and justice among all the Bantu-speaking peoples of South Africa. Citing himself and a handful of other studies, Isaac Schapera pronounced, "Incest, bestiality and other perverse sexual aberrations are similarly looked upon as ill-omened actions; and the people concerned are in most cases killed, often savagely"

(1956 [1937], 212). To C. K. Meek, Ibo girls who "donned a cloth like a male" (1934, 222) were sold into slavery along with other deviants of equivalent horror, such as girls who menstruated too early, twins, or breach-birth children. It appears that anthropologists who otherwise often implicitly admired Africans' tolerant, liberal-seeming attitude toward heterosexual sex education, and the relative sexual freedom or lack of guilt in African cultures, and who noted that cross-dressing rituals and the public transgression of norms under certain circumstances had a socially constructive role in village life, with rare exceptions were unable to credit Africans as capable of more than the crudest, dogmatic, and uniform hostility toward homosexualities.

Yet universalist claims about extreme intolerance of sexual diversity or gender variance clearly flew in the face of considerable other work. Numerous anthropologies from the 1930s onward, for example, took care to show how reluctant African societies were to impose extreme sanctions for criminal behaviors, especially the death penalty, in part out of anxiety about metaphysical consequences. Yet in this case, capital punishment was blithely asserted as a norm. Schapera simply ignored a dissenting view that he himself had previously cited (Falk, who had discussed evidence of same-sex sexuality and a tolerant attitude toward it among Bantu-speaking peoples as well as Khoisan). Likewise ignored in subsequent characterizations of West African societies as fiercely homophobic was Herskovits's finding that the punishments for homosexuality even among married men and women were "sly remarks and what is even more dreaded, deriding songs" (1932, 284). This suggests a powerful ideological blind spot at the heart of the discipline. That blind spot becomes even more striking in retrospect when seen against the growing evidence of new or "semicivilized" homosexualities that were emerging among Africans in urban contexts.

"CIVILIZED" VICE AND COLONIAL INSECURITIES

To the dismay and frustration of many anthropologists in this era, Africans did not stay still. They moved from timeless traditional to detribalized modern and from raw to semicivilized, in the parlance of the day. One manifestation of this flux was in new forms of same-sex sexuality among Africans that began to appear, and to be talked about on the margins of public debate, in the late 1890s and early 1900s. These included a male-male sexual relationship associated with industrialization and large-scale male migrant labor among Africans (so-called mine marriages, or *inkotshane*, in the case of southern Africa), military service (most notoriously in the "Bat d'Af" of French North and West Africa), and prison or criminal gang homosexuality (such as the so-called Ninevite system in the South African case).[16] In mine marriages, men took younger men or boys as servants and "wives" for the duration of their employment contracts. As Moodie (1988, 1994) and Harries (1990, 1994) explain, these temporary male-male marriages often served (and in fact were often self-consciously intended by the men themselves) to strengthen traditional marriage with women back in the rural areas. Boy wives allowed the men to avoid costly and potentially unhealthy relationships with female prostitutes in town (although mine husbands sometimes still went for those as well). Homosexual gangs and prison relationships were also usually construed as short-term expediency or a symbolic assertion of masculine power and identity in a context that otherwise crushed African men's sense of dignity. White officials suspected that a dangerously antiwhite, anticolonial, and antibourgeois ethic lay behind the homosexuality within these gangs (South Africa 1913, 236; Van Onselen 1984).

Publicity about such developments was potentially devastating to the companies that benefited from male migrant labor and colonial governments alike. What kind of civilizing mission was it that abetted "unnatural" and "odious" behaviors in the very people it was supposedly advancing? The damage in terms of public relations in Europe and in the voting population of the settler colonies and South Africa had to be contained particularly when, as in the case of alleged catamites among Chinese indentured laborers corrupting black workers in South Africa, the scandal could be leveraged for advantage by white workers and populist political parties.[17] The hushing was done by, for example, distracting attention from the scandal with noisy, repeated public campaigns against female prostitutes or (much scarier to white voters), Black Peril cases (McCulloch 2000). Small reforms in living and working conditions, plus discreet assurances to concerned missionaries or chiefs that everything possible was being done, also helped quiet rumors. Indeed, after an initial flurry of missionary indignation about mine wives in South Africa and Mozambique, even their public remonstrances fell silent in lieu of private sermons from the pulpit and in the mission schools.[18] Leland Bell, in his study of mental and social disorder in colonial Freetown, also unwittingly hints at a state campaign to suppress male prostitution around the port during World War II. This was apparently conducted in such opaque language that the real meaning would likely have escaped public attention at the time ("wharf rats," "mingling with the seamen," "threatened morals" — 1991, 105). Bell himself subsequently clearly did not notice a possible homosexual reference in this language.

Anthropologists, by and large, tacitly supported those efforts to suppress or contain the scandal. For example, to allay public fears that the practice of

mine marriage was spreading among African laborers, the government of
South Africa through the 1920s and '30s disingenuously maintained that it
was confined to Shangaan or VaThonga men from Mozambique. Supporting
this view was the massive ethnography of South African peoples built around
the photographs of Albert Duggan-Cronin in the 1930s. Henri-Philippe Junod,
the son of the very missionary who led the campaign against mine marriage
in the early 1900s, provides the only mention of "unnatural vice" in the entire multivolume collection in his chapter on the VaThonga (Junod 1935).
This was long after it was privately well known in official and missionary circles that many other ethnic groups were implicated and indeed that a common vocabulary concerning male-male sex had developed over a whole vast
region as far away as Malawi (Epprecht 2004). Another fairly glaring case of
collective professional aversion of eyes comes from Senegal. While the Wolof
either traditionally had a social category for men who did not fit sexual norms
(sometimes named *gor djigen* or "homosexual slave") or were anecdotally re-
puted by their neighbors and by European travelers to have been converted
to homosexuality over hundreds of years of commerce with the French and
Portuguese,[19] Niang and colleagues (2002, 2003) did not find a single anthropologist who studied the Wolof to have reported, commented on, or analyzed
the issue. Perhaps the ethnography took its cue in this from the former administrator in chief of French West Africa, Maurice Delafosse, who at the
heyday of the French *mission civilatrice* in the region emphatically asserted
how any deviation from nature was "extremely rare" among the black races
under his watch (Delafosse 1912, 92).

How to explain this reticence to investigate, or even to titillate, in the
pseudoscientific style of sexologists like Bryk, particularly when the issue was
already on the public record in some cases? In part it reflects an underlying
discomfort or disgust with the topic among anthropologists, stemming from
homophobic norms in Western European society. Across much of colonial
Africa, those norms were enshrined in laws that criminalized "unnatural offenses" and that meted out punishments ranging from many years in prison
or public flogging (or both) up to death (under Dutch and early British rule
at the Cape). Personal aversion is made evident in authors' choice of words
or analogies to allude to the behavior. Hence to the Belgian Gustaaf Hulstaert
(1938, 95) homosexuality was nothing less than "malice," while for others it
was a perversion on exact par with bestiality (e.g., Schapera 1956 [1937]). In
some cases, however, the authors hint not so much at their own homophobia
but at anxieties about their readers' sensitivities. In these cases it may have
been close social ties with colonial officials and missionaries, and the desire
to spare them embarrassment, that led to self-censorship. Moreover, the sex

itself was not necessarily the issue but rather the other behaviors that often attended the sexual relationship. In those places where same-sex sexuality was most visible to outsider observers and the state (mines, prisons, streets, criminal courts, ports, conscript armies, or police barracks), it was often accompanied by violence, abuse of power over children, extortion, alcohol abuse, and prostitution. These behaviors obviously reflected badly both on the men and boys involved and on the colonial system in general, the latter often being the anthropologists' major source of employment.

Africans' own denial, taboo, euphemism, insistence on respectful language, and "double-think" on the topic made turning a blind eye that much easier. Hints of this appear in passing over the decades in studies that focus both on rural and urbanized African populations. Monica Wilson, for example, who appended two short oral interviews about male homosexuality among the Nyakyusa of southwest Tanganyika, makes clear that her informants were breaking a profound code of secrecy by sharing their knowledge of these matters with her (1951, 196–97). Brian MacDermot also refers to his frustration in this respect when he saw a Nuer man dressed in women's clothes (and who he later learned was addressed as a woman and was married to another man). This was "so totally against what the Nuer had been telling me, that I questioned Doerdering [his translator] carefully, but this failed to produce any further explanation. Perhaps this goes to show how easily the people will accept the ruling of a prophet, or again *how easily their own rules can be changed should the gods be willing*" (1972, 119–20; emphasis mine). Thomas Beidelman, who mentions in a footnote that "a few men enjoyed homosexual relations" without compromising their marriages to women, remarks that it took him six years of living among the Kaguru before his informants entrusted him with this information (1997, 273n16).

Culturally Westernized African elites, with whom the anthropologists often worked closely and depended on for translation and networking, undoubtedly added to the effect.[20] Striving to appear respectable according to colonial standards, this most articulate group of Africans (usually men) reinforced the starting assumption that African dignity depended on the suppression of certain secrets deemed disreputable. Indeed, missionaries, white settlers, and colonial officials had often used crudely racist language to demean African integrity and to emasculate or effeminize African men. Anthropologists who felt empathy with "their tribes" may have been loath to be seen in that tradition, impugning their subjects with too close an enquiry into disapproved behaviors or implicitly compromised masculinity.

Very strong signals from Christian African intellectuals warning against racist or patronizing tendencies in European accounts of African sexual mores began to appear in print as early as the 1860s (esp. Edward Wilmot Blyden's attack on Burton, described by Richard Phillips 2006, 193). Phillips also draws attention to a Krio poem published in Freetown in 1907 that acknowledges and bemoans the moral corruption of African youth in town, which the author attributes not to African culture but to European influence. The publication of *The Bantu, Past and Present* by Silas Modiri Molema in 1920 was another important shot across the bow in this struggle. Molema was one of the first southern Africans to be fully qualified as a medical doctor, was a scion of the Protestant Tswana elite, and was a self-styled progressive who later became a prominent member of the African National Congress. He wrote primarily within the conventions of the missionary style, it seems, to a liberal-minded white audience. *The Bantu* is dedicated to Scotland and its "illustrious heroes," and throughout it Molema unambiguously embraces his Scottish teachers' hierarchy of barbarous, semicivilized, and civilized in reference to Africans. Yet he also roundly criticizes bigoted judgments by Europeans about African morality. Even in acknowledging the moral evils associated with too rapid urbanization, he castigates those who portrayed prostitution, alcohol abuse, theft, and other aspects of urban working-class life as innate to African culture.

Homosexuality is notably absent from Molema's list of the evils of "semicivilization." Whether this was due to his ignorance of such matters or to prudery is unclear. His more general point is nonetheless established: liberal-minded Europeans who ventured critical opinions about African sexuality did so at grave risk of inviting scorn and enmity from the most accomplished African intellectuals. The risk was high that even implicit offense such as might be taken by mention of African homosexualities could alienate reform-minded Europeans from their strongest African allies in any attempts to make colonialism more humane. It is thus difficult not to imagine that Isaac Schapera's subsequent selective account of the impact of migrant labor on Tswana morals (which makes no mention of male-male relationships) at least partially reflected his desire to tread lightly around an area of potential embarrassment to influential and respected Africans like Molema.

The very first African to be trained as a professional anthropologist illustrates this point even more clearly. Jomo Kenyatta studied at the London School of Economics in the 1930s under the mentorship of one of the preeminent figures in the field (Bronislaw Malinowski). His monograph on his own people, the Gikuyu, came out in 1939 to mixed reviews, in part because of its polemical tone. For example, he begins the book by mocking "professional friends of Africa" who might presume to contradict or qualify an authentic African interpretation of African tradition such as his (a photograph in the first edition has him posed in full warrior regalia). Then, during a long discussion of puberty, courtship, and marriage, he categorically denies the existence of same-sex sexuality in traditional Gikuyu society. His choice of language starkly limited future discussion, for who would want to suggest that Africans could be unnatural, abnormal, or irregular? "Any form of sexual intercourse other than the natural form, between men and women acting in a normal way, is out of the question. It is considered taboo even to have sexual intercourse with a woman in any position except the regular one, face to face" (1961 [1938], xviii, 159). Kenyatta supported the latter claim with that old colonial argument that homosexuality was "unnecessary" since the opportunity for heterosexual sexual play was so readily available, including for adolescents (162).

Gay Kenyans even today do not necessarily dispute, and in important ways corroborate, Kenyatta's claims about sexual taboo (e.g., Murray 1998; Mburu 2000; Kuria 2005). The Gikuyu quite possibly were at the far end of the spectrum of cultural attitudes toward these issues. What is significant here, however, is that the absolute power of the taboo was taken for granted by subsequent writers. The possibility that Africans could break taboos, and might have creative ways to deal with the consequences, was foreclosed by the authenticity and authoritative tone of the man who later became the first president of independent Kenya.

External forces were also at work that contributed to the gathering silence regarding same-sex sexuality in Africa in the 1940s to 1960s. As Lyons and Lyons (2004) argue in their overview of the history of sexuality studies in anthropology worldwide, the middle-to-late colonial period witnessed a generalized retreat from sexuality topics as anthropology sought to carve out a niche for itself as a "respectable" discipline within academe. In most cases this retreat was likely unconscious, reflecting an uncritical conformity with the dominant academic culture. In that culture, Politics, War, Economics, Kinship, and other obvious, big, male-dominated issues were identified as the sole legitimate areas of scholarly investigation. In other cases, however, the retreat was made under direct pressure from institutions and academic mentors who disapproved of what they considered salacious or marginal topics. Prudery and homophobia played a role here, but so did, as Price (2004) has demonstrated, the political paranoias of the Cold War era. Homophobia and biphobia were especially intense in that context. To publish something that showed too much interest in same-sex sexuality, or that did not cast it in a poor light, was thus a risky career move for professional scholars, particularly in the United States. There, anthropologists with too obvious a sense of social justice or with unusual sexual habits were specifically targeted for surveillance, blackmail, and manipulation by the Federal Bureau of Investigation.

Price notes at least one such incident pertinent to African studies in which personal slanders secretly passed on to the FBI affected a scholar's career (2004, 231). That scholar was Ruth Landes, who in 1940 had published an article on homosexuality in the *candomblé* cult in Brazil. Landes (1940), and others subsequently, had linked candomblé to Yoruba slaves brought to Brazil, implying a tradition of male-male sexuality imported from and likely still present in Nigeria. Melville Herskovits, the dean of African studies in the United States, not only secretly cast aspersions on Landes's integrity to the FBI but also publicly denounced her in misogynist terms.[21] Given that Herskovits himself had earlier posited the existence of same-sex sexuality in Nigeria and Dahomey, this hostility to Landes as a researcher suggests an opportunistic homophobia on his part in keeping with the political paranoias of wartime and postwar America.

A quixotic attempt by the South African government to consolidate African tribal identities in the 1950s and '60s may also have fueled the impression that homosexuality among Africans was a new manifestation in that country, imported or invented by whites. This endeavor was a series of new dictionaries that aimed to replace the old missionary translations and to draw clearer ethnic and linguistic distinctions between Africans to correspond with newly designated homelands, or bantustans. Headed by P. J. Joubert of the South African Broadcasting Corporation, the apartheid linguists offered innovative translations of *homosexuality, homosexualist, lesbian,* and similar terms that earlier dictionaries had eschewed. These translations were so forced, however, that no native speaker would easily recognize their meaning. *Homosexuality* in Zulu, for example, was rendered as *ukubhebhana kwababulili-bunye* (lit., two people of the same sex being intimate with each other (Joubert and Khubheka 1975, 158).[22] Tsonga was even more convoluted: *ku va ni rinavelo ra rimbewu leri a nga na rona* (Joubert and Nkuzana 1975a, 135).[23] To anyone who was actually paying attention to these clumsy shenanigans of apartheid ideologues, it would have provided proof that Europeans were indeed trying to impose homosexuality on Africans.

Tellingly, Joubert and his colleagues somehow managed to miss the fact that the Tsonga actually did have an indigenous word for "servant" that could also mean "boy- or mine-wife." *Bukhontxana* had been in common usage among working-class Tsonga men and boys since at least the early 1900s (H. A. Junod 1962; Harries 1994). How did Joubert overlook it, particularly as it had been adopted into many other languages in the region? We can only speculate. Perhaps his middle-class informants did not know the word. It is also possible that Joubert knew of it but found the negative connotations (pedophilia, child abuse, sexual slavery) too upsetting or politically charged to include. Or his informants may have purposely suppressed the word by claiming that it had been invented by whites to humiliate and discredit Tsonga culture. Similar claims can commonly be heard in the region today. A traditional healer in Zimbabwe, for example, has been quoted affirming that the derivative term in Shona (*ngochani*), had been coined by white settlers in reference to African prisoners. This alleged European provenance of the word then ostensibly proved that homosexuality did not exist in African culture (Weinstock 1996, 40).[24]

Throughout all these years, anthropology in Africa remained overwhelmingly predominated by Europeans and North Americans (and still is in many specific instances). A small cadre of professional African anthropologists did sometimes bring sophisticated insider perspectives that have contributed to our understanding of the subtleties and diversity of African cultures. On the issue of same-sex sexuality, however, there was typically a determined silence or defensiveness in tone that tended de facto to strongly confirm the old Burton-Kenyatta definitiveness. Silence and timidity extended across the middle decades of the twentieth century, even to those with radical inclinations. The Soviet-trained polemicist Alfred Nzula, for example, in an otherwise blistering attack on colonial rule and racial capitalism in the 1930s, could not bring himself to be more explicit about the effects of male-only hostels than to hint, "Workers do not sleep in separate beds in the compound" (Nzula, Potekhin, and Zusmanovich 1979 [1933], 81). Owusu in the 1970s entirely neglected gender, let alone sexuality, in his scathing critique of Western anthropology in Africa (1978). And African anthropologists in this period who did venture into discussions of gender and sexuality consolidated the pattern in some cases by romanticizing African heterosexuality. Anicet Kashamura's bucolic description of Tutsi sexuality (1973, back cover), commissioned by UNESCO, is a telling case. Kashamura was explicitly aiming at the "decolonisation of human sciences" in Africa and toward that end had harsh words for foreign researchers who imposed their prudish moral values on African societies. Yet other than fond memories of his own sexual coming of age, one of his main sources was Boris de Rachewiltz (1964), a man whose sweeping overview of "Black Eros" had almost nothing to say about the Tutsi and carries low credibility as serious scholarship. Kashamura meanwhile simply ignored the Belgian anthropologist who had found homosexuality to be "common" and "widespread" among both Tutsi and Hutu youth (Maquet 1961, 77–78). And, although acknowledging that girls taught each other to masturbate, he construed this only as preparing the girls for an orgasm-filled life with future male lovers (Kashamura 1973, 70–73).

Taken all together, this wide combination of factors produced a situation where discretion typically got the better of valor. As David Coplan frankly admitted when finally breaking the silence on male-male sexual relationships among Basotho mineworkers, "some of our colleagues would rather this aspect of migrant life be left unexamined" (1994, 137). The ability and courage to break the silence was made possible by the rise of the gay rights movement in the West, by the emergence of poststructuralist, feminist, and queer critiques of respectable ethnographic traditions, and, belatedly, by the appearance of a proudly out pan-Africanist gay rights movement.

GAY RIGHTS TO QUEER ANTHROPOLOGY

If the term *homosexuality* had all but disappeared in Africanist ethnography by the 1960s, times were already beginning to change in the wider world. This change included the decriminalization and destigmatization of homosexuality in law, psychiatry, and popular culture in the West. Destigmatization afforded the topic tenuous legitimacy as a research question across a range of social sciences. That question produced some unexpected findings when raised in Africa. Tanner (1969, 302), for example, was the first scholar to mention male-male sex in an African prison. His analysis remained largely captive to the old stereotype of homosexuality as essentially Other to presumably Real Africa (that is, done by the Arab and Somali prisoners in the prison he studied). His passing remarks about local Ugandan participants in homosexual relationships, however, actually contradicted that stereotype. Another striking piece of research from this time came from revolutionary Guinée, where French psychologist Pierre Hanry carried out the first self-consciously scientific study of same-sex practices among African youth. No less than 17 percent of his high school boy informants admitted to having participated in homosexual relations—not for money or because of rape, but for the experience and, presumably, for fun (Hanry 1970, 86). This and other findings pertaining to young men's and women's sexuality were so far out of line with prevailing stereotypes that they led Hanry to recommend radical changes to the sex education curriculum.

Political decolonization in this period removed one of the stumbling blocks to such enquiry. It also opened the door to trenchant self-reflection about the relationship between anthropology and colonial rule. An indication of that reflection is the growing number of anthropologists who revisited data they had previously ignored or suppressed. Evans-Pritchard's observations and explanations of "sexual inversion" (meaning same-sex relationships) among men and women in Azande provide perhaps the best known such case. Although he had done the research in the 1930s, he did not see fit to publish it until just before his death (1970, 1971). By that time, practices that were already said to have become shameful under the gaze of missionary and colonial regimes in the 1930s were presumably safely moribund. Similarly, Carlos Estermann, drawing on his observations as a Catholic priest in Angola in the 1920s through 1940s, published his findings on *kimbandas* (that is, the *chibados* or *quimbandas* of much earlier accounts) among the Kwanyama only after Angola gained its independence from Portugal (1976, 196–97).

Two articles by John Blacking (1959, 1978) neatly illustrate the shift to reevaluate earlier research. In both Blacking describes and analyzes a fictive marital relationship between Venda girls that he uncovered at high schools in 1950s South Africa. And in both articles the lesbianlike content of the relationships under study is thoroughly concealed by utterly innocuous titles. In the first, moreover, Blacking explicitly denies that the relationship involved sex play or was actively homosexual, despite noting that the girls "may sleep together under the same blanket as 'husband' and 'wife'" (1959, 157). In the later article, by contrast, he concedes that the girls "enjoyed intimate physical contact" extending to kissing, petting, and the use of home-fashioned dildos with each other (1978, 109). Did the girls' actual behavior change in the intervening years or was Blacking simply being more forthright? Gay (1985), who found a similar, well-established relationship among Basotho girls in the 1970s, suggests the latter.

The still tentative nature of most references to homosexuality in the early 1970s is reflected in the very cautious language that anthropologists employed. Among the first to venture into the sphere of controversy was Alan Merriam (1971, 94–95), who compared the *kitesha* role he found among the Basongye to the well-known *berdache* among American Indians, a conservative analogy reinforced by Merriam's opinion—contrary to the strong view of one of his Basongye informants—that no sex was involved. Christopher Hallpike (1972, 151), also writing on the cusp of anthropology's definitive break with its colonialist past, is another tellingly coy example of raising the issue. He noted four distinct words for "effeminate men" among the Konso of southern Ethiopia (suggesting that those men also had distinct words for the "normal men" who came to them for sex). While he singled out the term *sagoda* to mean a man known to play the passive role in sodomy, he wondered about the others: "I am strongly inclined to think that it [sodomy] is not confined to relations with *sagoda*."

Where the transfer of political power from whites to blacks was stalled, as in South Africa and in the self-declared Republic of Rhodesia, new research in the 1970s began to broach homosexuality in bolder terms. Partly this was as a strategy by politically left-leaning and antiracist scholars and activists seeking to sharpen the critique of colonialism, apartheid, and capitalism. When

South African church leaders began openly debating how to deal with mine marriage in 1970, for example, they largely blamed the phenomenon on the apartheid regime (Berglund 1970, 44). Charles Van Onselen, in a seminal study of African migrant labor in colonial Rhodesia, also argued from a Marxist perspective that male-male sexuality and bestiality in the mine compounds had been tacitly condoned and exploited by the mine companies from as early as the 1910s and 1920s (1976, 174–75, 307). In subsequent studies he characterized homosexual criminal gangs in early-twentieth-century Johannesburg as "*anti-social* bandits" on account of their violence and homosexual practices, again derived from and exposing the dehumanizing conditions of racial capitalism (Van Onselen 1982, 195, emphasis in the original. See also Van Onselen 1984).

There is nothing to suggest that this new interest in uncovering homosexualities in Africa could be related to the sexual orientation of the researchers themselves or their desire to use African evidence to promote gay liberation in the West. On the contrary, the most openly gay anthropologist in this period had almost nothing to say about homosexuality in his two most famous books. Colin M. Turnbull actually enjoyed an affair with his main Mbuti assistant (in 1957) and subsequently traveled to the field with his long-term African American lover, Joe Towles (who also became an anthropologist, after studying at Makerere University). Turnbull alludes to none of this in his scholarship, which was only revealed posthumously in his diaries (Grinker 2000, 203–4). While he was quite controversial for his unabashed lack of objectivity and the almost Manichean contrasts he drew between cultures he admired and those he did not, on this topic Turnbull basically conformed to the dominant tendencies in the ethnography and indeed may even have pandered to homophobic sentiments. His single reference to desultory mutual masturbation among Ik young men was clearly intended to buttress his harshly negative portrayal of those people (Turnbull 1972, 254).[25]

The most common response to such material was simply to ignore it. In other cases, intrusions of historical or sociological evidence about same-sex sexuality prompted an actively defensive reaction by anthropologists determined to uphold the heterosexual reputation of "his" or "her" people. Eileen Jensen Krige published an article, for example, whose categorical language sought to shut down speculation that there might be a sexual element in the famous woman-woman marriages of the Lovedu rain queen (1974, 34). Ifi Amadiume made an even stronger intervention in that respect when she lambasted African American lesbians for daring to co-opt woman-woman marriage to their political agenda (1987, 7–9). The language was strong enough ("prejudiced," "offensive," "totally removed from, and alien to the concerns of the mass of African women," "shocking"), and Amadiume's profile as an award-winning Nigerian woman was impressive enough, to be daunting. More than a decade passed before Western feminists or queer scholars dared to challenge her gatekeeping in print (esp. Kendall 1998, 238).

Van Onselen's history of migrant labor in colonial Zimbabwe also elicited a defensive response from a leading anthropologist of the Shona people, Michael Gelfand. This was a small (two-page) but significant intervention in that it was subsequently picked up by medical researchers to justify not pursuing research on male-male transmission of HIV in South Africa (see chapter 5). Although Van Onselen had placed the responsibility for the appearance of homosexual relationships and bestiality primarily on the European mine owners (who created the situation) and impoverished migrants from Malawi (who, superexploited, had no means to acquire female wives or prostitutes), Gelfand clearly felt compelled to protect "his" people from slur by association. The methodology of his research does not give confidence in his impartiality, particularly when one bears in mind that he conducted it during the height of violence in the struggle by black Zimbabweans to overthrow white rule. Gelfand (a white man) first interviewed four senior male Shona chiefs. He also studied the written transcripts of some of their native court cases (apparently unaware that homosexual crimes were normally handled in the parallel system of district courts). Not too surprisingly, he found homosexuality to be "rare" (Gelfand 1979, 202). A subsequent investigation involving interviews with fifteen male chiefs and a Shona colleague at the university found, "None was able to confirm the existence of either homosexuality or lesbianism" (Gelfand 1985, 137).

Gelfand's main intention with this uncharacteristically weak research was probably political in the sense of seeking to demonstrate solidarity between white liberals such as himself and moderate African elites at a time of intense struggle against institutionalized racism. J. Lorand Matory, drawing on the insights of Michael Herzfeld (1997), has used the term *nationalist allegory* to describe this kind of tacit collusion between foreign anthropologists and local nationalists. He illustrates the concept with cases from Brazil and Nigeria, the latter focusing on the changing ways that secretive aspects of the *orisa* religion among the Yoruba has been treated in the literature. Ever since Landes (1940), there had been suspicions that the homoerotic elements of Brazil's candomblé religion had their origins among the Yoruba, from whom many black Brazilians are descended. In trying to trace this link, Matory came across a respected Yoruba art historian who had twice personally witnessed a ritual act of anal penetration by one *orisa adé* (priest) upon another. What was of interest to Matory was not how common the practice was, or whether it had meaning to the men as a sensual or homosexual experience. Rather, the key issue was that a scholarly witness chose not to publish his dramatic observations. Matory attributed this self-censorship to "cultural intimacy," that is, the shared, albeit unspoken, desire among nationalist-minded elites to repress certain facts about national culture that could be construed as embarrassing in light of an imputed homophobic colonial or international gaze (Matory 2005, 333–34n47).

Postcolonial conditions, including economic distress, politically unrepresentative governments, and a new generation of bossy Westerners, added pressures to corral Africans into a reassuring nationalist allegory of exclusive heterosexuality. As noted above, this involved both rosy generalizations about sexually healthy and "normal" cultural traditions and unsubtle warnings against the pursuit of queer research questions. Homophobic scapegoating and intensified police or social repression were also widely reported from around Africa in connection to the economic and political malaise of the postcolonial era.[26] Despite this homophobia (or perhaps partly motivated by it) a new generation of African anthropologists began to produce work in the late 1970s that tentatively conceded and tried to explain same-sex sexuality in customary terms, especially as it appeared in cases of spirit possession. Harriet Ngubane (1977) and Wallace Bozongwana (1983), notably, identified some traditional healers among the Zulu and Ndebele as bisexual, homosexual, or transvestite. Additionally, small social spheres and informal networks of blacks who self-imagined and identified through the imagery of international gay life or gay liberation had begun to appear in major African cities as early as the 1970s (e.g., Pape and Vidal 1984, on Abidjan). Drawn into political activism by the liberation movement in southern Africa, by state- and church-sanctioned homophobia, and by the struggle against HIV and AIDS, a small number of Africans began to voice explicit challenges to traditional cultures of discretion (closets), which trickled into public debate beginning in South Africa in the mid-1980s.[27]

Western partisans of such gay rights activism turned to the existing historical and ethnographic evidence as a potential ally to be cultivated and coaxed into service. This was not always an easy or comfortable alliance. On the contrary, the first such interventions tended to be naive about the history of anthropology and colonialism. As such, they often treated the sources uncritically and threw due caution to the wind with regard to translation and context. Attempts to plug Africa into a global queer theory on the basis of such patchy evidence were consequently not always very successful or convincing. Thus, while Dynes (1983), Aina (1991), and Rushing (1995) raised valid questions about hidden bisexuality in Africa, they undermined their arguments by fail-

ing to offer significant new empirical evidence and by citing among their
sources unabashed racists and imperialists without providing appropriate context. Herdt (1997) also made important observations about same-sex sexuality in
Africa but, by generalizing about the whole of the continent from only four,
extremely diverse empirical studies, he loses credibility to an Africanist audience. Those sources are, to say the least, belabored—Herdt's summary of
Evans-Pritchard's famous article on the Azande (1970) is almost longer than
the original article. Both Bleys (1995) and Vangroenweghe (2000), meanwhile,
in several cases stretched the meaning of homosexuality so far in their reading
of scattered enigmatic and euphemistic accounts that a determined critic
could easily call the whole analysis into question.[28]

Yet for all its faults, the early queer or queer-influenced scholarship nevertheless made crucial contributions. Perhaps the biggest was to confound the
lingering Victorian-era assumption that same-sex sexuality somehow endan-
gered hegemonic heteropatriarchal gender roles and identities (effeminizing
men and masculinizing women and leading to the fall of civilization as we
know it). Judith Gay was among the first to show how wrong that paradigm
was and, indeed, that the exact opposite applied in her close study of the
fictive "mummy-baby" relationship she described among Basotho girls (1985).
Gay found that the girls shared enough physical intimacy to appear lesbianlike by Western standards of the erotic. But the mummy-baby relationship actually enabled successful and safer heterosexual dating by providing a relatively
safe way for the girls to practice and negotiate new notions of romantic love
and sexual foreplay. The girls themselves valued lesbianlike relationships
with heterosexual marriage in mind. Gay also showed that these lesbianlike
relationships sometimes continued beyond adolescence, where they helped
stabilize heterosexual marriages under severe stress by long-term male absence. Gay's seminal contribution was that she made the effort to ask the young
women directly about their views rather than extrapolating from European
models of "real" versus situational homosexuality.

Similar seeming contradictions emerged from studies of male-male sexuality, including Donald Donham's analysis of the *ashtime* role (or gender
identity) in Maale society of southern Ethiopia (1990). Ashtime (male
"transvestites" in Donham's translation) performed domestic labor and ritual
functions in the king's court. One of the latter roles, apparently, was to enable
the king and other men to avoid the supposed pollution of having sex with
women just before a major religious ceremony. The king, as "the male principle incarnate," had to be protected from even the merest whiff of female
sexuality at key moments in the ritual life of the nation. For men to sleep
with ashtime at those times was thus a means for them to help preserve the

symbolic, heterosexually virility of the head of the nation. In no way was penetrating an ashtime regarded as homosexual, bisexual, or unmanly. Again, what set this study apart from earlier passing references to cultural quirks, is that Donham devoted time to the analysis and linked it to closely theorized consideration of the social construction of gender identities.

Studies conducted by expatriate researchers were inevitably occluded by at least one and often more translations, as well as the heavy cultural and political baggage that the different interlocutors brought to the meaning of *homosexuality, transvestite, lesbian,* and so forth. A critical turning point in the history of African sexuality studies therefore came when African gays and lesbians themselves first began to speak directly to academic audiences about their experiences and perspectives. At first this primarily involved specific "coming out" stories, such as Nkoli (1994), GALZ (1995), Mburu (2000), as well as individuals described in Ndatshe (1993), Sibuyi (1993), Brooks and Bocahut (1998), and Donham (1998). There were also initiatives to theorize specifically black gay perspectives. Zackie Achmat (1993) offered a powerfully argued, erotically charged critique of white scholars (like Van Onselen) who suppressed or gave a functionalist spin to evidence of male-male desire among African men in their analyses. Achmat urged a new generation of scholars not to fear homophobic or heterosexist allegories about African identity, but to boldly seek evidence of the diversity of sensual desire among Africans as they might among any other group of people in the world. African feminists such as Zinanga (1996) and Nfah-Abbenyi (1997b), while not identifying as lesbian, also called for research that would challenge heterosexist and androcentric representations of African sexuality.

Over the following decade to the present this has resulted in a rich new queer anthropology of sexuality in Africa, often harking back to Foucault for inspiration but far more attentive to the subtleties of race and female sexuality than Foucault ever was. Njinge and Alberton (2002), for example, examined the lives of three female *sangomas* (traditional healers) and their female wives in black townships in South Africa, finally corroborating Herskovits's 1938 speculation about the theoretical possibility that woman-woman marriages could be sexual. Morgan and Wieringa (2005) have amply extended that confirmation and add new research into contemporary butch, tommy boy, and other lesbianlike relations among African women. This book is methodologically interesting as well. The editors (white, Western-trained anthropologists) recruited seven African women from around southern and eastern Africa for training in oral research methods and awareness of female-female sexuality issues. Those women, most of whom identified as lesbian or bisexual, then went back to their home countries, found women who were in sexual or conjugal relationships with other women, and interviewed them. The result is direct testimony from several dozen women from diverse backgrounds (urban, rural, middle-class, peasant, traditional healer, mixed race and more) from places not normally associated with the gay rights movement in Africa, including Swaziland, Uganda, Kenya, and Tanzania.

Much of the new anthropology has thoroughly and dramatically destabilized both the African-as-incorrigibly-lusty-heterosexual and the tired categories of heterosexual, bisexual, and homosexual. Gaudio (1998), for example, offers a sensitive analysis of nuances in meaning of male-male sex among the Hausa, including the unexpected "male lesbians." Kendall (1998) and Lockhart (2002) show how women and male street children may engage in same-sex relationships yet deny to themselves that these are homosexual (indeed, in Lockhart's case, strongly homophobic attitudes among the boys he studied actually led them to engage in high risk homosexual practices). Amanda Lock Swarr (Swarr 2004, forthcoming; Swarr and Nagar 2004) reveal complexities and conflict within same-sex subcultures, including tensions regarding self-identified straight or normal African women who exploit lesbians for sex.

The interviews in McLean and Ngcobo (1994), however, published as part of a rich collection of divergent voices from lgbti people in South Africa, remain among the most striking testimonies to the diversity of relationships and identities that formerly were subsumed within old silences and categories. McLean and Ngcobo's informants were black, female-identified, transgender men in Johannesburg known as *skesanas*. They charted a complex typology of male-male sexual identities, including *mapantsula* (supermacho gangster types who "accidentally" have sex with the skesanas), *injongas* (men who have sex in the active role with passive-role skesanas yet who claim to be heterosexual, even though in some cases they were formerly skesanas), and *imbubes* (men who have sex with skesanas and who claim to be heterosexual but secretly enjoy being penetrated. But then, what skesana would agree to take the active role with an imbube? Implicit in the imbube role were skesanas or perhaps injongas who secretly enjoyed penetrating a male-identified person). A skesana who never graduates to become an injonga may be a "real homosexual," also known as an *istabane*. "Chris" explained some of the difficulties: "I am in a relationship with a *skesana*. His name is Sello. I am an *injonga*, but my real secret is that I am an *imbube*" (McLean and Ngcobo 1994, 168). As for the sex itself, these highly sexually active young men did not consider mutual masturbation to be sex. Older men and injongas often saw even anal penetration as nothing more than play, joking, or an obligation due to them.

Skesanas are part of a specific scene in one specific city, one of Africa's biggest and most cosmopolitan. They do not tell us much about Africa as a whole. However, a scattering of studies from other urban centers shows that Johannesburg was not alone in having enabled a scene, or "milieu," to develop where men have sex with men in a variety of roles—Abidjan, Dakar, Mombasa, Kano, and more. Indeed, Niang and colleagues report a conversation with an msm in Senegal that closely echoes Chris' story above. After distinguishing between the traditional Wolof term for homosexual (or "man-woman"—*gor jigeen*), "boys' men," "gentlemen," "*yoos*" and "*ibbis*," the informant confesses: "In my case, I was exclusively *Yoos* at the beginning, until one day, out of curiosity, I wanted to know what it felt like to be an *Ibbi*, so I had a passive sexual encounter, and ever since, I can't do without. But I do it on the sly, and my regular partners still think of me as a *Yoos*" (Niang et al. 2002, 9).

3 ⤳ Ethnopsychiatry and the Making of Gay Shaka

BY THE 1920S MOST COLONIAL ADMINISTRATIONS had reason to take pride in their achievements. Overt African resistance had been almost entirely quelled and, indeed, hundreds of thousands of Africans served loyally in the military, the colonial police, and the increasingly bureaucratized local (so-called native or tribal) authorities. A modern transportation and communication infrastructure was taking shape over enormous technical obstacles. An expanding system of schools and hospitals had begun to improve the lives of millions of Africans. The numbers of Africans who embraced Christianity and self-consciously modern or Western values was on the rise. Mostly high commodity prices sustained a growing class of peasant agriculturalists and industrial workers who were directly engaged with the international economy as both producers and consumers. While instances of terrible working conditions and political repression remained, and while the Great Depression and World War II brought intense suffering through the 1930s and '40s, the worst abuses of the earlier concessionaire systems and forced-labor regimes were coming to an end. Indeed, the biggest scandal of the era in that respect took place in nominally independent Liberia rather than under more generally paternalistic colonial regimes.[1]

Despite these achievements, existential doubts about the colonial project remained pervasive. These doubts arose in part from long-standing cultural misunderstandings. The emergence of new stresses and social pathologies among Africans, particularly in urban settings, added to the uncertainty, as did new coping strategies or forms of resistance by Africans to colonialism and racial capitalism. Such resistance, from official and missionary perspectives, often appeared like intransigence, laziness, superstition, and ingratitude on the part of Africans. These and a whole host of other character flaws were presumed to be either intrinsic to "savage" society or arising from Africans' "semi-civilized" imitation of the worst aspects of European behavior. Particularly disturbing, including to African intellectuals, were manifestations of what was often referred to as neopaganism, meaning new social practices couched in the idioms of traditional culture. Sorcery, ritual murders, exaggerated machismo, and ambitious women were among the most common worries.[2]

Doubts had also begun to whittle away at once high confidence in the ability of anthropology to improve the efficiency of native administration. Indeed, a number of leading theorists and practitioners began to advocate a new approach to understanding "the African mind" that would compensate for evident deficiencies in the conventional anthropological approach, most notably its persistent blindness to or disinterest in the problems associated with modernity. The new approach, using tools and concepts borrowed from psychology, was proposed to mitigate communication problems between Europeans and Africans and thereby facilitate good governance and development in the rapidly changing environment.

At first glance, this blending of professional disciplines seemed like an easy marriage. Psychology and anthropology shared much in common but differed primarily in focus. Where anthropology placed the tribe or lineage as well as tradition or custom at the center of its analysis, psychology made the immediate family and individual behavior or feelings the principal focus. Also, where anthropology was tending to devote itself to "respectable" topics like music, production, ritual, and religion, psychology was ineluctably drawn to sexuality. Several prominent Africanist anthropologists in the 1920s and '30s thought the gaps between the fields were complementary and that a synthesis was both possible and desirable to tease out answers to questions that their own discipline seemed incapable or averse to resolving on its own. European psychologists, meanwhile, also joined in the debate and encouraged the blurring of disciplinary lines. Prominent theorists such as Marie Bonaparte and Carl Jung advocated applying their research methods to so-called primitive people as a means to gain insight into atavistic attitudes underpinning European social and sexual problems. Hence was born the new discipline of ethnopsychiatry (when applied to the treatment of mental disorder), which was also subsequently known as cross-cultural, or comparative, psychology (when referring to study of the same).[3]

Given the discipline's explicit concern (some said obsession) with sexuality and the unconscious, ethnopsychiatry would seem to have provided a natural breaking point from the silences and circumspection of anthropology concerning same-sex issues. Such a break did not occur. To the contrary, eth-nopsychiatry and successor mental health sciences clearly had a reaffirm-ing affect on the prevailing wisdom about an African sexuality defined by its supposedly heterosexual, promiscuous, and impulsive essence. This reaffir-mation represents a remarkable intellectual nonachievement. From early crude efforts to lend an air of scientific gravitas to ethnographic observation in the 1900s, psychologists and psychiatrists went on to attempt to understand "the African" using Freudian theory in the 1930s and '40s. More sophisticated analyses of sexual decision making came in the early postcolonial period (roughly to the mid-1970s), although highly regarded scholars were still able to overlook or misdiagnose key pieces of evidence about African sexualities in the process.

The supposed absence of homosexual desire in "the African mind" eventu-ally came to play a role in explaining a major series of events in pre- and early colonial history of southern Africa. These events, known as the *mfecane* (from Zulu) or *lifaqane/difaqane* (Sotho/Tswana), include the rise of the Zulu and several other important African states in the region in the early nineteenth century along with associated transformations in gender and class relations. A theory emerged in the 1920s that drew upon popularizations of Freudian psychological theory to explain the origins of the upheaval. It linked the re-puted propensity to violence by the great Zulu leader Shaka first to his alleged small penis size and then to imputed repressed homosexuality. These links were both popularized and discredited to make political arguments for and against racist ideologies in the 1970s and '80s. Thereafter they took on a life of their own in Western gay subcultures. I argue that the amateur psychohistory of Shaka, rooted in stereotypes and speculation and deployed for self-serving political ends, contributed in a small way to the limiting of research on social and sexual factors that were fueling HIV/AIDS as it burgeoned among blacks at that critical moment in southern African history.

PSYCHOLOGY AND COLONIALISM

Psychology introduced many powerful insights into the working of the human mind and how to relieve suffering caused by disorienting disjuncture between internal thoughts and external empirical conditions. However, it was never a science, as its more zealous proponents claimed. The methods of its preeminent founder and his "disciples" (as they are commonly described in the literature) are open to sharp criticism even as applied within European cultures, much less in cross-cultural, colonial contexts. Dream interpretation, notably, is subject to enormous culture-, class-, and gender-specific meanings.

Moreover, Sigmund Freud tended to extrapolate from middle- and upper-class central European individuals in order to make universal claims about human nature. When he did not approve of or believe the empirical evidence presented to him by his patients — most notoriously in the case of his female patients' therapeutic recollections of sexual abuse by fathers and other male relatives — he concocted rationalizations to dismiss that evidence. Ostensibly scientific enquiry in the days of his long dominance of the field (1900s–30s) was deeply riven by moralism, authoritarian censorship, and bitter, personal recriminations. Freud himself gave a hint of the pseudoreligious nature of his science when he referred to his ex-students Carl Jung as a "heretic" and Otto Rank as a "deviant" (Roazen 1971, 224).[4]

With specific respect to homosexuality, Freud left a mixed legacy. He advanced a fairly radical argument for the time by stating that all humans were born bisexual or "polymorphously perverse" (sexually stimulated by anybody and anything all over different parts of the body). As later elaborated in the work of Erik Erikson, this theory held that infants developed from the state of polymorphous perversion by passing through phases where sexual gratification centered on different parts of the body. The process began with the mouth, as mother's breast was the original source of pleasure. Oral-centered sexuality was followed by an anal stage as the child discovered that part of the body, followed in turn by the genitals. For girls, mature sexuality had a further phase, in which its focus shifted from clitoris to vagina, implying a move from selfish and potentially lesbian fulfillment to a heterosexual, childbearing vocation. Freud caused some scandal at the time by arguing that much of the development toward mature sexuality took place before puberty.

According to this theory, sexual dysfunctions in adulthood could largely be explained as arising from the failure to make smooth transitions from oral to anal to mature genital sexuality. Nature alone could not be relied on to ensure the desired transitions. On the contrary, the natural developmental process was enormously complicated by social factors — above all, the fact that a child's sexuality initially focused on the mother as sex object, from whom boys and girls had to be both physically weaned and emotionally distanced. Freud termed this mother-infant sexual bond the Oedipus complex, after the Greek myth that warned against mother-son incest. Unless the emotional trauma of breaking that mother-child bond was handled properly, lasting damage to sexual development could result. Homosexuality, notably, could be explained as a failure to resolve the Oedipus complex (that is, a manifestation of incomplete distancing from the mother as the object of sexual desire). The trauma of separation from the original love object was further complicated for the child by the intervention of a father figure as a rival for the mother's affection (hence the Oedipus triangle). Other factors subsequently identified as disrupting the normal transition to adult sexuality included improper weaning and toilet training, and inappropriate sexual contact between parent and child.

Freud once famously advised a mother not to blame herself or her son for the son's homosexuality since it could ultimately be traced back to a natural phenomenon, more or less intrinsic to the human condition. Many people today thus credit him with opening the intellectual path to battering down homophobic prejudices rooted in Christian dogmas. Yet Freud nevertheless still clearly regarded homosexuality as something that could and should be avoided, even if only because the dominant homophobic society made it almost be impossible for homosexuals to be happy or free from neuroses. Freud's followers subsequently developed that thinking into an explicitly stigmatizing analysis. Homosexuality was first listed as a psychological disorder in the 1930s, and then as an example of sexual deviance on an equivalent plane as sadomasochism and voyeurism in the 1950s. The authoritative American Psychiatric Association did not remove it from its list of "mental diseases" until 1973, after which it continued to be described in leading textbooks as a "deviation" or "perversion" well into the 1990s.[5] In other words, while Freud helped to take much of the old moralistic stigma out of homosexuality, his analysis prepared the ground for a new form of scientific stigma. This included stigma against the individuals who supposedly enabled homosexuality through bad parenting—above all, domineering, overprotective mothers and absent fathers.

On the positive side, according to this view, the legacies of bad parenting in the form of immature and misplaced desire could be rectified by psychotherapy. Through that process the dysfunctional or perverse adult revisited childhood memories, emotionally confronted the traumas, and resolved the underlying psychological problem. Mental and sexual health could be restored, although admittedly that could take years and had to be paid for. In practical terms therefore, professional psychotherapy long remained the preserve of the wealthy and upper-middle classes in Europe and America.

By comparison, African cultures tended historically to understand mental illness and sexual difference as manifestations of a wider rupture in social relations.[6] That rupture could be caused by any number of factors, including witchcraft (deliberate evil sent by one person against another), vengeful spirits (correcting an injustice done against a family), and ancestral ill will created by more generalized failures in the community (such as failure to honor moral obligations to ancestors, or to carry out rituals needed for proper custodianship of the land, forests, and sacred sites). Healing was therefore not a matter for individual, private psychotherapy. Healing required investigation by specialists into the broad social context and historical background of the disturbed person. To take a model that is commonly described in the ethnography and attested by a wide range of African authors, that process would normally include consultation with extended family patriarchs (who could identify previous occurrences of the disorder back in the family tree), herbalists and traditional healers (who might have medicines or advice to right imbalances of heat and coolness in the blood or to cleanse pollution from the body), and spirit mediums (who could identify sources of stress arising from social or political tensions, past and present). When a cause was identified, and resolution was required, the cure normally involved a public ritual to attenuate the stresses. A typical example of the latter would be the making of appropriate sacrifices, payment of compensation, public admission of harboring ill will, or entering into a state of spirit possession or trance leading to catharsis and resolution. A high degree of suggestion was implicit in this model. Specialists, empowered through their secret knowledge and aura of mystery, could elicit admissions of guilt and responsibility, sometimes from many people and retrospectively across generations.

People who were known to breach heterosexual norms and ideals represented one such potential threat to family and community, the latter including the ancestors and the unborn. As such, same-sex sexuality could have far wider implications than the unhappiness of the individual and his or her immediate loved ones. It was therefore critical that the cause of the breach be determined. It might be that the unusual sexual behavior was a legitimate manifestation of an honored spirit, contained within ritual space or approved social role (for example, a spirit medium). It might also be a relatively simple matter of youthful curiosity or tardy development toward adult sexuality that needed to be "cured" by family intervention or medicines. Other feared spirits could be involved, however, that could entail elaborate appeasement ceremonies. Flagrant or violent homosexual acts might even indicate that witchcraft was at play, in which case the danger theoretically warranted exile, mutilation, or even death.

Contemporary queer anthropology from around Africa suggests that most same-sex infractions or diversions from gender norms lay somewhere between these extremes. As such they could be dealt with through discreet, appearances-saving ceremonies or "compensation." Among the Shona of Zimbabwe, for example, if a public healing process was indicated, it could involve as little as the payment of a few beasts to the family aggrieved by a same-sex incident (e.g., a boy raped or seduced by a man; Epprecht 2004). Several of the ethnographies noted in the previous chapter suggest that community derision was sufficient to the task of restoring the public appearance of normalcy (e.g., Herskovits 1932).

Europeans and mission-educated Africans were often dismissive of traditional African healing systems, which they lumped together pejoratively as mumbo-jumbo, witchcraft, and sorcery. Traditional healers were, moreover, at the heart of a social system that seemed to valorize African men's exploitation of female sexuality through polygyny and many other patriarchal customs. Christian missionaries and African evangelists thus at first generally sought to suppress the practices, sometimes by seeking the support of the colonial state for direct legal prohibitions (such as criminalizing witchcraft accusations) but also by ridicule and propaganda. Yet over time a growing minority observed that African healing systems could be quite effective, particularly as anthropologists looked beyond the idioms of sorcery and sacrifice to unravel the underlying rationality or functionality of witchcraft beliefs. They revealed how in practice the mumbo-jumbo appeared to work, in many cases better than European medicine. Herskovits (1934, 77) opined that Africans (and South American "Bush Negroes") had especially well developed mechanisms for recognizing and therapeutically compensating for emotional tensions arising from repression (for example, polite repression of anger at a friend or family member). The first trained psychologist to publish on the issue also found that even traditional means of diagnosis were more effective than his own. Wulf Sachs deserves quoting for his observations of a traditional healer (*nganga*) in action in a modern psychiatric hospital in South Africa in the early 1930s:

> he extracted from the insane a wealth of information far exceeding any that I did. Most of the patients not only willingly submitted themselves to his interrogation, but also regarded his efforts with confidence and trust. John, with his bones, horns, magical formulae, and rituals, meant to them the real medical man. And I wonder if it wouldn't be advisable, from a psychological point of view, to employ *ngangas* in the treatment of insane natives. In any case, there is nothing to lose, for our methods fail lamentably. (1937, 193)

It also emerged from professional anthropology that early missionary scandal at the oppression and exploitation of African girls and women, and at the incorrigibility of African men's polygynous or adulterous streaks, had in many cases been overstated. Indeed, while sometimes imbued with a "noble savage" sentimentality, and while often suspiciously convenient to cynical colonial efforts to buttress the authority of loyal native authorities, a number of studies began to suggest that traditional African notions of gender and sexuality were actually psychologically healthier than European. They noted, for example, that African societies tended to be relatively frank in their direction of children's sexual development and did not inculcate a sense of guilt about natural sexual feelings. Stress on the immediate parents was relieved in that respect, since responsibility for sex education did not fall directly on them but rather on aunts and uncles or professional initiators. The overall effect of this lack of sexual guilt on morality and physical health remained a topic of much heated debate, particularly as the issues of promiscuity and prostitution came to the fore. However, a growing consensus through the middle decades of the twentieth century held that frankness, extended family, and formal coming-of-age rituals all helped to mitigate children's' underlying fears and anxieties about their burgeoning sexuality. What often particularly impressed many European observers was that there appeared to be no homosexuals and hence none of the neuroses around homosexuality commonly found in modern European societies (guilt, self-hatred, and depression, for instance). No less an authority than Jung waxed eloquent about the "utter naturalness," "confidence and self-assurance," and "stability" he perceived in African women as a result of the absence of homosexualizing factors compared to supposedly rational societies like Europe (Jung 1963, 247).[7]

Whatever their perspective on African notions about healing and sexuality, however, few contemporary observers disagreed that these were in flux in the face of the contradictions and brutalities of colonial rule, the spread of Christianity, and the spread of a cash economy.[8] Urbanization and contact with Europeans in particular were widely regarded as giving rise to detribalization and demoralization, in the language of the time. Detribalization and demoralization meant a loss of faith in the old ways, beliefs, kinship ties, and reciprocal obligations. In retrospect we can appreciate that for some people this could be quite liberating. But rapid social and cultural change also contributed to evidently increasing alcoholism, depression, family breakdowns, crime and youth gangs, and suicide. Previously rare or unknown expressions of "sexual perversion" were another widely lamented symptom of urbanization and the cash economy. These included prostitution, male-male (often pederastic) relationships in labor camps, criminal gangs, and carceral institutions, and "les vices solitaires" (self-masturbation among boys and girls, according to one of the leading polemicists on the issue: Cureau 1904, 644–45). These new expressions of sexuality in turn were seen to be rippling back into the rural hinterlands in a host of formerly rare social, sexual, and mental health problems. Indeed, according to one of the first experts to publish on the topic, a symptom ("self-abuse") was also likely a cause of increasing rates of insanity

(Greenslees 1895, 74). Other problems associated with the breakdown of traditional healing systems and the management of sexuality were young people's elopements, rape, increased rates of divorce or abandonment, and the rising prevalence of sexually transmitted diseases. How to deal with the effects of all this—other than through repressive means, which often only inflamed the problems—became one of the preeminent concerns of the early decades of the twentieth century.

The first attempts to apply Freudian ideas to the problem were unfortunately not very successful. Mental hospitals, where they existed, for the most part were scarcely distinguishable from prisons.[9] Theorization of African mental illness, meanwhile, was typically based on anecdotes, cursory observation, and secondhand accounts, overwhelmingly of and about men. The result was that so-called psychology in the first decade of the twentieth century tended simply to restate the ethnography in slightly modified terms. This had the effect of amplifying and naturalizing imputed differences between "savage" and "civilized" mentalities or, in Burton's terms, Sotadic and non-Sotadic zones. Dudley Kidd (1904, 1908), for example, used the rubric of psychology to "explain" the low intellectual achievement and progress by Africans. Apparently their "nervous energy" was drained away toward thoughts of sex, precluding much else. Adolphe Cureau (1904) also used the language of psychology to confirm a preexisting stereotype—the nonexistence of homosexuality in precolonial central Africa except where pederastic relationships existed as a legacy of the Turks (the Turks? In central Africa?). Richard Dennett tacitly made the same point in his study of "Bavili psychology" (1968 [1906], 65). Although critical of what he termed the "false modesty" prevailing in the anthropology regarding sexual offenses, and while tackling that issue with some brio, he defined sexual offenses in strictly heterosexual terms, as if nothing else were conceivable among primitives.

Cureau, who was the lieutenant-governor of Upper Oubangui (French Equatorial Africa), and Dennett, a missionary, both wrote with the benefit of considerable personal observation. This qualification did not always apply. One of the strongest proponents of applying Freudian theory to Africans in the 1920s and '30s, for example, was Charles Seligman, who frankly admitted he had no firsthand knowledge of "the typical African Negro" (1924, 27). Such lack of knowledge did not stop him from charting African personality types along with other cultures worldwide according to their receptivity to the power of suggestion, as reputed in the ethnography. Indeed, in a surprisingly tenacious belief, firsthand knowledge through interviews with African patients (de rigueur in Europe and America) was not even considered an advantage for determining individual case histories, let alone formulating psychological theories. Geoffrey Tooth's study of mental illness in colonial Gold Coast, for example, was based on home interviews of psychotic individuals supplied to him by family members and chiefs (Tooth 1950, 35, 41). Direct interviews may actually have been counterproductive in this view. As the government psychiatrist at Tanganyika's Mirembe hospital put it in 1956, "most Africans have an inadequate vocabulary to describe the mental symptoms they may experience and many arrive so mentally ill that they are incapable of giving any account of themselves or their illness. Leading questions are useless because it is characteristic of the African, when in doubt, to agree with anything that is suggested by a European. . . . Hallucinations and alterations in mood are fortunately easy to recognize as the African shows his feelings in his face" (Smartt 1956, 449).

Such generalizations about African psychology often turned quickly to rationalizing the need for more paternalistic colonial guidance, to creating tribal hierarchies, or to streaming African, "bastard," and European pupils for the ostensible improvement of both races (Greenslees 1895; Bryant 1917). Yet whites were also under psychological stress in colonial Africa, and so they too, and through them the whole colonial project, would benefit from psychoanalysis. This point was at the heart of an article by South Africans F. S. Livie-Noble and F. O. Stohr, among the first Africa-based medical doctors with formal training in the discipline. The gist of their argument was that expanding the provision of psychotherapy to whites on the continent would improve white stewardship of blacks, going so far as to recommend psychoanalysis as "a prerequisite for magistrates, teachers, ministers, and all such as have in their hands the mental health and virility of the [white] race" (1926, 1005). This suggestion included one of the first articulations of scientific homophobia in Freudian terms. Livie-Noble and Stohr believed "homosexuals and perverts" were "closely allied" to neurotics and ahead of criminals as categories of white people for whom psychoanalysis should be a priority. Following Freud, they offered hope for all but the rare "thorough-going" homosexuals: "a homosexual who detests and fights against his craving can [and should] be cured" (999). The two doctors did not elaborate on methods to achieve the cure, nor did they have anything to say about Africans. Their presumption was clear, however, that a mentally healthy and heterosexually disciplined ruling race would redound to the benefit of the ruled.

A twist on this argument was to apply the principles of psychoanalytic theory directly to "primitive people" in order to gain insights into the hidden recesses of the modern mind. For Marie Bonaparte that end could be achieved ("à mieux nous connaître nous-mêmes") by a specific focus on primitives' sexuality. They, more than civilized people, were imagined to reveal the innate human sexual instinct unencumbered by the niceties of etiquette, guilt, or repression. Understanding them would help us, she argued, not necessarily to make colonialism work more efficiently, but rather to make civilized people happier and more fulfilled in their sex and emotional lives. For Bonaparte and Jung this was particularly true for European women, whom they regarded as disproportionately bearing the costs and anxieties of modern life. But time was of the essence. "D'ici peut-être cent ans, mais peut-être même avant, les primitives que porte encore la terre seront ou eliminés, ou plus au moins entamés par nos civilisations. Ceux qui reste encore sont précieux et fugitifs témoins d'un temps disparu" (Bonaparte 1934, 25).[10]

The first serious attempt to apply Freudian psychotherapy directly to an African patient began around this time. It was clearly not in the nakedly Eurocentric school of Livie-Noble, Stohr, Bonaparte, and company. It nonetheless provides a telling example of how even researchers who were politically sympathetic to Africans' plight helped reproduce key elements of the colonial stereotype—native sexuality. Wulf Sachs was a South African Jew who had trained under Freud and who identified as an independent socialist (Dubow 1993, 523). From clinical observation during his work at the Johannesburg African Mental Hospital from 1928, he hypothesized that the causes, forms, and content of insanity were identical between Europeans and Africans—a radical argument for the time. He then sought to test his hypothesis through extended close psychoanalysis of a "normal" African subject living in the city—again a radical departure from normal practice. The subject he found (with the personal help of one of the pioneers of urban anthropology on the continent, Ellen Hellmann) was a Manyika traditional healer, or nganga, from Southern Rhodesia to whom Sachs gave the pseudonym John Chavafambira. Over two and a half years of almost daily sessions together, Sachs gathered insight into Chavafambira's psychological makeup using free-associative methods, that is, prompting the subject to talk about whatever came to mind. The title of his resulting book suggests the emotional turmoil and neuroses that Chavafambira revealed in himself: *Black Hamlet* (1937), later retitled for the American market as *Black Anger* (1947). It details Chavafambira's deep psychological angst including, above all, persistent, debilitating anger, sexual dysfunction, and anomie.

Sachs identified the inherent stresses of moving from a rural setting to an urban one as underlying factors in Chavafambira's neuroses. Rather than being inherent in the loss of some noble-savage stability, however, Sachs astutely distinguished poverty, humiliation at the hands of whites, and the tensions arising from the state's policies of discrimination and harassment against African women in town as causes of those stresses. It was an analysis that precociously implied the need for political change as a precondition for achieving mental health for Africans.

For our purposes, one other aspect of *Black Hamlet* is especially interesting. Given Chavafambira's admitted distrust verging on hatred of whites, he was surprisingly forthcoming to Sachs about his sexual difficulties. Chavafambira admitted to finding sex with his wife repugnant and that he had married her only for the appearance of respectability. While sometimes having extramarital affairs, he also found sex with women generally caused him disgust. He had erotic dreams of his mother. When he chose to remain celibate for long periods of time, he explained it as a "family tradition" necessary to protect his medicine and power as a healer (Sachs 1937, 161).

Sachs, in short, sketched Chavafambira very differently from the stereotype of promiscuous, hungry-for-white-flesh, and irredeemably selfish sexuality that then prevailed in colonial and missionary debates about African men. *Black Hamlet* can be justly celebrated for that achievement. Yet in one important way Sachs did not challenge, and in fact unwittingly condoned, that stereotype. He did not consider whether something to the effect of homosexuality might have contributed to Chavafambira's lack of desire for women. This although Chavafambira himself brought the subject up in an exchange that Sachs records without comment between him and another African employee at the mental asylum: "John had argued with N'Komo about the abnormal ways of love-making practiced by many of his patients in the asylum. N'Komo had used them as proofs of madness but John just laughed declaring that if this were true, hundreds of natives in the compounds and in the crowded city yards would need to be put into asylums, for in such places love-making between men was quite usual as it was between women also" (1937, 193). Chavafambira also recounted witnessing a white policeman in Johannesburg arresting an African man dressed as a woman, complete with fake breasts. But Sachs did not pursue either the topic in general or Chavafambira's obvious nonchalance toward that incident.

A second study from South Africa published in the same year had more to say but little to add on this subject. That is, Barend J. F. Laubscher's 1937 study of "pagan native" sexuality spends more time considering the possibility and meaning of homosexual practices among Africans than any study up to this point. It ends up, however, once again confirming the dominant prejudices of colonial ethnography by couching those prejudices in scientific-sounding jargon. Laubscher casually revealed one of those prejudices when he explained his motive for embarking on the research in the first place: "The commission of sadistic sexual acts on European women by detribalised natives living in towns led me to enquire into the frequency of the occurrences of sexual offences in the native territories" (1937, 257).

Laubscher was head of the psychiatric ward of Queenstown Mental Hospital in the eastern Cape Province. He based his book primarily on clinical observations of mostly Tembu or Xhosa patients under his care and through interviews with hospital staff, traditional healers (isanuse), chiefs, headmen, and other male elders in the surrounding rural areas. On the question of sexual offenses, he also established a baseline of "tradition" as understood by nineteen native commissioners around the country. For this he sent out a written questionnaire. Among other things, his informants reported back with complete unanimity that "homosexualism" among men "does not occur," was "unknown in the kraals," or was "practically unheard of" (257–58). Laubscher accepted this view on the grounds that there was "very little necessity for this type of offence" (257) and strengthened the reasoning with some thoughts of his own. In a society so entirely devoted to reproduction, with females subservient to the "phallic cult" and freely accessible to men from a young age, and where women's frustrated psychosexual needs were largely met through dreams of penetration by well-endowed spirits called tikoloshi, why would any native risk attracting opprobrium by engaging in homosexual practices?

And yet Laubscher had learned from his female isanuse informants that there were forms of overt homosexual behavior among Tembu women associated with spirit possession or witchcraft (31). Moreover, by his own estimation, 80 percent of male and female African inmates under his watch practiced some kind of homosexual sex, mostly mutual masturbation. That this apparently did not invalidate the ethnography or suggest the need for investigating the phenomenon is a telling example of the power of "African sexuality" as an explanatory model. Indeed, the widespread practice of homosexuality in the asylum (and, Laubscher notes, prisons and mines as well) could be explained quite simply in two ways. It was either the result of unavailability of appropriate sex object (celibacy or self-masturbation not being imaginable as a possibility for Africans). Or it was a "regressive phenomena due to the psychosis or defect" that had brought the inmates to the institution in the first place (258). For Laubscher, an example of such a defect was implicit in the fact that many of the male inmates had been to circumcision school but for unknown reasons had not been circumcised. In short, they had missed the ritual psychosexual completion of transition from childhood to normal adult masculinity and Tembuness or Xhosaness. But could it have been that the isanuse and circumcisers knew something about these boys that preceded the defect? Laubscher did not consider that possibility.

Laubscher set a standard to which the discipline largely conformed for roughly the next two decades and to which anthropologists paid close attention. Often the disciplinary cross-fertilization is unacknowledged but can be traced through shared terminology and, in a few cases, through direct personal connections. Charles Seligman, notably, was a medical doctor who began advocating cross-fertilization between anthropology and psychology fully a decade before publishing the results of his fieldwork in southern Sudan. His collaborator in that fieldwork and in promoting the use of Jungian dream analysis among "primitive peoples" was his wife, Brenda. A book in his honor (Evans-Pritchard et al. 1934) includes contributions by a virtual who's who of authorities in the two fields, including Marie Bonaparte. Indeed, one of the most significant personal connections in this formative period was between Bonaparte, Bronislaw Malinowski (a personal friend who also taught her son in his anthropology seminar at the London School of Economics), and Jomo Kenyatta (a promising African scholar, also in the same seminar).

Bonaparte was a Freudian psychologist whose primary interest was in the effects of clitoral versus vaginal orgasm. Like Freud, she believed that clitoral orgasm was a sign of immature sexual development that could have deleterious effects on women's emotional stability in marriage, their assumed natural vocation. Her primary contribution to contemporary debates was to advocate clitoridectomy as a way for modern, European women to achieve adult sexuality and, hence, emotional fulfillment (she had subjected herself to the operation). Malinowski, like her a strong proponent of psychology within anthropology, introduced her to Kenyatta, an outspoken defender of the Gikuyu practice of female circumcision. Kenyatta and Bonaparte had at least one extended meeting in Paris in 1935 to share their views on the benefits of clitoridectomy, plus further indirect discussion via correspondence with Malinowski (Frederiksen 2008). A meeting of minds is apparent in their subsequent publications. Bonaparte referred to African sexuality as a possible model for Europeans to emulate, while Kenyatta's opus is both unusually frank for the period in its treatment of sexuality and unusually Freudian sounding in its characterizations of Gikuyu sexual practices. He explains, for example, that Gikuyu self-confidence and sense of dignity could be attributed in large measure to a nonshaming and sex-affirmative sexual initiation (1961 [1938]). This in turn supposedly obviated the possibility of homosexuality.

Another important site for intellectual cross-fertilization between anthropology and psychology through the 1940s was at the Rhodes-Livingstone Institute in Livingstone, Northern Rhodesia. Its director at that time was Max Gluckman, another politically left-leaning South African Jew and a strong advocate of using psychological tools and theories to enrich the understanding of African culture and history. Gluckman deserves specific credit for enabling the ideas of John Ritchie to gain widespread, respectful attention. Ritchie was an amateur (a high school teacher), but he claimed both decades of observation of his Northern Rhodesian students and a "number" of formal psychoanalytic assessments of young Africans, presumably male (1944, 57). This experience enabled him to fashion a global theory about the origins of African personality traits that the Rhodes-Livingstone Institute published not once but twice, first as a booklet and then as an article in its academic journal. In his preface to the booklet, Ritchie states that it was Gluckman who first encouraged him to write up his theory and that Gluckman read two drafts of the booklet before publication (Ritchie 1943). For his part, Gluckman in his introductory note warns against exaggeration but overall praises Ritchie's study as a "confirmation of the Freudian theory."

The African as Suckling and as Adult (1943) and "The African as Grown-up Nursling" (1944) deserve extended attention as testimonies to the power of prejudice and presumption to co-opt scientific language. In them, Ritchie advanced the argument that "the African" first spent too long at "his" mother's breast. The African was then weaned so suddenly that it thwarted resolution of the Oedipus complex. This trauma made him excessively needy and compulsive in his sexuality, as if in that way he could recapture the bliss of the maternal teat. The fact that African women were all too ready to accommodate his needs from early adolescence onward only made things worse (what women's Oedipal problem was is left unclear). But in addition to the weaning trauma, Ritchie also invoked the Freudian concepts of repression (steadily increasing self-control over polymorphous perversity that was a sign of healthy maturity) and transference (applying that repressed sexual energy to productive, nonsexual pursuits). The African supposedly lacked these psychological attributes. This led to "too rapid erotic development" with harmful implications for sexual health and attitudes toward self-discipline, work, and savings. Ritchie's rendering of African sexuality further explained why the African was "pathetically" incapable of mastering the principles of mathematics, with all that that implied for development and good local governance on the continent (1944, 61).

It is worth quoting at length from The African as Suckling to illustrate the level of assumption and abstraction that passed as legitimate scholarly enquiry in the field of psychology in Africa in those days. Admittedly, the following quote is taken out of context, with some wordy connections deleted. But it does capture in one relatively concise passage the tone of the whole. Referring to the long-term psychological and social impacts of trauma generated in infancy by faulty African child-rearing practices, Ritchie wrote:

This is the time of "anal primacy," when the infant's erotic interests and phantasies are concentrated on the anal zone and functions of his own and his parents' bodies. Both their training and his fears compel him to repress his anal-erotic instincts prematurely, and he passes rapidly to the genital stage. . . . [One result] is that it confirms the paralysis of mental effort. A great deal of intelligent learning finds its details and its unconscious motives in infantile anal-erotic phantasies, and we have seen how undue repression of the original makes for inability to investigate the later interests. Further, as is generally recognised, full sexual gratification is the most intense pleasure of which man is capable. . . . So if this is available from later infancy through childhood and adolescence, it is natural that the African child and youth should have insufficient mental drive for the mastery of abstract studies. It is true that there are psychical energies which cannot be exhausted in sexual activity, but these are mostly on the anal-erotic plane, and in the African they are paralysed by dread, as we have seen. (1943, 42)

Needless to say, contradictory evidence could easily be found, even in Northern Rhodesia, let alone elsewhere in Africa. (Health officials in South Africa, for example, commonly complained about African mothers in town who weaned their children too early or who, in keeping with widespread practice, gave their children regular enemas (Natal 1951; Segal and Tim 1979).) But Ritchie's bowdlerization of Freudian theory found a respectful, sometimes enthusiastic audience. Another amateur, Colonel S. Davidson, also published in the *Rhodes-Livingstone Institute Journal*, put it succinctly in calling for an expansion of psychiatric studies of Africans in collaboration with anthropologists. After acknowledging Ritchie's pioneering contributions to the field, and applying Ritchie's model to the Bemba people, Davidson held that such research "will be of great value both to the Government and to the private industrial concerns" (Davidson 1949, 85). The benefits would include more efficient administration, reduced policing costs, better physical health and worker discipline, and an improved international image for enlightened colonial rule.

For men like Gluckman, the unspoken appeal was obviously different. Gluckman was a vocal political activist against racism in his native South Africa. Nothing in his biography suggests that he harbored hidden racist or sexual anxieties against blacks. Rather, the appeal may have been in the way that Ritchie's analysis treated Africans as being subject to basically the same psychological processes as Europeans. Rather than intrinsically perilous, as racists maintained, the analysis implied that African sexuality could be fixed through reforms in childhood socialization. It removed a modicum of the blame that overt racists placed on Africans for their perceived shortcomings and suggested that the colonial state needed to be more active in addressing social problems within the African population. Gluckman may also have felt that the analysis sent a discreetly reassuring message to his primary audience, assuaging Europeans' fears of African male sexuality. Cutting the black man down from a well-endowed black peril to an emotionally stunted suckling—all in the most objective, scientific terms—was unquestionably appealing to many whites in the context.[11]

A poignant marker of the consolidation of this theory in the discipline can be found in a comparison between the first and second editions of *Black Hamlet*. Sachs, it seems, was a personal friend of Max Gluckman's and visited him in Livingstone when Ritchie was promoting his suckling theory (Schumaker 2001, 88). The revised edition of his book published four years after Ritchie's suggests he was moved by the theory. In *Black Anger* Sachs deleted a long discussion of family tensions between Chavafambira and his in-laws. He inserted in its place an aside that used the Ritchie hypothesis to explain Chavafambira's "irrational fear" (Sachs 1947, 51). Sachs posited that Chavafambira might have been better prepared psychologically to deal with his family tensions and with the stresses of poverty and racism had he not been breast fed until the age of four only to be brutally cut off, and replaced in his mother's bed, by his father. Whatever the merits of the analysis, there can be little doubt that it took much of the sting out of Sachs's earlier pointed critique of colonial racism and hence almost certainly added to the appeal of psychology to politically conservative audiences.

To be fair, professional psychologists generally distanced themselves from crude service to the colonial state and from overly bald generalizations. In his overview of the state of the art of African personality studies at the end of the 1950s, the director of the National Institute for Personnel Research in South Africa, Simon Biesheuvel, actually singled out Ritchie for his "uncritical application of psychoanalytic theories relevant to Western cultures" (CSA 1959, 3). Yet with minor quibbles, the publications that ensued through to the early 1960s still tended to restate some version of Ritchie's thesis (and the nonexistence or exotic nature of homosexuality) as a starting point. Geoffrey Tooth, notably, in a government-sponsored monograph exploring mental health issues in the Gold Coast, first lamented the "orientation of the average African to sex" arising from childhood socialization. He then simultaneously asserted that homosexuality was rare in the Gold Coast and that "Moshies" (Muslim traders from the north) were to blame for importing it (1950, 31). To J. C.

Carothers, who for twelve years was director of the Mathari Mental Hospital in Nairobi and was regarded in the 1950s as the world leader in the field, ethnopsychiatry did nothing less than confirm "classical conceptions" and "popular stereotypes" (Carothers 1970 [1953], 85). In a book first published by the World Health Organization he stated that ethnopsychiatry showed how and why Africans were "happy-go-lucky." While they had an "aptitude for music and dance" they lived in a "pre-hypnotic state . . . 'twixt sleep and wakening" on account of faulty child-rearing practices, among other things. Contributors to the Scientific Council for Africa study on *Psychological Structures of African and Madagascan Populations* also noted how abrupt weaning "serves to retard personality development, or in some cases to cause fixation, or even regression, in later life, to a stage of primary narcissism" (CSA 1959, 10). In plain language, it created an obsession with personal sexual gratification that necessitated male orgasm to be achieved through vaginal penetration—only. Carothers made the latter point almost explicit when he pronounced, in appropriately scientific-sounding euphemism, that the "mental concomitants" of physical feminization in men had no relevance to African psychology (meaning, I think, that homosexual desire did not exist in Africa and therefore future psychologists should not waste their time looking for it or related anxieties—Carothers 1970 [1953], 114).[12] An isolated study that found evidence to the contrary around this time buried its findings in among dense survey statistics with no discussion (Schenkel 1971). In any case, the subjects here were *evolués*, Senegalese middle class whose assimilation to French values would explain the non-normative sexuality to anyone who asked.

The first generations of Africans trained in Freudian psychology did not necessarily dispute these notions, even when they implied a diametrically opposed politics. The Ugandan psychologist B. H. Kagwa (1965), for example, posited the relationship between weaning and supposed African dependency and passivity. Reformed breast-feeding practices would in this analysis engender men who were more emotionally suited to the responsibilities of political independence. With respect to homosexuality, the pioneering Nigerian psychologist T. Adeoye Lambo (1955) had nothing at all to say in his first blistering attack on Laubscher, Carothers et al. Then, as a contributing author to what is commonly regarded as the first scientifically valid epidemiological study, he condoned the descriptions of homosexuality as "sociopathic" and "extremely rare" (Leighton et al. 1963, 111). As late as 1994 Nigerian Tolani Asuni and colleagues placed the blame for "failure" mostly on improper motherhood. Boys, they suggested, were at risk from mothers who dominated passive fathers, hence setting a confusing example, while lesbians appeared to be the result of a mother who "is not satisfied with her feminine position"

(Asuni, Schoenberg, and Swift 1994 [1975], 150). This represents a remarkably conservative conflation of sexuality and gender role that Freud would likely have worried about but that, for all the other rhetorical gestures against Eurocentrism in the text, colonial administrators and psychologists would mostly have approved.

NEW DIRECTIONS, OLD TROPES

Challenges to colonial psychology and to scientific homophobia emerged beginning in the late 1930s. While mostly focused on whites, they had a long-term effect on popular understandings of African sexuality. Indeed, through their essentializing claims about the appearance, demeanor and behavior of white homosexuals, they helped to consolidate a caricature of homosexuality that Africans could subsequently point to as proof that the condition did not—and could not—exist in African culture.

Louis Freed, first, was a trained psychiatrist in the Freudian tradition that tended to underplay the personal stigma or blame attaching to homosexuality. His first important public intervention came during the 1939 trial of Carl Buckle, a young white Johannesburg man accused of homosexual rape (Achmat no date). Buckle's trial was one of the first arising from newspaper revelations that a homosexual prostitution ring existed for whites in Johannesburg. On the eve of a looming world war, the extent of the ring (involving up to one hundred boys) caused something of a panic about the young generation of white men's moral and fighting fiber. Church leaders, politicians, and police advocated various stern, punitive solutions to this assumed feminization of young South African white men. Freed, however, stepped in with the argument that Buckle's and other homosexuals' problem lay in a combination of physiological intersexuality and environmental conditions, above all poor mothering. The latter could be explained in part by lack of education and desperate economic circumstances. Buckle's and other white men's homosexuality was thus not necessarily a moral shortcoming of the men or the mothers but at least partially a reflection of the state's dereliction of duty to them. On that basis, Freed argued against imprisonment as punishment for Buckle.

The judge at that time was not impressed and sentenced Buckle to a relatively harsh eighteen months in jail. But at a subsequent trial for a repeat offense in 1942, the judge gave Buckle probation under Freed's care. Freed's study of this and other case histories of white male homosexuals provided him with considerable evidence to back his argument for broad reforms in the treatment of homosexuality. Indeed, in a letter sent directly to the

Commissioner for Mental Hygeine in the South African Department of Health after the war Freed further upped the rhetorical stakes by estimating no less than 15 percent of white men in the military practiced homosexuality.[13] Given how well South Africans comported themselves as soldiers during the war, this was a backhanded compliment to the men but a terrible indictment of the state for enabling the behavior.

Freed at this stage of his career was by no means a friend of homosexuals or sexual liberation. He condemned active and passive roles as "one being as harmful as the other" and laced his descriptions of specific homosexual acts with severe disapproval. On fellatio, for example, he wrote, "This unpleasant act is mostly indulged in by men whose depravity urged them to explore novel sexual malpractices" (Freed 1941, 14). Freed's treatment of lesbianism among white women was even less forgiving. In his 1949 study of prostitution in Johannesburg he affirms that lesbians were virile, hairy, aggressive, scheming, addicted, sexually desperate, frustrated, and/or "infantile," the latter presumably a reference to their failure to move from clitoral to vaginal orgasm (Freed 1949, 60–62). Their perversion led to actual physical decline such as pallid skin and "ill-defined features," and posed a sometimes direct menace to society including rough assaults and secret injections with morphia to seduce their victims. He again communicated that view directly to government with the recommendation that the state take action to rescue such women, although exactly how was not clear.

Over the course of the 1950s and '60s Freed's views moderated both in line with new international thinking and in response to the worsening local political situation. The latter arose from the electoral triumph of the National Party and the progressive consolidation of sexually repressive policies as part of its implementation of apartheid. Among the very first apartheid enactments was a law prohibiting interracial sex. Through the decades the regime sought to criminalize homosexuality and to suppress the discreet gay scenes that had emerged among whites in major cities since World War II. For example, proposed legislation would have made it illegal to possess dildos and to empower the state to prosecute lesbian sexuality. That same legislation would have enabled police to arrest suspected male homosexuals (rather than wait until evidence of the commission of homosexual acts). Overt Christian moralism meanwhile began to penetrate ostensibly scientific discourse: Don (1963, 484), notably, cites Deuteronomy 22:5 to support his analysis of four case studies that demonstrated the "hazards" and "difficulties" of transvestism, transsexualism, and homosexuality (and justified aversion and other psychotherapy). Louis Freed and a locally educated psychologist, Renée Liddicoat, emerged as the leading professional voices against these developments. Liddicoat (herself a lesbian) calmly catalogued the many variations of same-sex combinations across cultures, history, and in different species as an argument in favor of reforming the law to end discrimination against gays and lesbians (1962). Freed (1954, 1968), developed his argument that most homosexuality was not a menace to society but to a large extent symptomatic of a deeper social malaise. Cases where it was an innate condition (what we today call sexual orientation) were relatively insignificant in his view and could safely be left alone. Cases where homosexuality occurred through accident or circumstances could meanwhile fairly easily be cured by modern psychoanalysis and therapy. To use the law to repress homosexuality, he concluded, would only drive it underground and give rise to other, far worse psychopathologies like depression, alcoholism and suicide.

Opinions differed on the most effective therapies for curing suspected homosexuality, notoriously extending to the use of chemicals and electroshock aversion therapy in the South African military in the 1960s and '70s.[14] The professional discourse was united, however, by its almost total disinterest in nonwhites. The rare exception proves the rule. In an anonymous and undated (but likely mid-1950s) letter, for example, Freed discussed male-male sexual relations among Africans in Johannesburg. His proposed solution indicated that he did not believe real homosexuality was at stake. With better urban planning, he argued, situational homosexuality among Africans would quickly disappear (Freed no date). At the other end of the continent, meanwhile, Schenkel's pioneering study from Senegal was conceived precisely to address colonial ignorance and myths about "the sex life of Africans" (Schenkel 1971, 313). But it largely negated that objective by basing the research on culturally Westernized, professional-class Senegalese (acculturés). Homosexuality, from this perspective, was a recent phenomenon associated with nightclubs and white people rather than the traditional gor djigen referred to elsewhere (379; compare to Ken Bugul 1991, 58).

The weight of the scholarly output from elsewhere in Africa is also striking in this regard: not one of the specialists who contributed to a 1959 overview report on "basic psychological structures of African and Madagascan populations" (CSA 1959) mentioned homosexuality. Andor (1983) subsequently annotated over three hundred articles and books published between 1960 and 1975 on "abnormal and clinical psychology" among Africans, and hundreds of others that measured or assessed African attitudes to heterosexual sexuality, prostitution, and social changes associated with urbanization. Not one of these studies made same-sex sexuality the focus of investigation, even though homosexuality was considered a mental illness throughout this period internationally. Mallory Wober's sweeping synthesis of the history of psychiatry in

Africa from its origins up to the mid-1970s (1975), by contrast, did make a sole allusion to homosexuality and to the psychological and emotional stresses its repression might create. But he did this by citing a single article by a medical doctor in Liberia that is frankly bizarre. That doctor had posited the existence of gynaecomastia among Temne men (the development of breasts and a presumed "feminoid tendency" in personality), which he attributed to chronic malnutrition and cirrhosis of the liver. From this scanty evidence, Wober surmises that such men might have psychological disorders since "presumably the cultures [all of them, all over the entire continent?] effectively discourage active homosexual behaviour" (Wober 1975, 209–10; citing Davies 1949, 677).

The extent of the triumph of such presumption in the field is also indicated by the very first psychology monograph on the topic of male homosexuals in Africa, published in 1992. Isaacs and McKendrick succinctly explain interpretations of psychological theory that destigmatize homosexuality with the objective of humanizing the men involved, hence contributing to debates about the transition to democracy and a culture of human rights in South Africa. But the book drew its empirical evidence almost entirely from Cape Town, probably the most European-looking city on the continent, with a gay scene that was overwhelmingly white and coloured. Virtually no evidence is admitted for the rest of South Africans, even though by that time anthropologists, and even a few scattered psychologists, had begun to raise challenges to the orthodoxy.

The work on homosexuality among whites was eventually noticed by black gay rights activists (Achmat n.d.; Achmat and Lewis 1999, for example), and used to effect. Freed thus in a small way may have contributed to the achievement of overturning homophobic laws in South Africa in the 1990s. But elsewhere, and indeed among blacks opposed to gay rights in South Africa as well, another psychiatrist from the era of anticolonial struggle had a far more significant influence in precisely the other direction. That was Frantz Fanon, a black man from Martinique whose youthful faith in Enlightenment values was shattered by his experiences of pervasive racism in France and subsequently during the Algerian war of liberation against French colonialism. Fanon emerged and is justifiably renowned as a passionate critic and theorist of racism, colonialism, and neocolonialism. He played a major inspirational role to a whole generation of radical African and African diaspora intellectuals. On the issue of homosexuality, however, he effectively promoted some of the hoariest and racist stereotypes in existence in the postwar era and in that way played an important role in legitimizing homophobia on the antiracist political left.

Fanon had footnoted the lack of an overt presence of homosexuality among blacks (in Martinique but by extension to Africa and other colonial situations) in his analysis of colonial psychopathologies, *Black Skin, White Masks*. This lack, he suggested, was likely the result of the lack of an Oedipus complex in blacks that presumably could be accounted for by the parents' (mainly mothers') nonshaming attitudes toward sexuality. Black male transvestites did exist, Fanon conceded, but he believed they led "normal sex lives" since they could "take a punch like any 'he-man'" (1967 [1952], 180n44). He went on that where black men did engage in homosexual relationships, it was not for "neurotic" reasons but simply to earn a livelihood, prostitution being one of the few good-paying jobs for blacks in a colonial setting. Hence, blacks became homosexual only when they traveled to Europe, where they were "always passive." This experience was necessarily degrading to blacks, in Fanon's view, but to Fanon the worst effect of homosexuality in such a setting was on whites, whose racism against blacks was inflamed. "Negrophobic man is a repressed homosexual" who vented anger at his mostly unconsummated lust for African men through racist acts of violence (156).

Fanon never qualified or retracted this cursory and prejudiced analysis in his later work. In this way he became unwittingly complicit in a cultural intimacy that united a disparate group of colonialists, white liberals, African chiefs, and African revolutionaries. The secret to be protected or denied was that Africans out of their own initiative and desire might not always conform to sex and gender expectations. One could take a punch like a he-man, in other words, but still privately enjoy sexual intimacy with males. Or one might not be hairy and aggressive as Freed's early stereotyping of lesbians would have it, but nonetheless still desire sensual closeness with females. That this secret could persist for so long is even more remarkable given that at least two other contemporary psychological studies provided compelling contradictory evidence. These two studies attempted, first to quantify, and then to understand same-sex desire among Africans in Africa using tried-and-true psychoanalytic methods. Both studies are entirely overlooked in Andor's compilation *Psychological and Sociological Studies of the Black People of Africa* (1983) as well as in leading academic monographs.

The first of these two studies came from a very different tradition from that of Freud, Jung, and Erikson within psychiatry. Pierre Hanry, a French professor of philosophy and psychiatry based in Conakry from the mid-1960s, took his primary inspiration from Wilhelm Reich, a former member of the German Communist Party who had developed a specifically Marxist interpretation of Freud. Reich's approach actively promoted frank sexual education and initiation from an early age. He also saw sexual emancipation from bourgeois or other oppressive mores as critical not only for individual mental well-being but for wider social transformation. The emancipation of female sexuality in particular, Reich argued, was elemental to the task of building a truly revolutionary (classless and democratic) society. He also saw repressed homosexuality as a factor in the rise of the cult of hypermasculinity that underlay fascism and militarism. Hanry was the first to adopt this analysis in his contribution to the development of socialism in revolutionary Guinea. While he wore his anticolonial and antiracism politics as defiantly as Fanon, he appears also to have been the last to do so.

Érotisme africain (Hanry 1970) was based largely on the results of a detailed questionnaire that Hanry administered to several hundred upper-level high school students in Conakry. Hanry also conducted key informant interviews. His goal was to learn what young Africans really did and thought about sex as a first step toward designing a radical sex education curriculum. Hanry's findings were startling, seemingly even to himself. For example, the consensus among his informants was that homosexuality was not practiced in Guinea, although it was thought to be widespread in neighboring Senegal. That clarified, more than one out of six of the boys conceded to having had homosexual relations. Twenty-one percent admitted to continuing regular masturbation notwithstanding its association with homosexuality, high peer pressure against it, and intense socialization to engage in early heterosexual intercourse. Even among the girls, despite enormous stigma, four out of eighty admitted to lesbian relationships. In addition, while most of the girls had been "circumcised" (their clitorises had been excised), many of them still practiced and claimed to enjoy clitoral masturbation. How this was possible was not explained, but it is possible to imagine Marie Bonaparte turning in her grave.

These numbers surely warranted attention, at least to problematize some of the balder generalizations about African sexuality then in play. Yet despite publication by a reputable press, Hanry's book generally escaped notice. It (and the issues it raises) failed to elicit even a passing nod in the overviews of the literature: Mallory (1975), Andor (1983), or Westley (1993). Most of the pages of the copy of *Érotisme africain* I consulted at an important research library remained uncut, thirty-five years after publication.

The other idiosyncratic study from this period is in some ways even more striking than Hanry's for the high quality of its interviews with African subjects and for the relative open-mindedness of the researchers. Beginning in 1955 three Swiss psychiatrists trained in classical methods took a series of sabbaticals from their successful Zurich practices with the aim of testing Freudian theory in a cross-cultural setting. With candid naïveté about Africa and colonialism, husband and wife Paul Parin and Goldy Parin-Matthèy plus colleague Fritz Morgenthaler first read a few books and talked to a few colonial officials to decide which people to study. After an initial sojourn among the Dogon of

Mali, they settled on the Anyi, a Twi-speaking branch of the Akan peoples in eastern Côte d'Ivoire. This choice came about in part because, as they admitted, the main Anyi villages were conveniently located on a good road and the people there were relatively fluent in French (Parin, Parin-Matthèy, and Morgenthaler 1980, 4). Primarily, however, the Swiss team chose the Anyi because their matrilineal kinship system was so different from the European family model that Freud had worked from. The Oedipal conflict apparently did not exist among the Anyi on account of this matrilineal system. Nonetheless the Anyi clearly and self-admittedly suffered all kinds of emotional traumas, including depression and intense suspicion and rivalry between males. The Anyi thus seemed to offer a fertile field to test whether Freud's insights into these kinds of traumas might be applicable despite radically different processes of childhood socialization. The methods the Parin team used to do so included observation of daily life, interviews with traditional healers, Rorschach tests (visual stimulation of free association), and nearly three hundred hours of psychoanalytic interviews carried out on seven volunteer patients intermittently over several years.

The Swiss were apparently unaware that Africans were not supposed to have doubts about their heterosexuality. They quickly established that "disturbed love relations" between adolescent boys were not only commonplace but that the boys' mothers actually approved and tacitly encouraged sex play among them, including group masturbation. The boys simply ignored their fathers' sporadic, ineffectual threats and whippings intended to stop them. Although boys were ultimately directed by their mothers to focus their adult sexuality on women and marriage, apparently long-term ambivalent tendencies remained. Morgenthaler, for example, complained of one of his subjects' persistent "homosexual wooing of me" (181). They also found that grown men sometimes joined in the masturbation circles, and reported a male "sorcerer" who attempted to seduce one of the male clients. A consensus emerged among the team that "bisexuality may be even more common in women" (204).

Hanry and Parin's team worked in isolation from each other and had little impact on the formation of African professionals. Africans who began entering the field of academic psychology in this period tended instead to align themselves with Fanon in their politics and priorities. The first Yoruba psychiatrist, T. Adeoye Lambo (1955), for example, and the Senegalese Alfa Ibrahim Sow (the first African to publish a monograph on psychology—Sow 1980) offered trenchant critiques of the inadequacies and false assumptions of Western nosology or categorization of illness. Yet like Fanon, Lambo, Sow, and others of their generation could be both strongly critical of Eurocentrism in the field yet at the same time replicate some of the very clumsiness and blindspots of their mentors. This included, notably, generalizing from the experience of boys and men to the entire population. More to the point of this chapter, African authors in the discipline through the 1990s had virtually nothing to say about the possibility that same-sex desire might be a complicating factor in African sexuality, childhood socialization, or mental health. By their silence, even when acknowledging possible tension between taboo and tolerance or between adolescent and adult sexuality, they strongly affirmed the old stereotypes: "sexual deviations are almost unheard of in most traditional African communities" and where they exist, it seems to be the Muslims to blame (Asuni, Schoenberg, and Swift 1994, 150). Sylvester Ntomchukwu Madu et al. (1996), billing their work as the "first investigations" by African professionals to address "various lacunae in psychotherapy" in Africa, do not manage a single reference to same-sex sexuality notwithstanding chapters on traditional healing, HIV/AIDS, and cults where mention was due.

THE STRANGE CASE OF GAY SHAKA

Early efforts to psychologize Africans' sexual behavior were clearly hugely problematic. As with the early ethnography, the field of ethnopsychiatry was populated by apologists for colonialism, male chauvinists, homophobes, and barely disguised racists. Much of the research they self-consciously conducted in the name of science scarcely rose above the level of conjecture or extrapolation from anecdotes and already dubious European models and stereotypes. The publications that resulted were in many ways even more colonialist than the colonialist ethnography. Directly reliant on the fieldwork and the presumptions of that ethnography, but typically lacking even the limited language skills that anthropologists aspired to, the first generations of ethnopsychiatrists interpreted their evidence through quintessentially Eurocentric models. Their sources and methods, including dream analysis, third person accounts, and observation of psychotic people, were notoriously vague and open to manipulation. In most cases, the research did not include reflection on the researchers' subjectivity or their power relationships over Africans, while in some cases it unabashedly aligned itself with the colonial state. Moreover, they often appeared in journals and in a style of language that were so arcane as to frequently escape the attention even of fellow professionals, let alone other interested audiences. Small wonder that psychology as a field was largely bypassed by Africans in the period of expansion of universities in the immediate postcolonial era (Nsamenang 1995).

Debates about "the African mind," and by extension African sexuality, nonetheless trickled into popular culture in innumerable ways. Amateur psychology was central to the creation of a film industry for colonial Africa, for example. The first attempts to use film to teach Africans Christian morality and how to be modern had often foundered on African laughter or seeming incredulousness at inappropriate moments. How then to fashion screen images that could penetrate Africans' consciousness in the desired edifying way? A British medical officer based in Nigeria named William Sellers proposed sweeping generalizations about African psychology that, if catered to properly, he promised would result in more effective cinema. In that way Sellers established an orthodoxy of method in filmmaking for Africans that dominated the continent from the 1920s through the 1950s. Indeed, as James Burns has noted in his study of Rhodesian documentary films, Sellers's brand of colonial pop psychology still resonated in the southern African advertising industry well into the 1990s (Burns 2002, 46; Sellers 1941).

Amateur psychology permeated European and settler literature about Africans as well, most commonly to explain and justify white domination. The work of Ethelreda Lewis is a noteworthy exception in that she wrote from a liberal, feminist perspective that was critical of racism against Africans. Lewis in fact played a significant role in promoting African trade unionism throughout southern Africa in the early 1930s (Couzens 1984, ix). In her best-selling novel *Wild Deer* (1984 [1933]) Lewis employed Freudian imagery and concepts to illustrate the modernizing potential of (somewhat) liberated sexuality for Africans. The novel is careful not to recommend interracial desire, but it does suggest that Africa as a whole will be uplifted by sexual union between culturally Westernized male Africans or African Americans and "raw," or pre-Oedipal, female Africans.

Few Africans are likely to have read *Wild Deer*, although, interestingly, echoes of Lewis (and Wilhelm Reich) are recurrent in several of the antiracist and antiapartheid novels from the 1970s and '80s.[15] Probably more significant by far than such novels was the impact that amateur psychology had in the historiography of southern Africa. This foray into psychohistory involved an attempt to understand the decision-making process of a prominent African leader in terms of his traumatized and repressed sexuality. That leader was Shaka, the humble, illegitimate boy from the small Zulu clan who rose to forge an "empire" between 1818 and 1828. Shaka was already a mythical figure before the end of the nineteenth century, a Black Napoleon, whose reputation subsequently served in diverse patriotic histories. Most accounts of his bloody career variously stressed his ruthlessness and cruelty as well as his military and social innovations (Hamilton 1998; Wylie 2000, 2006). His *impis* (warriors) became synonymous with African fighting élan, while the Zulu today are the largest single ethnolinguistic group in South Africa in part because of his wide-ranging conquests and assimilations. Refugees from Shaka's state in turn formed sometimes powerful states, modeled on his methods, that by the 1840s had spread like a ripple as far as present-day Zimbabwe (the Ndebele), Zambia (the Kololo or Lozi), and Tanzania and Malawi (the Ngoni). Shaka in the twentieth century also came to play an iconic role in pan-African ideology, disproving the racist lies that Africa had no history and no men of genius. According to Dorothy Blair in her study of francophone African literature (1976, 97), the legend of Shaka was pressed into service as far afield as West Africa, where Leopold Senghor, for example, characterized him as a "black martyr," and others as a prophetic advocate of Malian socialism. To David Chanaiwa (1980), he was nothing less than a revolutionary whose promotion of meritocracy and gender equity was not unlike that to which the Zimbabwean ruling party rhetorically aspired in the early 1980s.

Shaka existed as a real historical persona who may have been or done some of the things attributed to him. But could the heroic, tragic, symbolic founder of so many nations and an icon of pan-African and even diasporic black masculinity have been queer? Not only has the possibility been asserted in several international best-selling popular histories over the decades (esp. Morris 1965). A leading African nationalist also put it forward as a cautionary tale about African leadership (Mazrui 1975; see below). The same idea has recently been seriously discussed by a prominent international economic management psychologist for much the same reason, that is, Shaka's propensity for violence and arbitrary or tyrannical leadership may have been outward expressions of inner sexual turmoil (Kets de Vries 2004). Shaka has meanwhile been appropriated by queer scholars in a positive light (e.g., Desai 2001) and by lgbti groups in the West straightforwardly as a gay man. The KwaZulu-Natal theme park Shakaland, where the television series *Shaka Zulu* was filmed, is now being marketed as a tourist destination for African American gays.[16]

In his new biography of Shaka, Dan Wylie dismisses such claims about Shaka's sexuality as "speculative rubbish" (2006, 325). Aside from rehashing select second- or thirdhand anecdotes about Shaka's heterosexual impetuousness, however, Wylie does not justify such a harsh judgment. Nor does Wylie consider why, if indeed it is rubbish, what factors have contributed to the longevity and wide distribution of the homosexuality thesis. If we are to avoid giving succor to the sentiment that automatically rejects research that even skirts this topic, and if we want to gather insights into Africanist writing about African sexuality, we need to take the psychological speculation (and its appeal and deployment for such diverse polemical purposes) more seriously. How exactly did a modern, distinctively Western identity such as homosexual come to be projected so far back into the past and onto such a prominent individual? To answer that we have to go back to the earliest accounts of Shaka, written long before the words *psychology* or even *homosexuality* had been coined.

Early accounts of Shaka were penned retroactively by British traders and adventurers after his assassination. We know now that these men stood to gain financially by exaggerating Shaka's ferocity and the chaotic conditions of war and famine that he had supposedly caused. They hoped in this way to invite British imperial rule over the area that would consolidate their trading privileges and land claims at Zulu expense. A relatively minor element in this narrative was Shaka's cruelty to women specifically and his unusual fascination with (and desire to control) other people's sexuality. Henry Francis Fynn (1950, 30) also noted that Shaka shared a peccadillo (feigning menstruation) with his mentor, Dingiswayo. But what exactly caused Shaka and subsequent Zulu despots to be so cruel and irrational hardly needed commentary in these early accounts. They were Africans, after all, and from the dominant colonial point of view at that time, that meant cruel, libidinous, and woman hating by definition.

Since the 1980s, historians have shown how tendentious the early descriptions of Shaka were and how, over the nineteenth century Christian propagandists progressively inflated the horrors of his rule to create a trope of heathen savagery against which to measure the progress of Christian civilization.[17] The emerging historiography of Afrikaner nationalism also made use of this imagery to promote their own national identity (Christian heroes in a savage land) and to justify their claims over vast swaths of territory (allegedly depopulated by Shakan depredations).

African historians did not at first refute those exaggerations and slanders. On the contrary, the earliest recorded oral histories tended to corroborate that Shaka was indeed capricious and cruel. The missionary James Stuart, who gathered an archive of about 160 interviews from Zulu men and women at the turn of the nineteenth century, includes recollections stretching back to the wars and other disruptions of Shaka's times (Webb and Wright, 1975–2001). These interviews are full of contradictions, even about Shaka's physical appearance, on top of which there are worries about the effect of Stuart's translation and Christian politics on the archive. Nonetheless, a degree of consensus emerges in the testimony. Shaka's Zulu contemporaries were clearly alert to a sexual component in Shaka's success as a leader. He was remembered for having made several dramatic innovations concerning gender relations and sexuality (and for punishing people severely for disregarding them). For example, he abolished the traditional initiation schools in favor of age-regiments where the boys grew up and received disciplined military training together.

They remained a cohesive fighting unit for the rest of their warrior lives, which ended only either by death in battle or when Shaka determined that they had fought bravely enough to warrant the reward of marriage. Shaka also abolished the practice of *hlobonga* (nonpenetrative sex play among unmarried young men and women) as a strategy to co-opt the boys' frustrated youthful sexuality to military service. Stuart's informants also populated their recollections with numerous influential and sexual women, suggesting a degree of respect for women's power and sexuality that seems to stand at odds with heteropatriarchal norms.

Stuart's informants often tempered their criticisms of Shaka's violence or capriciousness with sympathy for his lonely childhood and the humiliations he and his mother were said to have suffered from his father, among others. Those humiliations stemmed from his illegitimate and foreign status in the village he grew up in, a theme that recurs in the first literary interpretations by African authors (notably Fuze 1979 [1922]; Mofolo 1981 [1931]). Christian missionaries who used the trope of an irredeemably savage Shaka were displeased with this interpretation to the extent of first repressing and then insisting on substantive editorial changes to Mofolo's manuscript (Dunton 1990). But a more subtle strategy to keep Shaka co-opted to the Christian cause also emerged in the 1920s. This was to put forward an analysis that situated Shaka's distemper directly in his troubled, and implicitly pathetic, sexuality. The author of that interpretation of history was Alfred Bryant, the first to draw upon Freudian theory to make his point.

Bryant wrote extensively on Zulu history and customs with an unwavering didacticism to promote the march of Catholic moral values in Africa. Typically he wrote in florid, melodramatic language, but he also turned to objective-sounding science where it served to underscore the moral lesson (Wylie 2000, 15). Bryant had toyed with ideas emanating from Freudian psychology as early as 1917, when he posited a profound decline in African boys' intellectual ability at the age of puberty that he linked to a cultural failure to instill sexual discipline. His magisterial *Olden Times in Zululand and Natal* (1929) then developed the analysis to explain Shaka, and the spread of an atavistically macho ethic in Zulu-influenced cultures throughout the region. The problem was, Bryant wrote, that Shaka as a boy had been tormented by other boys because of "the marked stumpiness of a certain organ" (1929, 62). This trauma had left him with a permanent psychological insecurity about his masculinity that manifested itself in fear of pregnant women. It also fueled a burning desire for revenge against the traditional patriarchal and gerontocratic system that had exposed him to the humiliation in the first place. Having climbed to power, Shaka's social and political reforms then transferred his neurosis as an individual to a whole generation of young Zulu men and, through constant wars against their neighbors, to Africans throughout the region.

Bryant identified his sources for his stunted-penis claim only by saying, "Many stories are extant" (62). In fact, after sifting through the hundreds of pages of jumbled testimony in the Stuart archive to which Bryant had access, I assume that he fixed upon a single, fleeting, and ambiguous reference to justify the claim. The evidence came from one of Stuart's informants, named Jantshi, who had just related to Stuart his recollections of the stories his father had told him about Shaka's boyhood. Jantshi was moving on to describe Shaka's rise to power when he interrupted himself with an afterthought about a childhood quarrel that Shaka had had with another boy living in a foreign village. According to Jantshi, that boy insulted Shaka with these words: "What sort of little Ntungwa is this, the one with the little half-cocked penis?" Ntungwa was a disparaging reference to the Zulu, but, as Jantshi explained, the rest of the insulting words "were similar to those the Lembe people had formerly used *in respect of his [Shaka's] ancestors*" (Webb and Wright 1975, 180; emphasis mine). In other words, if the incident ever even happened, it was a generic sexual insult by one boy *and others in the past*, against a whole category of people to whom Shaka was related.

From this inauspicious debut, the "historic insult" took on a life of its own. After Bryant, long-serving colonial official E. A. Ritter essentially plagiarized Bryant's story for his book, adding for good measure a colorful imagined quotation from the offending boy: "Look at his penis; it is just like a little earth worm!" (1957, 14).

Ritter's embellishment of the story was likely intended to titillate and to improve sales of a book that was unabashedly aimed at a popular, white audience. Matters became serious, however, when a highly respected academic intervened—Max Gluckman. By the early 1960s Gluckman had moved on from the Rhodes-Livingstone Institute to found the so-called Manchester school of anthropology. This school emphasized the importance of historical and applied political consciousness in anthropological research, and Gluckman made no secret of his commitment to anticolonial and anti-apartheid politics within and without the academy. Yet he also clearly maintained his earlier fascination for psychological explanations of behavior, and in his later career he argued that psychology was critical to offset dehumanizing tendencies in the structural functionalist analysis then in vogue in the discipline (Gluckman 1974). In this he was a pioneer of Africanist scholarship that sought to place African agency and dignity as people at the center of the analysis.

How then to explain Gluckman picking up and expanding on Bryant's theory in a baldly speculative manner that would probably have been offensive to most educated Africans and that, historically, had been used by Christian and colonialist propagandists to undermine African claims about their own history? Yet that was exactly what he did in a prominent article in one of the top international scientific journals when he claimed that Shaka "was at least a latent homosexual and possibly psychotic" (Gluckman 1960, 168).

As with Gluckman's earlier promotion of Ritchie's musings on African sexual incontinence, it may be that Gluckman saw a subtle antiracist value in psychologizing Shaka's sexuality.[18] The context in which he wrote had worsened considerably for blacks in South Africa since the early 1940s. The apartheid regime was broadcasting its ultimate goal to entrench distinct African tribes that could be legally and politically disenfranchised once and for all. Clumsy anthropologies that reified difference and stability in traditional cultures were being elevated to state doctrine. If nothing else, therefore, the idea of Shaka's homosexuality threw a wrench into the project of stereotyping all Zulu or all Bantu according to such potted ethnography or Afrikaner nationalist myths. Moreover, since even repressed homosexuality was still generally regarded as a moral shortcoming, almost across the social, political, religious, and ethnic spectrums in South Africa, this version of Shaka by implication valorized a deep commonality between the Zulu/African moral universe and that of responsible whites.

According to Daphna Golan (1994), Gluckman privately expressed doubts about this assertion.[19] With his solid reputation as an Africanist scholar who was publicly sympathetic to African political aspirations, however, and given that he published this claim in such a high-profile *scientific* journal, others relied on him implicitly. Donald Morris, first, restored Shaka's physical phallus to generous proportions. But, following Gluckman, he retained the explanatory power of Freudian theory by conjecturing its nonperformance: "despite the fact that his genitals had more than made up for their previous dilatoriness, so that he always took great pride in bathing in full public view, he was probably impotent" (1965, 46). When prominent African nationalist academic Ali Mazrui next uncritically embraced the claim by citing Gluckman, it was then well on the way to becoming a "fact."

Mazrui's intervention in 1975 in one of the premier Africanist political science journals is especially significant in that it connected Shaka's purported sexual problems to a popular interpretation of Frantz Fanon's homophobic antiracism. In this view, the "demasculation" of African men that had taken place under colonial rule was continuing under humiliating neocolonial and apartheid conditions. Such ongoing demasculation necessitated the assertion of a heterosexually virile African leader in proud, remasculinizing opposition. Mazrui pointed to Uganda's lusty Idi Amin as an exemplar of the latter while putting forward Shaka as the bad example. According to Mazrui, Shaka had failed as an African leader and should not be regarded as a nationalist icon because the cruelties and excesses he had committed could be traced back to his homosexuality. While the homosexuality was blameworthy in itself, even worse, it indirectly opened the way for white conquest of southern Africa. Other than "Legend has it" (as he put it), Mazrui cited Bryant, Ritter, and Gluckman plus one other critic (who actually rejected the idea) as his sources (Mazrui 1975, 74).[20]

Mazrui's apologetics for heterosexual despotism were not the nadir in Shakan historiography. On the contrary, while the 1980s witnessed a series of radical revisions to the Shakan and the wider mfecane historiography at the level of professional scholarship, little was done to pin down Shaka's shifting sexuality through meticulous research. Silence left the field open for a remarkable piece of apartheid propaganda that, almost certainly unintentionally, elevated Shaka to the level of international gay icon while at the same time playing on some of the oldest colonial stereotypes about African savagery, machismo, and female heterosexual looseness.

Shaka Zulu (Faure and Sinclair 1987) has much discreditable about it in the way it constructs a racial hierarchy. As art, however, the film clearly transcends the standards of its genre. Its treatment of the character of Shaka is an especially enduring aspect of that achievement. Put simply, the camera cannot feast its eye enough on the exquisite physique of the man recruited to play Shaka. Henry Cele, a soccer star, rarely appears on screen in more than a loincloth. The plot has him possess and impregnate his nubile concubine, in accordance with conventional accounts dating back to Fynn and Stuart. The film also sticks to convention in its flashbacks to Shaka's suffering from bullying as a boy and to his growing volcanic rage at the injustices of clan and family politics. Throughout the long narrative, however, uncountable naked breasts and black bodies sway in regular periodic dance scenes to create a constant erotic tension (remember that soft pornography, and even the Beatles, were banned under apartheid censorship laws). Cele/Shaka scarcely seems to notice. In short, while no direct hints in the script lead the viewer back to Bryant's or Gluckman's theories, the visual aesthetic that the film creates is as gay as the Village People.

The principal intended audience for *Shaka Zulu* was never in Africa but in the United States, where the antiapartheid campaign was then picking up momentum. The government of South Africa hoped that the movie's depiction of crazed, whirling savages and calm white men would deflate some of the American public's support for the transition of power to blacks in South Africa. It did not, and in fact it was roundly panned in the American media as the racist propaganda that it was. But something else unexpected did happen: Cele's beautiful glistening torso and campy posturing found an audience. The politics of HIV/AIDS and race in the United States at that specific moment unquestionably played a role in this development. African American lgbti had become the focus of intense, explicit demonization in the rapidly emerging genres of rap and hip hop music. At the same time, in the panicky discourses about "gay plague" in the relatively affluent white gay community, African American lgbti were largely airbrushed out of the picture. A gay Shaka in that context was a powerful affirmation of pride against homophobia in their own communities and against invisibility in the wider body politic. Over the course of the 1990s, *Shaka Zulu* thus became one of the most popular miniseries ever to be screened on American television. Today it circulates internationally as a DVD, marketed as a classic historical adventure story without the slightest reference to its provenance as apartheid propaganda.[21]

꙳

None of the foregoing discussion resolves key questions raised by the literature. Perhaps Shaka was tormented by ambiguous sexual feelings and repressed desire. Perhaps weaning practices in African societies do have an effect on adult sexuality something like Ritchie described. Perhaps it does make a difference to the prevalence of same-sex sexuality in a society if that society is matrilineal as opposed to patrilineal. Perhaps for a man to have sex with another man or boy or for a woman to have sex with a woman or girl was so insignificant to his or her understanding of personal identity or psychological well-being—right across the whole of Africa and over all time—that it does not warrant investigation by professional psychologists. The kind of trauma and homophobia coming out of rape experiences described by Gear's and Ngubeni's informants (Gear and Ngubeni 2002; Gear 2005, 2007), or the mixed emotions revealed in African literature and film (see chapter 5) suggest not, but admittedly the research simply has not been done to be entirely confident.

One thing we can say for certain, however, is that the way these questions were asked and answered in the past is of considerable interest. Indeed, if the ethnopsychiatrists and psychohistorians did not solve the riddles they perceived about African sexual decision making, their work, at least until the mid-1970s, does tell us that future research will have to be more careful. Taken as a whole, the early attempts to psychoanalyze Africans provide a sobering lesson on the ease with which self-described science can elide to almost the baldest racism. This history also helps explain why African intellectuals might have had difficulty perceiving the relevance of key concepts of homosexuality to their own societies. For example, when science said women who had sex with women were lesbians and that lesbians were defined as follows, who can blame Africans for not recognizing the type and disregarding the literature: "they wear low heel shoes, costumes with an almost masculine cut; they are fond of wearing men's slacks; their hair is cut short. They smoke and drink and sport a monocle" (Freed 1949, 60). And, for a more recent example, what does Kets de Vries mean when he says that Shaka conformed to "the etiology of homosexuality" except that "Shaka is sometimes purported to have sometimes behaved like a stereotype of closeted gays in a particular period of history in the West" (90)?

This history does not give confidence in the rigor of ostensibly scientific enquiry into and constructions of African sexuality as it unfolded through the middle decades of the twentieth century. When the issue reemerged with a vengeance in the footsteps of HIV/AIDS in the 1980s and '90s, many Africans were simply unwilling to believe that a new generation of Western scientists had definitively put those old prejudices behind them.

4 ~ Slim Disease and the Science of Silence

I HAVE SO FAR EMPHASIZED HOW SCHOLARSHIP that claimed to be scientific was in many cases scarcely more than self-serving prejudice. Bad or sloppy science in colonial and apartheid Africa thus often amply merited popular mistrust, particularly when the results were deployed for invidious ends. Anthropology and psychology, notably, were commonly used to argue for maintaining or expanding privileges for whites within colonial systems, while biomedical science was used to justify the racial segregation of neighborhoods and cities, leaving a lasting imprint on Africa's urban infrastructure. Biomedical research involving human subjects, to be generous, was not always conducted ethically under the prevailing conditions.[1]

This history is highly pertinent to understanding popular responses to HIV/AIDS in the present. Indeed, a striking aspect of the HIV/AIDS pandemic is the ability of people to deny scientific evidence of its existence and to rationalize not changing behavior in the face of what objectively looks like a dire threat. This ability existed from the onset of the disease among highly educated gay men in big urban centers in the West, and remains a persistent problem worldwide. However, the denial of AIDS in various forms has emerged as a particularly disturbing theme in the recent history of Africa south of the Sahara, where the sheer numbers and rippling calamitous impacts of illness are so huge. A proliferation of folk explanations and "cures," and of charlatans, pseudoscientists, faith healers, witch finders, conspiracists, and other opportunists, has arisen, offering to fill in the explanatory gaps left by science. Notwithstanding that science has made huge strides in the decades of research since the outbreak began, that biomedical interventions such as antiretroviral therapy now have directly and almost immediately observable health benefits, and that rigorous biomedical research and guidance are now universally accepted by African governments as crucial to fighting the disease, often profound misunderstandings, ignorance, distrust, and cynicism toward science continue. Such attitudes are not confined to the poorly educated fringes but have been displayed at the highest levels of state. A case in point was when the deputy president and former head of the National AIDS Council in one of the most heavily infected counties in the world testified under oath in April 2006 that he had knowingly had unprotected sex with an HIV-positive woman. Jacob Zuma of South Africa went on to explain how he took a shower afterward to mitigate the risk. His minister of health's first public response to this admission was to castigate not Zuma but the media for its coverage of the issue.[2]

Ignorance or obtuseness on such a scale is a real threat to efforts to contain HIV/AIDS, and indeed, Zuma subsequently apologized for the harm he may have done to public education. But Zuma's and others' startling views nonetheless raise the question of whether prejudices and blind spots inherited from colonial-era science have percolated into scientific enquiry and public discourse in the postcolonial period. We can pursue that question by interrogating the early scientific literature on the transmission of HIV among Africans. It is a literature that has been closely scrutinized before and challenged for insidious racist assumptions. Gisselquist and colleagues (2003), notably, found scientists to have been overhasty in ruling out unhygienic needles as significant in the African epidemic, in part due to strong prior assumptions about African promiscuity. Tellingly, however, they did not consider whether that same rush to orthodoxy happened in the case of msm or "hidden bisexuality." Yet even a casual eye must note how rapidly orthodoxy was established and how cursory was the research in this regard. Less than two years and a handful of questionable empirical studies passed between the first tentative acknowledgment that an AIDS-like disease was present in Africa to definitive statements that homosexual transmission did not merit investigation in any of the forty plus countries in question. The literature clearly warrants another closer look.

SEXUALITY AND HEALTH IN COLONIAL AFRICA

The sexual health of Africans was a major concern to colonial regimes and Christian missionaries across Africa from the late nineteenth century. The unchecked spread of sexually transmitted infections, above all syphilis, was a humanitarian crisis. Syphilis before the late 1940s was effectively incurable. It frequently resulted in insanity and a horrible, humiliating death, including for wives infected by their husbands, with all that that implied for stable family life. There were also material and political implications to the disease. Even less debilitating infections like gonorrhea undermined the viability of a cheap African labor force in that the resultant sickness and absenteeism imposed significant costs on industry. The existence of sexually transmitted diseases on such a scale also exposed to public debate the sordid underpinnings of the so-called civilizing mission. The male migrant labor system, the legal and institutional apparatus erected to minimize women's and children's presence in towns and to prevent normal urbanization, and the proliferation of prostitution that often flowed from these policies, brought condemnation of colonialism from critics as wide ranging as Christian missionaries, African intellectuals and traditional leaders, African Americans, European feminists, and the Comintern.[3]

Colonial medical interventions to address the crisis often did put humanitarian concerns to the fore. Funding and personnel, however, were never remotely adequate to the task. Moreover, often operating under extremely primitive laboratory conditions and in the face of unfamiliar tropical diseases, European medical interventions almost inescapably drew on poor or flatly wrong empirical research. The extent of the syphilis epidemic around the turn of the century, notably, appears to have been hugely exaggerated due to confusion between the very similar spirochetes that cause syphilis and yaws, the latter being endemic in much of Africa and nonsexually transmitted (Jochelson 1999, 218–19).[4]

Medical interventions concerning sexual health further suffered from high levels of morally normative language and presumptions. Indeed, the majority of the early health care providers were missionaries or lay Christian doctors and nurses. Their understanding of African sexuality was profoundly colored by the vocation that had brought them to Africa in the first place: to convert "barbarous" or "lascivious" Africans to a model of "civilized" gender relations and sexuality such as they idealized about their own societies. Disease in this way became a rhetorical crowbar to pry Africans away from customary practices and understandings of puberty transitions, courtship, marriage, and even specific sexual acts. As evident in the writings of the doctors who dabbled in psychology, and as appears as a persistent theme in colonial medical reports, secular health care officials often expressed a similarly blaming or manipulative conception of African sexuality. Their professional intentions may have been laudable, but their frustrations with promoting Africans' sexual health fed directly into an old colonialist tautology. That is, high levels of sexually transmitted infections "proved" the natural proclivity of Africans to unconstrained heterosexual activity. This then proved that authoritarian forms of government were needed to save Africans from themselves. Paternalistic regimes, often built around an alliance between colonial power and reactionary "tribal" patriarchs, were needed to inculcate the moral core of sexual discipline thought to be necessary for good governance. Until that happened, Africans could not be trusted with even basic acknowledgments of shared humanity such as city planning and labor regimes designed to enable stable family life. Yet without the latter, prostitution (or what looked liked prostitution) prevailed in the demographically skewed cities. The logic looped back upon itself.

In practical terms what all this meant was that medical interventions purportedly on behalf of Africans' sexual health were frequently punitive, deeply humiliating for the recipients, and either useless or actually counterproductive to preventing the spread of diseases. The practice that the Shona people termed *chibeura* was one of the more notorious examples (L. Jackson 2002). The government of Southern Rhodesia condoned chibeura as a corporate and municipal practice in the 1920s whereby police would intercept women they suspected of being prostitutes before they could get into town. The women were then compelled to submit to a vaginal examination, often with male African police constables in attendance. If found to have a sexually transmitted infection, they were given a measure of treatment. The main point, however, was that they could then be summarily deported back to the rural areas, where they would not infect the precious male workers in town. Suspicion of being a prostitute often meant little more than not having proof of permission to travel to the "white man's town," such as a letter from the male legal guardian (husband, father, headman, or son).

In other settings, men who did not report symptoms for treatment faced a prison sentence—or were fired and deported to rural homes—if discovered (Jeeves 2001, 2). And discovered they would be, since many of the large employers subjected their contract African laborers to mandatory genital and anal examinations as a precondition for employment or reemployment after every short-term contract.

The colonial medical establishment through the first half of the twentieth century also de facto supported the view that male-male sexuality among Africans either did not exist or was not a potential health concern. Some doctors may have simply accepted the prevailing wisdom about Africans' simple heterosexual nature and not even considered homosexuality as a possibility. Others may have felt the same misplaced confidence in the progress of "respectability" as, for example, the influential anthropologist E. E. Evans-Pritchard. This view recognized the existence of certain homosexual-like rites or relationships in traditional culture but felt (as the anthropologists' African informants assured them) that such practices had become moribund in the face of the march of civilization and Christian missionary propaganda (Evans-Pritchard 1970, referring to research conducted in the 1930s). But at the same time, medical professionals were unquestionably aware of new situational forms of msm. Doctors were often called as witnesses in criminal cases of indecent assault or sodomy, for example, and were likely abreast of the work of prominent authors like Cureau, Henri-Alexandre Junod, and Laubscher. The fact that medical health officials did not write more about the situational sex that Cureau and others described thus reflects the fact that it simply was not perceived as a public health concern. It may even—though not to be admitted in public—have been regarded as an actual public health good.[5]

How could men from a culture that otherwise criminalized and scorned homosexuality have construed msm among Africans as a desirable behavior? The simple answer is that anally transmitted sexual infections were almost never observed in the dominant forms of msm practiced by African men, and indeed, the men themselves claimed that anal sex was not allowed according the prevailing etiquette, even among the fiercest criminal gangs. The participants in these relationships for the most part clearly were not turning into "real homosexuals" to disturb social decorum. In the context of the times, the male-male thigh sex or masturbation that Cureau and others alluded to were also obviously less risky activities than male-female prostitution. As a discreet (and discrete) temporary expedient they probably helped preserve men's marriages to women and social stability back home in the rural areas, not to mention protecting white women from the assumed scourge that might result from unrequited black male lusts (so-called Black Peril). Male-male sexuality associated with long-distance porterage, prisons, mine hostels, and other modern institutions was thus somewhat embarrassing to colonial health officials but could be tolerated or even tacitly condoned.

Public health not being at risk, and moral education being largely in the hands of the missionaries, colonial states thus made scant movement on this issue beyond guarding against obvious breaches of the peace and public decency.[6] The first noteworthy health intervention I was able to uncover was not until the late 1930s or early 1940s. In that instance, the South African government lent its support to an International Red Cross initiative. The intent was to teach African working-class men the health benefits of abstinence, self-repression, and self-masturbation. The pamphlet they circulated to men on the mines in southern Africa was principally concerned with averting sexually transmitted infections acquired from female prostitutes. However, it also vigorously denounced homosexuality ("This unnatural act, repulsive to all healthy minded men, must be strenuously opposed and eradicated"). It underscored this point by anchoring itself in reference both to modern medical science and to the ethnography of ancient African cultures. Indeed, without noticing any contradiction with its masturbation advice for grown men (or that white doctors had previously berated African mental patients for "self-abuse"), the authors swathed themselves under the mantle of respect for African traditions: "Tribal Laws of the Bantu provided drastic penalties for sexual irregularities." (Red Cross Society, no date).

Vaughan (1991), Summers (1991), and Jeeves (2001) have all shown how other antisyphilis propaganda in eastern and southern Africa from the period was similarly crude, hectoring, and both fickle and so hubristic about the wonders of Western science that African audiences were probably largely alienated from the key public health messages. A medical breakthrough, however, eventually made the ineffectiveness of education somewhat moot from a narrowly utilitarian perspective. This was the discovery and widespread availability of low-cost, effective cures for syphilis after World War II. Anxieties about heterosexually transmitted infections, and state hostility to women in town as purveyors of disease and immorality, remained strong throughout the 1950s. The sexual health crisis of the prepenicillin days, however, was largely contained and managed with the new medicines. The change is evident in colonial and apartheid health reports in the 1950s that emphasize tuberculosis and poor housing as the principal enemies of African health.

Yet even as this medical achievement was being accomplished, a new aspect of the crisis—and of African sexuality—was revealed. Perhaps the state's antiprostitute campaigns and missionary antipromiscuity propaganda were having some impact after all, or perhaps African men on their own initiative started to bend their own rules about no anal sex. In any case, the first-ever systematic attempt to determine the numbers of African men engaging in penetrative male-male sex in an urban context was reported in 1949. It turned up an unexpected result. Dr. Louis Freed found that nineteen out of his sample of 211 syphilis patients had an anal infection. To the doctor, this suggested that no less than 9 percent of African men in Johannesburg were engaged in receptive homosexual anal sex, or just about double the rate he found among white men in the same study. Freed did not us tell much about his sample. The complete lack of evidence from elsewhere of a white john/black male prostitute scene, however, points to other black men as the source of the anal infection, presumably prisoners or coworkers in the mining or other industrial compounds.[7]

Startling as they were, Freed's numbers did not inspire any follow-up studies. On the contrary, the weight of other opinion in the scholarship and popular discourse made them appear so anomalous that they were effectively ignored. The consensus that msm among Africans was not a health or other issue actually strengthened in the two ensuing decades in keeping with the gathering definitiveness of assertions about African sexuality elsewhere on the continent. Lindsay Clowes and Kenda Mutongi have examined how this unfolded in the advice columns in the popular style magazine *Drum* (Clowes 2001, 2005; Mutongi 2000). But as we saw in the previous chapters, the scientific literature and the rhetoric of the anticolonialist, antiapartheid movements also supported that view. Jomo Kenyatta's polemic on the topic, for example, had been conceived and written in the 1930s but it acquired a wide readership only after Kenyatta became president of an independent Kenya in 1966. More explicitly revolutionary writing such as Frantz Fanon's asserted an even more homophobic construction of African sexuality, which similarly gained its first wide audience in the 1960s and '70s. These powerful works carried a resonance among African intellectuals that far outweighed the obscure publications of white doctors in South Africa. Apartheid obsessions about the state of white male sexuality meanwhile further served to downplay the existence of msm among nonwhites in public debates in South Africa through the 1960s and '70s (see in particular Retief 1994 and Schiller 1998). Freed poured his own energies into the struggle to resist the South African state's attempts to criminalize homosexuality among whites in the 1960s, abandoning his earlier research on black msm.

It may also be that the period from the 1950s to the 1970s witnessed an empirical decline in the frequency of homosexual relations among black working-class men that added to the disappearing effect. Improved conditions for men in single-sex institutions, notably, started to undermine the mine marriage "system" in those decades, as presumably had "stabilization" policies in the Belgian Congo and Northern Rhodesia. An influx of women into towns in those years also brought a relative diminution of risks normally associated with a scarcity of female prostitutes (increased demand, high rate of infection), making it easier and less costly for the men to establish heterosexual relationships in town. It may even be that African nationalist enforcement of heterosexual sexual discipline contributed to the reduction in msm, or at least in the practice of anal sex. Dlamini (1984, 132) alludes to as much in his account of homophobic violence instigated by the Pan Africanist Congress on Robben Island in the 1960s. But whatever the combination of causes, the next survey after Freed's to raise the issue brought his estimate on the prevalence of homosexual anal sex down considerably. A survey of 362 African men with syphilis, outpatients at the Johannesburg Native Hospital (currently, Chris Hani Baragwanath Hospital), positively traced homosexual contaminations in six cases, a bit less than 2 percent of the total (Dogliotti 1971, 9). Again no discussion or investigation followed this finding, at least in the professional journals.

It would be a mistake to invest too much in the meaning of these or other numbers pertaining to the sex lives of Africans in town. The real point is that between the late 1940s and mid-1970s virtually no dedicated, methodologically sound research on the question was done. Early attempts to survey African opinions directly did debunk many colonial myths about African sexual brutishness and naïveté but still at most only barely skirted the issue of homosexuality. Schenkel's study (1971, 341–43, 378–79), for example, refers to it only obliquely in reference to Senegalese informants' understanding of male impotence. Symington (1972) also captured the spirit of the times in a study that, while clearly aspiring to Alfred Kinsey in sociological methods and style, simply did not ask his Harare township subjects about same-sex sexuality or even masturbation. In this, Symington reflected how far the inability to conceive, let alone publicly to broach the topic had firmed in popular and academic discourse. Significantly, hints of that reticence or incomprehension also began to appear around this time in the political sphere. When a German journalist questioned Tanzanian president Julius Nyerere on the issue in 1973, for an important example, Nyerere first maintained that homosexuality was unnatural and should be illegal. He then declared that, as an African, he was "amazed" by liberal European attitudes toward homosexuality: "I can't even begin to talk about it."[8]

Yet before the decade was out, Tanzanian traders who later admitted to having casual sex with males and females would be implicated in the introduction of a fearsome new disease into Uganda.

MSM AND SLIM DISEASE

The above history needs to be borne in mind if we are to understand people's responses to three shocking discoveries over the course of 1983–84. First was the discovery that HIV/AIDS had already become well entrenched in Africa before the first cases were even identified. By the time doctors arrived in the Rakai district of Uganda, whole villages had been depopulated by "slim disease," while people reported having been aware of the mysterious killer at least three or four years before. Among select groups tested elsewhere in the region, such as prostitutes and truck drivers, rates in 1984 were found to be already in the double digits—and in some cases a majority of the sample—barely months after the first confirmations of HIV infection. As this finding represented far higher rates than anywhere else in the world to that point, it implied that efforts to contain the pathogen's spread had to be even more urgent than had been the case in the West.[9]

Second was the discovery that men and women in Central Africa were almost equally infected. Since its appearance in North America in 1981 the new disease had been primarily associated with gay or bisexual men. Even considering the other "risk groups," as they were identified (intravenous drug users, hemophiliacs and other recipients of blood transfusions, and Haitians), the disease in the West in 1983 remained overwhelmingly concentrated in the male population. The equal ratio between men and women in Central Africa thus suggested a very different and far more dangerous pattern than that in Europe and North America. As one of the first World Health Organization studies found, 90 percent of the African AIDS patients did not belong to any of the then known risk groups (Quinn et al. 1986, 956). This meant that rather than a potentially self-limiting epidemic among relatively small minorities, Africa might be facing a catastrophic pandemic in the majority population.

And third was the discovery that HIV appeared to be a genetic adaptation of simian immunodeficiency virus from apes to human hosts. As if stigma and AIDSphobia were not already complicating political responses to AIDS in the West, racists there immediately seized on the new evidence to slur Africans with accusations of bestiality. Even otherwise sober media made comments that fueled an existing popular perception of Africa and Africans as a source of disease and a looming threat to the West.

Conscious of the political uproar and moral panic that HIV/AIDS was causing in the West, but likewise horrified at the prospect of uncontrollable pandemic, the first scientists to propose its existence in Africa tried to appear as calmly empiricist as possible in publishing their findings. The very first letter to alert medical professionals that AIDS was present among blacks in Africa referred to a married Zairean woman and concluded, simply, that "AIDS is not restricted to homosexuals and drug users" (Offenstadt et al. 1983, 775). Another early letter, whose lead author went on to become one of the foremost researchers in the field, ventured only that "Black Africans, immigrants or not, may be another group predisposed to AIDS" (Clumeck et al. 1983, 642). Thereafter, as studies began to report an almost equal number of black women as men testing positive for HIV or showing AIDS symptoms, researchers first wondered ("Is there something unusual about the sexual mores of Kinshasa"?—Greenwood 1984, 294) and then carefully tested their logic. The evident absence of risk groups as then understood could mean only three things: either that African AIDS was a different disease from what appeared in the West, or that it was being spread to women through needles infected in the health care system, or that it was being spread through heterosexual intercourse among Africans.

The first possibility was quickly ruled out by genetic analysis (although, significantly, different clades, or subtypes, of the virus predominated in Africa compared to America and Europe). The second hypothesis took a bit longer but, notwithstanding the often chaotic state of health care systems in Central Africa, infected needles were soon also ruled out as a major mode of transmission. This left oral sex and heterosexual intercourse, either through vaginal or anal sex. Both oral and anal sex were ruled out through interviews with African patients and healthy controls alike, almost all of whom often strenuously denied any sexual practice other than vaginal intercourse. African informants apparently did not mind admitting to multiple partners in that activity, however. On the contrary, Africans in the most affected areas like Rakai themselves intuitively connected the disease with the breakdown of traditional mores that had valued (and enforced) heterosexual restraint. As Hooper reports, many Ugandans rued the new disease as metaphysical payback for their self-admitted decline in sexual morality (Hooper 1990).[10]

Several studies from 1983 through 1985 appeared to corroborate that admission or intuition by demonstrating a close correlation between vaginal intercourse with multiple heterosexual partners and HIV infection. Hardly more than a year after the first cautious alert, therefore, scientists posited—and then began to unambiguously assert in positive terms—that men's frequent use of female prostitutes and the prostitutes' "highly promiscuous" behavior were the key variables in the spread of the disease. Van de Perre et al. (1984, 65) added that living in the city and having a "reasonable standard of living" (which compared to rural poverty enabled promiscuity) were also probable risk factors.[11]

But could it be possible that the men who infected the female prostitutes had been infected by other men? Although there was obviously no gay scene in the cities first affected by HIV/AIDS, the first studies in Kinshasa, Kigali, and Kampala nonetheless did tentatively inquire about the possibility of covert homosexual or bisexual activity. In some cases they left the question open. The pioneering article by Van de Perre et al. (1984, 65), for example, did not exclude the possibility that one of the seventeen men in their study may have had homosexual contacts during his three previous years in prison. Mostly, however, male African informants vigorously denied such activity and their interlocutors saw no reason either to dispute them or to reask the question in more subtle ways. The consensus thus moved very quickly to discount that possibility out of hand, that is, without bothering any more to ask about it or to consult pertinent local publications.

Summing up the evidence after the first two tumultuous years, a key article published in the *Lancet* in 1986 thus concluded, "The sex ratio of cases does not support homosexual distribution and, furthermore, most Africans, both male and female, adamantly deny homosexual activity" (Biggar 1986, 81). The predominantly heterosexual nature of transmission was further, definitively asserted in *Science* magazine the same year by four of the top medical scientists in the field. Despite offering tantalizing evidence to the contrary, Quinn, Mann, Curran, and Piot set the dominant tone for the next two decades by not even listing homosexual intercourse as a mode of transmission in Africa (Quinn et al. 1986). Occasional calls for caution and more careful research notwithstanding, this omission was established as so strong an orthodoxy that by 1988 it typically did not require a footnote to substantiate or qualify. When Botha and colleagues described the first two cases of South African women with AIDS, for example, they did not include a single citation to back their flat claim about "heterosexual promiscuity" in Africa (Botha et al. 1988). Writing in 1989, Hooper even suggested that scientists who had left the door open to homosexual or bisexual transmission in their early publications quickly regretted or were embarrassed by the caution (1990, 347). With Caldwell, Caldwell, and Quiggin's sprawling and influential synthesis of the research on African sexuality published that same year, same-sex sexuality entirely disappeared as an object of enquiry. The number ninety, meanwhile, which had first been cited by the WHO as the percentage of symptomatic Africans in the category "no known risk factor," came by default to be understood as quantifying the dominance of heterosexual transmission.

The first systematic Knowledge, Attitudes, Beliefs and Practices (KABP) surveys came soon *after* certainty about heterosexual transmission was established. These were begun by the Global Programme on AIDS of the World Health Organization in 1988. By 1991, collaborative (international and local) research teams had completed surveys in eighteen African countries with sample sizes ranging from 1,600 to 3,000 informants. The summary of the findings reported all kinds of intimate details about sexual activity outside of marriage and traditional relations as revealed by African men and women, including mean age of first intercourse, how many partners on average, frequency of "casual sex" and condom use, risk awareness, and much more. Same-sex sexuality does not merit a single mention (Caraël et al. 1991).

National HIV/AIDS control programs or committees began to be put in place around this time in line with the scientific consensus. Without a cure or vaccine, this meant that attention focused first on securing the blood supply by proper screening and safe transfusions. Next came national prevention and education initiatives. A strong tendency to blame and to fan fear or despondency was often apparent in the early official rhetoric (Iliffe 2006, 67). For the most part, however, state prevention and education campaigns quickly came to adhere to the World Health Organization's practical antidiscrimination philosophy. That position explicitly recognized the important role of secrecy and taboo in abetting unsafe sexual practices, and it advocated developing an approach to sex education that used frank language. In keeping with the scientific orthodoxy of the time, however, the latter almost never spoke frankly about or even conceded the possibility of African msm. On the contrary, national AIDS campaigns focused virtually exclusively on reducing high-risk heterosexual contacts by promoting the use of condoms and a reduced number and frequency of sexual partners: "zero grazing" (no sex outside marriage) was the catchphrase of Uganda's relatively successful initiative in the late 1980s. Gay white South Africans did on their own initiative introduce HIV/AIDS education directed in their own small, out communities, but nothing in the academic or scientific literature suggested that their concerns were regarded as pertinent to nonwhite, nongay audiences. As late as 1992, the very first scientific monograph on male homosexuality in South Africa abetted the impression that both homosexuality and HIV/AIDS were white, essentially urban phenomena by its flat disinterest in nonwhite msm (Isaacs and Mc-Kendrick 1992).

As logical and persuasive as this orthodoxy may have seemed at the time, it was evidently ineffective in addressing the public health crisis. With the sole exception of Senegal, where adult prevalence of HIV/AIDS was kept below 1 percent, the disease confounded every national AIDS program—in some cases, notably in southern Africa, spectacularly so. Adult prevalence shot up from around 0.7 percent in South Africa in 1990 to nearly 25 percent in a decade (Abdool Karim and Abdool Karim 2005, 56), and as high as 37.5 percent in KwaZulu-Natal and in neighboring countries by the early 2000s.[12] No serious observers doubted that heterosexual intercourse remained at the heart of the disaster and that every effort needed to be made to protect girls and young women in particular. This could be attempted through, among other things, frank sex education, such as how to put on a condom properly. But one has to wonder, did an understanding of "frank" that stubbornly did not allow talk about the full range of human sexuality add to the mystery/disaster? A profound naïveté about social science research extended to clumsiness in the broaching of questions about sexuality and to haste in accepting informants' nos at face value. Heterosexist logic, disciplinary blinkers, self-censorship by African gays and gay rights activists, and the politics of appeasement toward homophobic political leadership, both in Africa and in the United States, also played a role in overdetermining the blind spot.

CONSTRUCTING "HETEROSEXUAL AFRICAN AIDS":
A DISCOURSE ANALYSIS

In retrospect, the orthodoxy about the nonexistence or insignificance of homosexuality and bisexuality to the struggle against HIV/AIDS in Africa surprises not only for the unscientific rush to generalize about a vast place based on extremely limited research samples, but also for ignoring anomalies in the empirical record. Even South Africans—coming from a country with an established gay rights movement, a dense and relatively richly supported research environment, and a long history of public acknowledgment of African msm in male-only hostels (indeed, an explicit, if not lurid account of male-male anal sex was published on the cusp of the epidemic in that country—Mathabane 1986, cited in the introduction)—seemed incapable of connecting the dots. The very first comprehensive overview of AIDS in South Africa epitomized this inability. Ijsselmuiden and colleagues warned that densely populated single-sex dwellings such as the one Mathabane had visited were among the "social and economic factors intrinsic to our society which may enhance the impact of HIV infection" (1988a, 457). The danger was not, however, because of the type of activity described by Mathabane. Rather, male-only hostels in Ijsselmuiden's analysis were dangerous because they gave rise to *hetero*sexual prostitution and promiscuity.

Overt homophobia among doctors and scientists themselves does not appear to have been a factor in ruling out the requisite scientific research, although it may well have been a factor in driving msm underground or misrepresenting their sexuality to disapproving medical professionals (Isaacs and Miller 1985). Naïveté and heterosexist logic, however, are apparent right from the beginning of AIDS research in Africa. A commonplace false assumption was that if a man were married to a woman or went to female prostitutes, then he was heterosexual. That category was assumed to be stable enough over time not to require further investigation. The doctors who reported the first Zairean woman with AIDS thus did not think it necessary to establish the sexual history of her husband. We know only that he was not a drug user but have no idea whether he had ever had unprotected sex with a man (Offenstadt et al. 1983). Similarly, the studies of men who admitted to going to female prostitutes assumed that this admission alone established their 100 percent heterosexual credentials. The first two reported cases of South African women with HIV/AIDS also simply noted that they had engaged in prostitution in one case and cohabited with a Malawian migrant laborer in the other. The men's sexual histories were not questioned, on the assumption that they must have been exclusively and permanently heterosexual since they had engaged in sex with a woman (Botha et al. 1988).

The first large-scale survey of sera conducted in South Africa made a similar unspoken assumption about heterosexual normalcy and stability when it established a control group of unselected black and white patients to contrast against a small group of self-identified white homosexuals. No effort was made (or at least none was reported) to establish the actual sexual histories of these ostensibly normal men, nor was a footnote inserted to alert readers to uncertainties such as closeted or situational bisexuality. The obvious operating assumption was that men who did not explicitly identify as homosexual were exclusively heterosexual (Lyons et al. 1985).

Efforts to establish whether African men's sexual histories were more complicated than appearances might first suggest followed a pattern first established in 1983. That is, either the pertinent question of sexual history was not asked, was clearly token, or was expressed in a way that unintentionally elicited negative responses. The first report of a black man in South Africa with apparent AIDS symptoms, for example, simply noted that "sexual orientation was unknown," implying that no one asked about it (M. Hayes et al. 1984, 226). Here, as commonly elsewhere in the literature, use of the passive voice obscured the research gaffe. The twenty healthy Rwandan men against whom Van de Perre and colleagues controlled their prodromal AIDS patients "were not known to be drug abusers or homosexuals or bisexuals" (1984, 63).

As for the early cases turning up in Europe, mostly from francophone Central Africa, we are left to assume that sexual histories were established through interviews in French. That language, however, like English, did not convey much subtlety in capturing nuances of meaning or avoiding pejorative associations. Reports about extremes in the homosexual and bisexual subculture in San Francisco and New York unquestionably reinforced those pejorative associations in the popular media, including in Africa, where the press often picked up stories that showed "the West" in a mocking light. Meanwhile, no mention was made of what, if any, indigenous terms were used to translate "homosexual" and "bisexual" in interviews and on the questionnaires administered to Africans in Africa to determine their sexual histories. On the contrary, readers are led to assume that these concepts are transhistorical, stable, and self-explanatory categories, unaffected by language. An important case in point was a report written in English by Dr. Fred Kigozi based on thirty-minute interviews with forty-eight Ugandan hospital patients. This was the very first study to attempt to determine sexual behavior in Uganda in a scientific manner (Kigozi was a professional psychologist). Kigozi did not identify the language used in the interviews, although it was likely mostly luGanda. Nor did he note that none of the indigenous languages of Uganda contained proper words for "homosexuality, oral or anal sex"—all of which the informants are nonetheless reported to have denied experiencing (Carswell et al. 1986, 7). This research then became a substantive cornerstone for subsequent studies, including an authoritatively worded article, "HIV Infection through Normal Heterosexual Contact in Uganda" (Sewankwambo et al. 1987).

Many of the most widely cited articles in the emerging canon demonstrated the same obliviousness to the power of language. Van de Perre and colleagues (1984, 63), for example, interviewed twenty-six patients with AIDS symptoms at the Centre Hospitalier de Kigali. Interviews were conducted in Kinyarwandan only "when necessary," suggesting that French was the default language of choice. The ability to capture nuance and subtlety on such a delicate topic is also put in doubt by the methodology described in a follow-up study by Van de Perre and colleagues (1985). This involved administering a baseline questionnaire to thirty-three women (passive voice, again) "who were understood to be prostitutes," twenty-five men getting treatment for sexually transmitted infections who admitted to going to a prostitute at least once in the previous three months, and a control group of sixty women and men who denied being or using prostitutes. No details are given about the Rwandan investigator other than his name (Elie Nzabihimana, the only Rwandan out of the listed authors). But one has to wonder, how would Rwandans in a stigmatized group have responded to a series of highly personal questions in a public space (the state hospital)? The reliability of answers is further called into question given the (unacknowledged) fact that the Rwandan state in the mid-1980s was an ethnic dictatorship with a long history of repressive government facilitated by Belgium, whence came most of the doctors conducting the research.

A sense of reluctance or even duplicity in African informants' responses to this line of research comes through in one of the first serious studies of msm in African prisons. The discrepancy between what the men admitted about themselves (3.8 percent engaged in penile-anal sex while in prison) and what they estimated about their coprisoners (nearly 60 percent felt that many or almost all were involved in such sex) is so pronounced that it indicates a distorting effect in the question or questioners themselves (Simooya et al. 2001, 1742). That 3.8 percent bears an eerie similarity to the figures Van de Perre and colleagues (1985, 525) determined about their Rwandan informants who admitted to anything other than vaginal intercourse.

A suggestive possible parallel also can be seen in the Haitian experience around this same time. In the 1970s Haiti had been a destination of choice for American and German white gay sex tourists (who may in fact have introduced HIV to the island). The international gay guide to tourism actually recommended Haiti as late as 1981 on account of the relative ease with which white men could enjoy sexual relations with black men and boys (Farmer 2001, 118–23). When Haitians in New York were identified later the next year as one of the four so-called risk groups, researchers rushed to Haiti to find out why. The first comprehensive study done there indicated that "bisexuality" was indeed the most important risk factor among AIDS patients, cited by 38–50 percent of the sick Haitian men surveyed up to 1983 (Pape et al. 1986). The men themselves did not necessarily identify as homosexual or even bisexual but claimed to have engaged in sex with foreign tourists for the money, not pleasure. Nevertheless, the government immediately responded by criminalizing homosexual activity and making it punishable by six months in prison, plus six months of so-called rehabilitation. Known or suspected foreign homosexual tourists were deported. Not unexpectedly, as social opprobrium of Haitian men who had sex with men grew inflamed, the number of Haitian AIDS patients who willingly admitted to such behavior dropped precipitously. By the time the next systematic surveys of risk behaviors took place, self-identified "bisexuality" had dropped from up to half, to less than 10 percent of all cases of HIV infection (Farmer 2001).

Researchers in Africa unfortunately do not appear to have paid much attention to Haiti. Nor did they appear to reflect on evidence coming out of the West and from white South Africans that indicated serious problems with the stability of the categories of homosexual, bisexual, and heterosexual. An urgent letter to the *South African Medical Journal* in 1988 was a breakthrough in that respect. It reported in almost panicky terms a case of an HIV-positive white gay man who made it his practice to seduce men who regarded themselves as heterosexual (Knobel 1988, 617). The author of the letter did not identify the race of the young partners who "liked showing off their virility," leaving readers to assume that they were white as well. His key point, however, was that doctors and AIDS educators needed to be aware that a little alcohol, some flattery, and some pornography seemed to be all that was needed to destabilize exclusive heterosexuality. This alert passed without subsequent comment, let alone substantive follow-up research in the journal.

Also apparent in the early studies were fundamental misunderstandings about the meaning of the word *sex*. European, American, and white South African researchers predominated in the production of knowledge about HIV/AIDS in the early years and evidently brought to bear on their research culturally specific assumptions about what exactly sex was. Freud had been hugely influential in that regard with his notion of polymorphous perversity, that is, the idea that humans experience sexuality in many, perhaps all parts of the body irrespective of such details as penetration, orgasm, or fertilization. Such a broad conceptualization obviously included genital-genital contact (male-male, female-male, and female-female), genital-anal, oral-genital, oral-anal, mutual masturbation, and many other forms of intimate physical contact. Revelations about the range of combinations and activities among gay men in San Francisco and New York at the start of the "gay plague" confirmed the appropriateness of understanding sex in such a wide-ranging way, as indeed the World Health Organization advocated (Shilts 1987; Bayer and Oppenheimer 2000).

By contrast, we now know that this broad understanding of sex was not historically widely shared in African cultures, at least as documented (and often rued) in the ethnography and psychology discussed in previous chapters. Restrictive understandings of what constitutes sex in popular discourse are also demonstrated in a growing body of contemporary research informed by years of fluency in African languages. An important article alerting HIV/AIDS researchers to this disjuncture was Anne-Marie Jeay's deconstruction of Malian ways to connote what she as a European would unambiguously regard as sex acts (mutual masturbation, and maybe more). These included Bambara euphemisms equivalent to "reposer le corps" (to relax the body), "se détendre" (to loosen up), "bien-être" (well-being), and "massage" (Jeay 1991, 66). Studies from Lesotho and Tanzania similarly revealed a common understanding that sex was procreation-minded, penis-in-vagina penetration, only. Other activities involving genitals and orgasm did not necessarily fall within that definition but had their own distinct terms or euphemisms (Lockhart 2002; Kendall 1998). Camerounian sociologist Charles Gueboguo has also argued that traditional cultures in his country enabled widespread "pseudo-homosexuality" and "sex games," including female-female masturbation. These took place as symbolic acts, rites or play without at all compromising the meaning of *sex*, which remained in the popular imagination as an act that took place between men and women leading to children (Gueboguo 2006a). This would have made it possible for a man who had had penetrative anal sex or mutual masturbation with men to say no in all honesty when asked, "Have you ever had sex with a male?"

In the rush to pronounce homosexuality a nonissue, cautionary notes about such possible cross-cultural research problems were generally ignored. A letter published in the *Journal of American Medical Association*, for example, wondered if the rarity of Africans who admitted to bisexual or homosexual contacts "could be based in fact, but could also reflect cultural or methodological biases in the interviewing technique. . . . Low African ratios could be explained by a higher proportion of bisexual compared to homosexual men in Africa than in the United States" (Padian and Pickering 1986, 590). As with Knobel's worries about the instability of heterosexuality in self-identified heterosexual men, no response or rebuttal to Padian and Pickering's point was ever published, as also seems to have been the case with Jeay's article.

Keeping cultural dissonance in mind, and recalling that Zaire, Rwanda, and Burundi were heavily evangelized by the Roman Catholic Church and that huge moral stigma consequently attached to *homosexual* and *bisexual*, it is almost amazing that some Africans actually did admit to behavior in those terms. That they subsequently disappeared from the analysis is thus all the more curious. In an article on African AIDS patients in Europe, from 1981 through 1985, for example, Jean Sonnet and H. Taelman (1986, 80) noted that one out of forty-two patients in their study admitted to not being heterosexual, about 2.5 percent of the total. The WHO study noted above found even more. Out of 117 African patients in Europe who were tested in the first nine months of 1986, 5 percent were found to have contracted HIV through homosexual or bisexual transmission, and a further 1 percent either that way or through intravenous drug injection (cited in Quinn et al. 1986). These figures are very low compared to the epidemic in Europe and America. But they can more usefully be compared to what Alfred Kinsey found in American men in the days before gay rights (that is, 4 percent admitting to homosexuality as a predominant orientation). They can also be compared to the ratio of men from the Caribbean who so identified in the same WHO study (8 percent), and to the numbers of Haitian men who admitted to sex with men in the period of homophobic and xenophobic backlash following the AIDS outbreak (falling to near-negligible).

It could be argued that the HIV-positive Africans living in Europe had been corrupted and infected by homosexual Europeans (cf. Fanon 1967). A possible exception to the use of the former colonial languages in interviews about sexual history, however, hints at something else. This reference appeared in the first substantive study of slim disease to come out of Uganda. Its findings were based in part on interviews with fifteen Tanzanian traders who were suspected of having introduced HIV into the most heavily affected region of the country. As usual, the authors of the study did not think it important to identify or reflect on the language they used in their interviews. In this case, however, we can safely surmise it was kiSwahili. KiSwahili is the historical lingua franca of trade and cross-border traffic throughout much of east Africa. It is also one of the few major African languages that possess a vocabulary distinguishing individual types of sexual preference without necessarily suggesting an immoral or imperialist agenda (Amory 1998). That might explain why, if indeed they were asked in kiSwahili, the traders "admitted to *both heterosexual and homosexual contacts*" (Serwadda et al. 1985, 852; emphasis mine).

Serwadda and colleagues did not break down the fifteen interviews to determine how frequent and what kind of homosexual contacts these were. The more germane number from my perspective, however, is zero. That is, while the article was subsequently widely cited as a pioneering work of scholarship on the emerging pandemic, this particular clause of that particular sentence of Serwadda's was not once reiterated or pursued by systematic research into hidden male-male sexual practices. Nor does an article purporting to synthesize research to that point on the "social context" of HIV in Uganda mention the complicating claim—either to contest or to discredit it (Adeokun et al. 1995).[13]

How then did the tentative conclusion that homosexuality was insignificant so quickly solidify into unquestioned fact? To be blunt, the repetitive citation of a handful of crude investigations to the exclusion of contradictory evidence played a big role. Quinn, Mann, Curran, and Piot (1986, 958) were thus incorrect when they claimed that "multiple studies performed in Africa by both national and international experts in sexually transmitted diseases" had definitively ruled out the possibility of male-male transmission. In fact, the studies they cited typically referred only to each other's assertions rather than to any original and culturally sensitive research on the topic. One of the very first descriptive articles of cases appearing among blacks in South Africa, for example, baldly stated that "homosexuality is not a factor" (Sprackle et al. 1985, 139). This was not based on interviews with South African men or local studies, like those on anal syphilis by Freed (1949) and Dogliotti (1971). Rather, Sprackle and colleagues supported this claim about blacks in South Africa with a footnote to a single study on HIV among female prostitutes from Zaire as proof. The authoritative proclamation of the heterosexual nature of "African AIDS" in the *South African Medical Journal* (Ijsselmuiden et al. 1988b, 466) required only the five most commonplace references to Rwanda, Zaire, and Uganda as proof, including Serwadda and colleagues (1985), whose data, as noted above, actually contradicted the nonexistence of male-male sexuality.

Quinn and colleagues themselves provide one of the more sobering illustrations of that incestuous tendency in scholarship. They back their statement that "African AIDS patients rarely report a history of homosexual activity" (1986, 958) with three footnotes, all of which refer to works that draw largely on the research of the coauthors themselves. One reference to coauthor James W. Curran (an expert on the U.S. epidemic) is especially weak in that the article by him and colleagues scarcely refers to Africa at all, beyond a sentence that claims heterosexual transmission only (Curran et al. 1985, 1352). That claim is backed by citing two of Curran's coauthors (Piot and Mann) plus the famous Van de Perre et al. article on Kigali prostitutes. Besides the obvious huge difference between "rarely report" and "actually do," this is a remarkably empty substantiation.

The former medical officer of health in what is today one of Africa's most heavily infected cities got her introduction to the field in Uganda in the 1980s. She was but one of many in an expanding cohort of medical professionals tackling the crisis, and perhaps is not representative. However, her recollections about the learning process from the time seem to fit the same pattern:

ME: How did you come to understand that male-male transmission was not an issue among black people in Africa?

JULIE DYER: As a medical student in Liverpool most of our discussions focused on Uganda and Kenya and the truck drivers/prostitutes culture as a vector of the disease. I had been in the region before, hitchhiking around. And I got a feel for that scene where the men just hung around and had prostitutes or girlfriends at every stop.

ME: But did you know that there had been an article published in the *Lancet* in 1985 that referred to traders in Uganda who admitted to both heterosexual and homosexual sex?

JD: I don't remember that. Heterosexual transmission made a lot of sense, it was logical to assume. Why would men need to go with men or boys when there were so many women readily available?

ME: They say some people don't necessarily differentiate that seriously.

JD: Well, we never really even considered that possibility. And there was a difference in the type of the virus from what homosexuals were getting in the U.S., no?[14]

Compounding this accumulating logic was the problem of disciplinary blinkers, itself likely exacerbated by the difficulty of access to secondary (published scholarly) material in the field in Africa. Among contributors to the major scientific journals, such disciplinary blinkers appeared to rule out the consulting of nonscientists for background or historical, cultural context, a consultation that might have explained localized sexual subcultures or Africans' attitudes toward Western experts inquiring about sexual secrets. Most noticeable is the almost systematic tendency to overlook or ignore the history of sexual health interventions and ethical abuses under colonial rule, as well as the ethnography of African societies. Indeed, it was not until 1985—two years into the known epidemic—that any of the scientists noted above referred to the ethnography at all. This was in the study by Van de Perre et al. (1985), which contains a reference to a Belgian anthropologist who studied *femmes libres* (free or loose women) in Kigali. The effort here was clearly not to find out if there might be hidden practices or discourses around same-sex sexuality that complicated getting an honest answer to bald questions about such matters. Rather, the authors needed to justify their methodologically unusual decision not to have controlled for marital status in their tests for HIV infection. The anthropologist in question simply demonstrated to their satisfaction that all women of the ages in question in Central Africa were heterosexually active regardless of their marital status (hence no control group was needed—Van de Perre et al. 1985, 524).

Lack of interest in anthropological or historical research into sexuality in Rwanda enabled Van de Perre and subsequent researchers to take their patients' (and their African collaborators') claims of no homosexual or bisexual activity at face value. But had they at the very least read Jacques Maquet's classic anthropological study of Rwanda (1961) (or looked in the index, p. 196) they would have had to have been more careful. Based on two years of field work carried out from 1949 to 1951, Maquet found that "homosexuality was widespread among Tutsi and Hutu young men" (77) and "common" among Tutsi elites (78).[15] Beyond Rwanda, moreover, anthropologists, historians, and other social scientists were by this time revealing significant male-male sexual subcultures that existed side by side or were hidden within the heterosexual norms. For example, Tanner (1969) had broached the topic of prison sex in Uganda, Hanry (1970) in Guinean high schools, and Van Onselen (1976) in the industrial compounds around mines in colonial Zimbabwe. Even Michael Gelfand's amateurish attempt to demonstrate the ostensible infrequency of same-sex sexuality in Shona traditional culture tacitly conceded that more was going on in the cities and industrial compounds than met the eye (1979, final sentence). An open secret was starting to be outed to those who chose to listen. As Mathabane later reflected on his own experience, "Little did I know then that what I vowed to keep secret until I died was actually an everyday occurrence known to every adult in Alexandria" (1986, 74). Every adult except, it seems, visiting epidemiologists.

Researchers in Central Africa meanwhile had little interest in what the premier English-language medical journal published in Africa had to say, and understandably so. Indeed, the South African Medical Journal contributed almost nothing of relevance to the rest of the continent until the end of the 1980s. For the first two years after its initial mention of the existence of the new disease (interestingly, in an editorial written in Afrikaans, not English—Anon. 1982), the journal characterized the disease as an almost exclusively white male homosexual phenomenon. Before 1985 it made almost exclusive reference to studies from the United States and Europe. Travel to the United States was cited as a key risk factor in these early articles (e.g., Anon. 1983a; Ras et al. 1983). On the surface, this appeared to be empirically justified, given that the first deaths attributed to AIDS closely matched the profile. However, the journal's lack of interest in the rest of Africa continued even after the first report of a possible case of a black South African man with AIDS (M. Hayes et al. 1984, referring to a case in March 1982). Ras et al (1984) made no mention of the emerging material from Central Africa about heterosexual transmission but continued to contextualize AIDS in South Africa with studies from the West. Isaacs and Miller (1985, 329) did identify "black men and women in contact with carriers from Central Africa" as one of the risk groups in South Africa, but then nothing at all was published on HIV or AIDS among black Africans in the journal in 1986 and 1987. As late as 1987 the South African Department of National Health and Population Development based its predictions entirely on the U.S. epidemiology, notwithstanding the presence in South Africa of hundreds of thousands of Africans from north of the Limpopo. This myopia allowed the department to counsel a highly misleading complacency just as the epidemic began to transform (South Africa 1987).

Remarkably, government complacency sparked but one lonely protest in the journal in response. Noting the almost total ignorance about condom use among his black patients with sexually transmitted infections, N. O'Farrell (1987) advised his fellow South African doctors to pay more attention to the rest of Africa than to the United States, alas to little apparent avail. An editorial later that year for the first time used the term "African AIDS," in distinction to Western AIDS, and warned that it could become a major public health disaster for South Africa (Anon. 1987). But it pointedly did not mention homosexuality or bisexuality as possible factors in its epidemiology among blacks. Rather, it deferred to the orthodoxy already established from the Central African research.

An element of self-censorship—conscious or unconscious—may have contributed to the gathering orthodoxy and associated blind spot. Such self-censorship can be traced back to an apparently unexpected obstacle encountered in the initial research project—Africans' memories of colonialism, and in particular of its punitive and paternalistic sexual health campaigns and associated rhetoric. Suspicions by African leaders of a Western conspiracy to dredge up old colonial slanders about African sexuality were evident from the earliest days of epidemic and, without question, media coverage in the West was sometimes so unbalanced, inaccurate, and almost frankly racist that it understandably raised hackles in Africa. Inflammatory, apocalyptic language seemed intended to pull the rug out from under very fragile economies right across the continent, whether AIDS had been identified in a country or not (Hooper 1990; Putzel 2004). The fact that the very first learned conference on AIDS in Africa was held in the capital city of one of the most reviled former colonial powers (Brussels, November 1985) and that more than nine out of ten of the participants at that conference were non-African did not help with appearances. The impression created was that many of the delegates regarded Africa as a single country and that the history of racism or colonialism was not an issue. Both were insulting if not infuriating views to most African leaders. Moreover, eminent professors and doctors at the forefront of the research were not incapable of overstatement. Generally this happened in a passive manner by failing to contextualize or qualify their generalizations about African promiscuity. In some cases, however, most notoriously Nathan Clumeck's remarks about "the unbridled sexuality of Africans" ("la sexualité débridée des Africains") in *Le Monde* in 1987 (cited in Fassin 1999, 47n2), the prejudice was made explicit. Public ruminations by white men about timeless, thoughtless promiscuity among blacks produced a sharply defensive reaction by African leaders on key fronts in the battle against HIV/AIDS.

That reaction did not at first explicitly extend to homophobic denial. Rather, it manifested itself primarily in accusations of sensationalism and racism against Western researchers, in African officials' denial or huge understatement of the looming crisis, and in bureaucratic or police harassment and obstructionism against research. An apparent death threat and deportation were carried out against at least one prominent scientist—Wilson Carswell, coauthor of several of the pioneering reports and articles on the Uganda epidemic (Hooper 1990)—while a team of Belgian, French, and Burundian doctors were first prohibited from publishing their findings, then in 1987 "brutally" closed down by the Ministry of Health (Kocheleff 2006). On the academic and activist front as well there were shrill accusations of racism against Western scientists. Richard and Rosalind Chirimuuta (1989), notably, made important points about the sloppiness of Western research and reporting about AIDS in Africa. But their polemic went on in such strong language that it could easily be read as a blanket condemnation of the whole project and as an appeal for Africans to resist Western scientists' AIDS education and prevention advice.[16]

Western researchers and activists faced a real dilemma in this context: to speak the truth as they saw it and to probe into painful and sometimes embarrassing matters or to calm the reaction by underplaying the most controversial aspects of the disease. It is also possible that scientists restrained themselves out of a desire to protect their subjects from homophobic or racist reaction. A hint of such strategic self-restraint comes through in the first study by a Nigerian team of the prevalence of HIV in prisons. They note the obvious ("it is probable that some kind of homosexual intercourse was occurring") but then, "In order to avoid trouble or hurt we did not press the matter further" (Orubuloye, Omoniyi, and Shonkunbi 1995, 125). Since the men had already volunteered that they were sexually active, and the wardens had confirmed it, one has to wonder who exactly was at risk of trouble or hurt—the authors themselves?

The absence of effective and cooperative government significantly exacerbated such dilemmas, as it implied dependence on civil society groups both to disseminate HIV prevention information and to get researchers into affected communities. Yet in the African countries most affected by HIV/AIDS in the mid-1980s, civil society scarcely existed beyond church, mosque, and elders. Uganda had barely begun its recovery from the devastation of the dictatorship, invasion, economic collapse, and civil war, the latter still very much alive in the north of the country. Rwanda and Burundi had brutal dictatorships with institutionalized links to the stridently homophobic Catholic Church. Zaire was a kleptocracy teetering on the verge of collapse, while Kenya groaned under the deeply corrupt and ethnically divisive regime of Daniel arap Moi. With the exception of Rwanda, all these countries made homosexuality illegal; punishments, inherited from the colonial regimes, extended up to fourteen years in prison in Kenya's case. Popular sensitivities under such conditions could preclude frank interventions on HIV/AIDS in general, let alone on homosexuality. According to John Iliffe, even Nelson Mandela was compelled to retreat into silence from an attempted "bold" discussion of HIV/AIDS in response to popular anger among his rural audiences in 1991 (2006, 67) and, in his own reported words, his desire to "win the elections" (Nattrass 2007, 40).

An insight into the kind of difficulties the political environment created for the conduct of research is provided by Dr. Julie Dyer. As the epidemic in South Africa moved into the general population in the late 1980s, a virtual civil war prevailed in parts of the country. Direct repression by the apartheid state constituted a big part of this, but violence was also intense between black supporters of the main liberation groups (United Democratic Front, African National Congress) and supporters of "tribal" movements like the Zulu-based Inkatha. The political schism was reflected in social divides as well, with the UDF and ANC strongest in the townships and Inkatha strongest in the rural areas and the male-only hostels. Dyer remembers the effect that the violence and these schisms had on the free flow of ideas about public health in a place that was popularly notorious for male-male sexuality:

> We visited one of the big hostels in 1988 as part of our course learning about hygiene and social conditions. Ten thousand men lived there in bunk beds. I suppose if it were England, we would have asked. But here we never discussed the possibility or the risks of homosexual transmission of HIV. We didn't even consider it. Instead, the focus was on female prostitutes who were either just outside the hostels or sometimes right inside. There was very little control at the time. There was so much lawlessness and violence that we actually feared to ask sensitive questions, even afterwards in privacy to our teacher.[17]

In this fraught context foreign researchers and donors were under enormous pressure to enlist the leadership of political allies in Africa. Downplaying the most sensitive, and seemingly tangential, issues was an obvious gambit. The first indisputable success in that respect was Yoweri Museveni, who came to power in Uganda late in 1986. High officials in both the previous regime and in Museveni's new government had amply made their displeasure known toward supposedly racist Western researchers (Hooper 1990; Putzel 2004). Museveni himself, however, soon showed willingness to listen carefully to scientific opinion and eventually (1988) moved decisively to muster civil society in line with scientific advice. He was able to do that in part because his radical (antitribal, anticlass) politics were balanced by a social conservatism that appealed to the Christian ministers and Muslim imams who comprised the backbone of Uganda's attenuated civil society. Museveni's social conservatism did not at the time extend to the public expression of homophobic sentiments, which he revealed only in speeches in the late 1990s. But it is hard to imagine that Western researchers did not intuit his (and his powerful wife, Janet's) implicit homophobic streaks in their views on family and monogamy. Censoring themselves on the topic of same-sex sexuality, or more commonly making unduly strong claims about the nonexistence of male-male sexual transmission in Africa, made sense in the effort to keep a critical African ally on board against those who would obstruct the research entirely.

Retrospective admissions of such self-censorship are in fact starting to come forth from lgbti activists in South Africa. As noted earlier, HIV/AIDS first appeared in that country among gay white men. Its epidemiology seemed to conform to that of the United States and Western Europe, and it met with much the same official callousness and homophobia. As late as 1987 the South African director general of the Department of Health basically shrugged at the need to provide safer-sex education for the only men then thought to be at risk. Cynically suggesting that his government had the interests of the African majority at heart, he claimed that because "homosexuality is not accepted by the majority of the population" it was the gay community's "own affair" and that they were apparently welcome to die off if they chose (in Jochelson 1999, 235).

This was a rare point where the National Party could win kudos among blacks. Indeed, although UDF leader Simon Nkoli had come out with his homosexuality in 1986, and the ANC had informally committed itself to protect the rights of sexual minorities in a future democratic government as early as 1987, the antiapartheid movement still contained some prominent vocally homophobic leaders. Most infamously, Winnie Mandela, "the mother of the nation," sought to portray black boys in the townships as under threat from white homosexuals in her defense against charges of kidnapping and murder in 1990 (Holmes 1994). It was not an auspicious time to voluntarily draw attention to oneself as a potentially infectious, deviant population in the popular consciousness.

The instinct to keep a low profile was encouraged by the dominant thrust of lgbti activism in the West. From the onset of the disease lgbti activists had seized upon (or co-opted) "heterosexual African AIDS" in their own struggles against homophobia and AIDSphobia in the West. Heterosexual African AIDS made it impossible to blame the disease on a despised sexual minority and hence helped create political space for mainstream leaders to commit to fight the disease (Patton 1999). White South Africans, a deeply suspect group in the West by this time, were not welcome to disrupt such a useful narrative even had they been inclined.

That said, white gay rights activists from the onset did take their own initiatives to inform themselves of the disease and to organize education for prevention within their communities. In 1984, the Cape Town branch of the Gay Association of South Africa established an AIDS Action Group—the first HIV/AIDS association to be formed on the continent (Gevisser 1994; Pegge 1994). But tensions about race within the gay scene and gay rights groups frustrated efforts to bring nonwhites into the movement (Hoad, Martin, and Reid 2005). Black lgbti and white activists who stressed antiracism over anti-homophobia politics took their struggles elsewhere and actively sought to distance themselves from the existing white-dominated scene, including the anti-HIV initiatives. Zackie Achmat, one of the first black intellectuals to come out as gay and as HIV positive, suggests that this was at least partially a conscious decision. Downplaying homosexuality helped to win credibility, first in the wider antiapartheid struggle and then, after 1994, in the majority population affected by HIV/AIDS. Compared to the West, he notes how:

> In Southern Africa, the taboos [against overt homosexuality] were stronger, the economic and social power and influence of the lgbti community weaker. And, it was further weakened by the moral failure of the white lesbian and gay community with very few exceptions to speak against apartheid and racism. So, when the HIV/AIDS epidemic hit our shores, we all scrambled against direct association with our lgbti communities. We feared association with the racist lgbti communities and we wanted to protect the broader lgbti community from discrimination. We did not actively campaign for the direct needs of especially vulnerable communities—the gay community, sex workers, prisoners, women, children, substance users and so on.

We dissociated HIV/AIDS from the lgbti communities as sources of infection to reduce discrimination and danger [by African populist reaction] very effectively but we failed to identify our own real physical and social vulnerability.[18]

DEMOLITIONS

By the late 1990s and early 2000s, the nonexistence of homosexuality in Africa was so firmly entrenched in mainstream AIDS discourse that it did not require explanation. As Achmat describes, even black lgbti activists focused their attention on the presumed heterosexual majority, to the neglect of their own specific needs. And yet, even as heterosexual African AIDS was being asserted with such confidence, the dogma was already beginning to unravel. The successes of the gay rights movement in South Africa in the early 1990s, and the subsequent emergence of smaller associations elsewhere in Africa, as in Zimbabwe and Namibia, first made African lgbti visible. Visibility in turn precipitated a flurry of demagogic attacks on gays and lesbians by African leaders (Long, Brown, and Cooper 2003). By so dramatically raising public debate and by so implausibly linking African lgbti to Western gay imperialist conspiracies, these attacks stimulated new research into same-sex practices in Africa. They also stimulated interventions by or about African lgbti in countries where public discussion of the issue had hitherto been almost nonexistent (e.g., Teunis 1996; Brooks and Bocahut 1998; from Senegal and Côte d'Ivoire, respectively). At the same time, a whole generation of orphans and the impacts of prolonged, wrenching structural adjustment programs made preexisting problems of high-risk (mainly msm) sex among heterosexuals clearer than they had been in the mid-1980s: street children and a crisis of overcrowding and underfunding in the prison system. The sheer overwhelming and unremitting extent of the health and social calamity in Africa began to undermine ideological denial and resistance to research on taboo topics. This facilitated a tentative alliance between gay rights, antiracism, feminist, and AIDS activists to cohere, beginning in South Africa in the late 1990s. Zackie Achmat and Jonathan Berger, for example, moved from being leaders in the antihomophobia Equality Project in 1998 to found what quickly became two of the most spectacularly successful civil society groups in African history: the Treatment Action Campaign and the AIDS Law Project. Since then, TAC and the ALP have scored victory after victory in securing access to low- or no-cost antiretroviral drugs, in promoting research, in improving access to dignified health care and death for people living with AIDS, and in exposing AIDS denialists and charlatans to public scorn (Robins 2004; Hoad 2005). TAC now counts a membership in the thousands and has established links with sister organizations around the continent.

The leadership role of openly gay people in these broad struggles has won respect for their ostensibly narrower concerns about sexual rights and sexual identities and has helped to insinuate those concerns into HIV/AIDS and feminist activism throughout Africa in the 2000s. This development coincided with pharmaceutical triumphs and education campaigns that by the late 1990s had succeeded in containing or turning back the HIV/AIDS epidemic among homosexual and bisexual men in much of the West. While homophobia remained a significant issue for HIV/AIDS activists in the West, it was no longer a central or dominating concern compared to harm reduction for intravenous drug users and systemic racism against marginalized communities. Indeed, gay rights activists riding in part on the strength of their victories in the struggle against HIV/AIDS, scored enormous legal, political, and social victories in the late 1990s and early 2000s, including the right to marry and to receive child custody, and the ability to be elected to high political office. The political value of heterosexual African AIDS to Western activists fairly quickly diminished as a result. The hesitancy to raise the profile of (and risks faced by) sexual minorities diminished along with it. A new generation of researchers stepped forward to begin to erode the determined blindness to same-sex sexuality in mainstream AIDS discourse in Africa.

Several of the first of the new generation of studies to tackle taboo sexual topics came out of Tanzania. Ranjani and Kudrati (1996), notably, first documented the existence of so-called *kunyenga* or "comfort sex" among male street children in the central Tanzania city of Mwanza. Kunyenga activities included gang anal rape, anal penetration by one boy of another sleeping boy, and mutual, usually nonpenetrative sex "play." Kunyenga was not regarded as real sex, hence, in the boys' minds, no condoms were necessary and they were not used. Another study in the same city revealed that 9 percent of girls reported that their first sexual act with boys was anal sex and that half of all girls had been initiated into sex through force (Matasha et al. 1998, table 1).

These studies were then followed up and linked in analysis with a stunning piece of anthropological research by Chris Lockhart (2002). Lockhart, fluent in kiSwahili but also employing a former street kid as cotranslator, conducted close, extended interviews with seventy-five street boys aged eleven to eighteen in Mwanza. He "spent extended periods with them at all hours of the day and night" on the street. He compared the observations with previous ethnographic interviews. What he found following this meticulous methodology was nothing short of dynamite: no less than 92 percent of the boys cited physical and sexual violence as the first reason for leaving home to live on the street,

76 percent participated in kunyenga activities at least once a month, and nearly half did so at least once a week. The boys had deeply homophobic attitudes toward "real homosexuals" and, because they regarded self-masturbation as a sign of real homosexuality, kunyenga was their preferred means to perform *hetero*sexual normalcy to their peers. One hundred percent of the boys subsequently moved from predominantly kunyenga activities to heterosexual relations with girlfriends, which, as Lockhart reminds us, included significant levels of anal sex and forced sex. Kunyenga thus represented "a critical bridge for the transmission of HIV/AIDS between the general population and the population of street boys" (Lockhart 2002, 307).

Simooya et al (2001) and Gear and Ngubeni (2002) also alerted the research community to another potential bridge from male-male sexual activity to the general population and vice versa. They do not report statistics as to how frequent high-risk anal sex was among the men in their studies but it is clear from their interviews that neither prison regulations against homosexual sex nor supposed gang prohibitions against anal sex were well enforced. The "old road" (anal penetration) was in fact a preferred activity including in cases of gang rape in the Johannesburg prison. Moreover, because of the high levels of violence, the extreme gender hierarchy of "bitches" (*wyfies*) to "warriors," and the sense of powerlessness arising from the whole prison milieu, men leaving prison often carried intensely homophobic and violently misogynistic attitudes with them into the community. The fact that all this was discovered to be occurring in one of the best-funded and -administered penal services on the continent suggests that prison sex for favors and food could be endemic in critically overcrowded and underfunded systems elsewhere (as indeed Orubuloye et al had intimated about Nigeria in their 1995 study but had deferred from investigating).

Research has also begun to trickle in from West Africa, where intense stigma and denial had previously largely precluded it. For example, a team based at the University of Dakar produced a report that identified a significant subculture of msm at high risk both for homophobic intolerance or violence (or both) and for infection by HIV and other sexually transmitted diseases (Niang et al. 2002; Niang et al. 2003). Dr. Dela Attipoe of the National AIDS/HIV/STI Control Programme, Accra, also published results of a survey that deeply unsettled popular stereotypes about the uniform heterosexuality of Ghanaian men. Attipoe analyzed 150 questionnaires and interviews of self-identified msm in Ghana. He found that youth were actively being drawn into msm activities, including many from a very young age but also a significant number of mature married men (8 percent of the survey). They lived throughout the country, not just in the big cities, and came from all walks of life and different ages. Their sexual choices were homegrown rather than imported—that is, prostitution to foreigners was insignificant. Among the attractions to sex with males was the belief that anal sex is safer than vaginal sex. While HIV transmission was not necessarily clearly demonstrated in the male-male sex, other sexually transmitted infections were, with big implications for the women they also slept with. Indeed, nearly half the informants identified as bisexual but even those who considered themselves gay often had girlfriends to conceal their secret. As one informant put it, "I like to have both vaginal and anal sex because two ways are better than one, and people will not suspect what is going on" (Attipoe 2004).

Attipoe went on to make several strong recommendations, including decriminalizing homosexuality, providing public education to remove social barriers that drive msm underground, educating all sectors of the public, especially youths, about the full range of human sexuality, rewriting national documents on HIV/AIDS to give recognition to gays as a vulnerable group and msm as a potential mode of HIV transmission, and mobilizing resources "to support programmes including the management of MSM related health conditions and NGOs working with gays and youths" (Attipoe 2004).

These studies have not yet demolished the orthodoxy of "no homosexuality in Africa." They are in fact routinely ignored in mainstream AIDS and even sexuality scholarship. Nonetheless, they demonstrate not only that research into hidden same-sex practices can be done but that there are Africans among those who are doing it. Far from being essentially homophobic or conservative on this issue, African researchers like Attipoe, Niang, Gueboguo, and others are quite capable of drawing conclusions and making recommendations that would still be considered radical in many jurisdictions in the West. Their findings put the silences and certainties of the dominant discourse into stark relief. They also raise burning questions about future strategies for research, prevention, and education strategies. For instance, the prison research has huge implications not only for harm reduction within the prison system, but also for ex-convicts' female sexual partners on the outside. At any give time there are roughly three-quarters of a million persons in prison throughout Africa south of the Sahara, most of them men. They move in and out, sometimes with only a few hours or days passing before they return to communities and sexual relationships on the outside. It is at least worth investigating whether the huge differences in rates of incarceration between West and Central Africa (less than fifty inmates per 150,000 population) versus East and southern Africa (up to 360 per 150,000 in the case of South Africa) might contribute to the huge differences in HIV seroprevalence between the regions.[19]

The possibility that female-female prison sex might also affect women's postincarceration sexuality also needs to be investigated. For example, does co-erced, lesbianlike sex make women more susceptible to high-risk heterosexual sex once they get out of prison (for example, influenced by alcohol abuse, need to "prove" sexual credentials, and so forth)?

Such research has been painfully slow in coming compared to other regions of the world. Many factors have contributed to the tardiness, and the unscien-tific overeagerness, of scientists to accept each other's naive enquiry and un-critical repetition of "heterosexual African AIDS" as a definitive fact. We can be generous about this. Above all, it was empirically correct that African women were at higher risk for HIV through heterosexual transmission than anywhere else in the world yet encountered. With the need to move urgently to address that fact in the face of desperate shortages of resources, it made sense not to overspend energy on what probably looked like a research dead end or minor distraction. Moreover, issues that today seem obvious and criti-cal, such as street children or the collapse of funding for public institutions like prisons, were not yet imaginable on the scale that was to come. Cutting short methodologically difficult enquiry into same-sex sexuality can be under-stood in part as a kind of research triage in a situation of grave danger for the heterosexual majority.

By now, however, this cultural intimacy among a diverse group of scientists, political and religious leaders, and lgbti activists in Africa and the West is al-most certainly contributing to the present sexual health crisis. A shared desire by diverse authors to enable a politically expedient untruth (no homosexuality in Africa) can no longer be sustained. Pointing this out is not to promote the counter-untruth that same-sex sexuality is a major factor in the transmission of HIV. It is simply to say that more determination is needed to tease out com-plicated truths from the sometimes reluctant or contradictory evidence.

5 ∽ Alternatives and Ambiguities

African Voices in Literature and Film

SO FAR I HAVE TRACED HOW Western authors across a range of professional discourses contributed to the notion of an African sexuality that was almost exclusively determined by or structured around reproduction and family. In this view, same-sex sexuality, were it even conceded to exist at all, tended to be attributed to exotic cultural influences. Significant contradictory evidence was overlooked, dismissed as being of little interest and, in some cases, even suppressed along the way. By the time AIDS appeared in the mid-1980s, the presumptions about African heterosexuality were so strongly reinforced in ostensibly scientific scholarship that top researchers conducted only perfunctory enquiry into alternatives or complicating factors.

African scholars played an important role in fashioning this consensus, whether from ignorance, homophobic disapproval, or simple conformity to the dominant academic standard. African nationalist sentiments almost certainly added to the effect. Indeed, in colonial and Cold War contexts, where homophobia was almost a civic duty and where Africans commonly encountered patronizing attitudes from whites, African scholars may have feared that to produce evidence on the topic, or even to show curiosity about it, might be taken as a reproof of African dignity. Hence when African scholars wrote about sexuality at all in the middle decades of the twentieth century, even those who were otherwise sharply critical of Western scholarship in Africa tended either tacitly to accept or to actively promote this one specific aspect of it (no homosexuality in Africa). A fairly direct intellectual path can thus be traced from Western adventurers and ethnographers in the late nineteenth and early twentieth centuries through Freudian psychology to African authors like Jomo Kenyatta,

Frantz Fanon, and Ali Mazrui up to the 1970s. HIV/AIDS researchers who today scoff at the possibility of male bisexuality or hidden homosexuality as a factor in the transmission of the virus follow in the same intellectual tradition.

This scholarly literature, with its unsuspected echoes of Western middle-class prejudices dating back more than a century, has in its turn trickled into public discourse in unexpected ways. It provides to African leaders an important element of apparent scientific credibility when they extol "African values" as a means to combat homosexuality, to resist improving public awareness about homosexuality, or to refuse to allow health interventions that might be interpreted as condoning or promoting supposedly deviant and un-African behaviors.

Yet not everyone shared in this cultural intimacy. As we have already seen, isolated references in the ethnography attest to some Africans who willingly acknowledged a range of exceptions to heterosexual norms, not all of which were frowned on provided they remained discreet. Beginning in the early 1950s a diverse group of African authors also pushed the limits of conventional representations of African sexuality by creating fictional African characters who engaged in same-sex practices or expressed same-sex desire. The first critical discussions of this literature by Daniel Vignal (1983) and Chris Dunton (1989) found that African novelists often treated same-sex sexuality in didactic or schematic ways that largely conformed to the consensus that homosexuality is exotic. In Dunton's terms, "homosexual practice is almost invariably attributed to the detrimental impact made on Africa by the West" (1989, 422). But both Dunton and Vignal also noted exceptions and ambiguities in the texts they analyzed, and concluded that African artists were not consistently and dogmatically homophobic or heterosexist in their work.

This begs the questions that will be pursued in this chapter. What subtleties are revealed in the short stories, novels, plays, and more recently in the cinema and videos created by African artists that belie the stereotype of a timelessly heterosexual and homophobic Africa? Moreover, there have been discernable changes in the ways that homosexuality has been characterized in novels, plays, and cinema in the more than two decades since Vignal and Dunton wrote (that is, since the emergence of HIV/AIDS and of an African gay rights movement). What can a historical perspective on these changes tell us about the stability of African sexuality—and the resilience of some scholars' loyalty to the concept—that may be pertinent to contemporary debates about sexual rights and sexual health?[1]

STEREOTYPES AND DEPARTURES

The first published African memoirists and novelists were Christianized graduates of the Atlantic slave system in the late eighteenth century or, in the nineteenth and early twentieth centuries, direct products of mission schools in Africa. Culturally assimilated to Christian and colonial respectability values, and writing under the stern gaze of their missionary mentors and editors, they often portrayed their ancestral cultures in a negative light (Carretta and Gould 2001). Tendentious depictions of traditional African gender relations and sexuality thus advanced a polemical argument for these authors. Olaudah Equiano, notably, painted an idealized picture of modesty and respect governing the culture of his childhood in what is now southern Nigeria. This stood in sharp contrast both to the immodesty of the women of his African enslavers and to the foppishness and moral corruption of aristocratic European men encountered in the Caribbean. This portrayal of Christian-like dignity among Equiano's people provided a subtle reiteration of the overarching abolitionist argument of the book (Equiano 1987 [1969], 26–32; Nussbaum 2001). Thomas Mofolo's treatment of Shaka in his historical novel (1981 [1933]) is also noteworthy. Mofolo tempered the monstrousness of the heathen Shaka's political violence with a female love interest drawn in terms of demure and almost Protestant-like respectability.[2]

Yet however much they sought to promote or slur certain groups, cultures, or morals, not one of these early African authors invoked same-sex sexuality among Africans as a rhetorical device. Not a hint can be found even in melodramas about the immorality of urban life and the loss of supposed tribal innocence in the burgeoning cities. The dominant trope, rather, was the wayward man whose bad choices about alcohol and loose women led almost invariably to tragedy. O. R. Dathorne and Willfried Feuser, in their overview of African prose from 1896 to 1969, describe this silence in understated terms as "a certain reticence amongst Africans towards the issue of homosexuality" (1969, 262), suggesting a tacit common understanding to keep a secret. Such reticence closely parallels that described above in the ethnographic literature and mental health sciences. The first generations of African scholars and African political leaders avoided the topic as they sought to establish legitimacy or respectability in the eyes of both African and European audiences, with rare exceptions.

European authors in the colonial era, by contrast, sometimes did allude to male-male sexuality among Africans, typically casting it as one of the most deplorable effects of Western decadence or amoral capitalism.[3] The Swiss missionary Henri Junod's novel *Zidji* (1911) is the earliest such example. It tells the story of Zidji, a naive young Shangaan boy who travels from his village to the mines of South Africa and back again. Zidji encounters and surmounts many trials and tribulations along the way, including male-male sex among African mine workers. The immanent danger of the latter is first introduced in the novel through a cynical, Mephistophelean character replete with a suave fedora and menacingly wreathed in cigarette smoke. Junod then sketches a predatory homosexual character using even more demonic imagery such as bloodshot eyes and dark, dark skin. That character is partially thwarted in his hellish desires for boy thighs by the superior intellect and self-confidence of the novel's young, Christian protagonist.

The same trope was subsequently used in a number of novels set on the mines in South Africa (e.g., Scully 1912, 1923; Lewis 1984 [1933]; Poland 1993).[4] The men here are often portrayed as afflicted by alcoholism, depression, and other woes of too-rapid transition from rural idyll to urban anomie. The sex itself, while generally only hinted at in passing and in euphemistic language, is brutal and egocentric. It provides an immoral counterpoint against which ideals of loving, Christian marriage, and masculine self-discipline could be upheld for both Africans and Europeans. Indeed, since the readership for these novels was mostly European, the portrayal of corrupted African sexuality served primarily as a lesson to whites. Ethelreda Lewis's best-selling *Wild Deer* is an obvious case in point. The story attributes blame to the African men who engage in homosexual relations on the mines. The real weight of the author's condemnation, however, falls on the Europeans who first created the conditions under which such relations could flourish. As one of her European characters explains to a visiting African American character:

> Not a savage boar, not a venomous snake, not a cannibal spider, not a carrion vulture, not a lascivious baboon but is cleaner than primitive man forced by his chains to defile the laws of Nature. There is only one creature lower, and he is the white man who, in pursuit of gold, will thrust a young savage into the atmosphere of perversion, the life that is lived for choice by the decadent civilised; by men and women who practise perversion as a fashionable foible, or to gain the dirty pence of the only notoriety they can attract. (1984 [1933], 111)

The first African author to tackle this issue in novel form appears at first glance to be writing in the same literary tradition. *Blanket Boy's Moon* was actually coauthored in 1953 by British journalist Peter Lanham and A. S. Mopeli-Paulus, a Mosotho chief living in South Africa. We do not know how much the story was influenced or even actually written by Lanham (Dunton 1990). The novel rings true, however, especially in retrospective light of queer-influenced ethnographies of the Basotho (e.g., Coplan 1994). Moreover, Mopeli-Paulus independently raised the issue of male-male sexuality in his serialized autobiography in *Drum* magazine in 1954. In that venue he wrote in unambiguously homophobic terms about his personal observations of

Johannesburg prison life (Clowes 2001). That view is reflected in an early scene in the novel. The protagonist there is named Monare, whom the authors introduce as a naive young migrant from rural Lesotho. The plot unfolds with Monare just arriving in the big city only to be robbed and unjustly arrested. Thrown into jail, he is stunned to witness male-male sex among his fellow prisoners, a practice he describes as "sordid," "depravity," and "bestial lust" (Lanham and Mopeli-Paulus 1953, 77). Strikingly, however, Monare quickly qualifies the lesson in his internal reflections. He divides male-male sex into that which, at least implicitly, can be forgiven and that which cannot. In the former category is male-male sex that legitimately results from long-term sexual deprivation caused by the prison itself. In the latter are African men who "would obviously behave with the same wickedness outside its walls."

Blanket Boy's Moon is even more groundbreaking in the genre; it offers two further alternatives for male-male sexuality. First, out of jail and struggling to find happiness in the city, Monare acknowledges and then forgives himself for "minor adventures in homosexuality" in his youth with Koto, his "heart's friend" (132). "These two had been boyhood friends in far-off Lesotho; close friends such as there are in boys of all nations—a David and Jonathan pair. The love between them had endured until the time of Monare's marriage" (56). A second, less (but still forgivable) lapse in heterosexuality happens when Monare is unable to find a wife in the city. Driven by loneliness and under the influence of marijuana he falls prey to sexual infatuation with young male hustlers. "There he lay, dreaming his wicked dreams, consorting with such handsome boys as would play his wanton game without danger—poor, poor Monare!" (134).

Monare is eventually rescued from this predicament and heterosexual norms are re-established in time for the plot to move on to the more substantive issue of political corruption and neopaganism in the native authority. The novel nonetheless achieved a significant first in African literature. The existence of African male prostitutes or hustlers outside the context of male-only mine hostels and prisons is established as a commonplace of African urban life in Johannesburg. That an African chief made the point, even as a coauthor, makes the relative nonchalance of some of the key passages all the more significant.

Mopeli-Paulus's story is anomalous, as indeed were South Africa and Lesotho in the mid-1950s. Elsewhere in Africa colonies were mostly moving faster than expected toward political independence. As elsewhere in the world, the associated process of nation-building involved the assertion of patriotic and patriarchal myths about shared identity. These generally left little room for women and men outside stereotyped roles and models, and showed little interest in sexuality other than as a foil to racism and sexism under colonial rule. Hence, while homoerotic curiosity and tensions are intimated in such novels as *Houseboy* (Oyono 1966, first published in French in 1956 as *Une Vie de Boy*) and Mongo Beti's *The Poor Christ of Bomba* (Beti 1971, first published in 1956 as *Le Pauvre Christ de Bomba*) the prime target of their satire was the heterosexual misbehavior of white women and men in Africa. The Heinemann African Writers' Series launched in 1962 also tended to reflect a counter-machismo by African men against Europeans at the cost of allowing or exploring ambivalence in African perspectives or experiences with same-sex sexuality or even self-masturbation. For example, the series facilitated the articulation of much pent-up rage at the colonial experience that often took the form of romanticized, androcentric portrayals of the pre-colonial, pre-Christian past. As Florence Stratton (1994) meticulously illustrates, the fathers of modern African literature were often sharp in their attacks on the racism of European missionaries, colonialists, and authors of definitive ethnographic tomes about Africa and Africans. But otherwise, men like Chinua Achebe (founding editor of the African Writers Series) replicated many of the same old patriarchal generalizations and tropes about women, gender, and sexuality. These included portraying the geographical Africa in feminized language—being raped or dominated by masculine outsiders—and depicting African men reduced to metaphorical boyhood at the hands of racist whites. The "remasculinization" of African men in this body of literature is often attempted through heavy-handed portrayals of African men's heterosexual virility. In some cases it occurs through the symbolic sexual domination of white women and in a rhetorical style that closely recalls the writing of anticolonial revolutionary Frantz Fanon.[5]

A strand of African nationalist literature also began in the 1970s to employ some of the same or directly inverted homophobic and xenophobic constructions of male-male sexuality as European authors had—and indeed as Fanon had done in an important footnote. Unwittingly echoing ethnographers and polemicists as far back as Sir Richard Burton, this literature presented Africans as victims of morally corrupt and racist foreigners. Christian and colonial hypocrisy was a prime target in this genre, and no doubt deservedly so. Kole Omotoso (1971) of Nigeria and Cyriaque Yavoucko (1979) of the Central African Republic, for example, portrayed European priests who attempted to seduce or rape the African protagonist. By their lusts and abuse of power, they enabled the African characters to make speeches about the virtues of their own traditional cultures. For Williams Sassine (1976) of Mozambique it was Portuguese settlers who used their power under the colonial system to corrupt and exploit Africans, while for Saido Bokoum (1974) the corruption occurred when the African character traveled to Europe.[6] Wole Soyinka (1976 [1965]) of Nigeria, Ayi Kwei Armah (1974) of Ghana, and Abdoul Doukouré (1978) of Mali added a further potential danger to African heterosexual integrity by introducing obnoxious gay Americans, symbolic not of the crude exploitation of the old colonialism but of more subtle neocolonial relations and cultural imperialism. To Gibson Kente (1992 [1963]) of South Africa it was not foreigners as individuals who perpetrated homosexuality, but the oppressive system and penal institutions they built that turns Africans into sexual deviants.

A stark illustration of both the stigma attached to homosexuality and the displacement of blame for homosexuality among Africans away from Africans can be found in D. M. Zwelonke's *Robben Island* (1973). In this case, the idea of homosexuality is introduced when the protagonist of the novel, Blacky, is brutally sodomized in prison by another African, a thug called Bra Kit. In that scene, Zwelonke first takes care to establish Blacky's heterosexual and proudly African nationalist credentials. This is achieved through an expression of profound homophobic revulsion: "He [a real African] found it horrible. . . . The mess of beastly semen, like a mess of jelly on his thighs, was a sight so disgusting as to make him want to vomit. His blood, his nerves, his shrinking muscles, all rebelled against the whole act. He tried to associate it with his own masturbation, to diminish its impact on his mind, but he could not control his revulsion" (21). Yet Zwelonke then almost immediately exonerated the African man who had committed this atrocity, as well as the other black thugs who subsequently fought to take Blacky as their wife when the chance came up. The real problem, it seems, was the white captain in charge of the prison. Apparently whites condoned or actively encouraged the situation. "When a [white] warder has once been a homosexual, as many are in the barracks, he can find peace of mind only when he knows that [black] convicts do it too. What kind of convict, a kaffir, and a small chap at that, would rebel against this when he, the captain, did it?" (22).

This trope was not confined to colonial or apartheid power relations. On the contrary, some of the strongest (most homophobic) expressions in the literature reflected authors' anger at postcolonial abuses, particularly in West African nations with unresolved frictions between Islam and Christianity or indigenous religions. A long history is implicit in this anger, stretching back to the Arab-dominated slave trade but greatly inflamed by colonial systems of governance that tended to entrench the powers of Islamic elites. That anger is most palpable in Armah's novel *Two Thousand Seasons* (1979). Armah depicts African sodomists in two harshly drawn stripes. They are either *askaris*, or "zombies" (blacks who were ordered to service their Arab masters) or "cripples" (African rulers who had converted to Islam). Armah graphically describes their homosexual acts, involving abuse of children, pain, and blood, to cause the reader maximum revulsion against this foreign corruption (22, 65). Conflating homosexuality with pederasty and pedophilia serves to rhetorically underscore the criminality of Arab invasion.

Wole Soyinka's *Season of Anomy* (1973) is more subtle and ambiguous in that the main Muslim character in the story is actually a defender of his country's independence from neocolonialist white interlopers. Nonetheless, Soyinka depicts that man and his girlish boy concubine as part of the local Islamic authority, a cruel and arbitrary cog inherited from the British and consolidated in the corrupt, northern-dominated postcolonial regime. Mariama Bâ's *Scarlet Song* (1984, 70) touches on a similar tension in Senegal when, in one brief scene, a mother bemoans the development of her son into a "pansy" whose destiny in life appeared to be the role of *gôr djiguène*, a specialized but despised servant to a high-class courtesan. It is left unclear if either the courtesan or the clients she entertained were specifically associated with Islam, but it is clear that the boy's fate was to be a plaything for sexually decadent elites, a cause for despair in the parents and of pity in the neighbors.

This schematic distancing of homosexuality, authentic Africanness, and emotional wholeness was not always crudely and cursorily achieved in the anticolonial or anti-neocolonial genre. Soyinka, notably, spent considerable time fleshing out his homosexual character, Joe Golder, in *The Interpreters* (1976 [1965]) , including allowing him to show some sympathetic qualities. Golder is an intelligent, articulate, and once idealistic black man who is attracted to black men in postcolonial Nigeria. Soyinka's Golder nonetheless ultimately conforms to the schema, not merely because he is an aggressive and sometimes whiny outsider. While said to be African American and while earnestly desiring to be accepted as a fellow black by the African characters, Golder is so light skinned that he can pass as white. His attempt to discuss his sexual orientation with the African character Sagoe thus allows Sagoe (and Soyinka?) to compare the United States unfavorably to Nigeria. Golder's mocking response to the claim that Nigeria is "a comparatively healthy society" (that is, free from homosexuality) is meant to deflate Sagoe's self-delusion. But at the same time Soyinka protects that self-delusion by having Golder hark back to the theme of Muslim moral corruption: "Do you think I know nothing of your Emirs and their little boys?" (199).

In all these cases, the authors portray homosexuals with different levels of pity or revulsion. They use a range of descriptive terms, from the stereotypically effeminate ("long lashes," "giggled," "minced," "daintily"; Soyinka 1973, 120, 127–28) to aggressively discomfiting ("ploughing the predators' arsehole"; Armah 1979, 22). Aside from the pejorative, depersonalizing meaning, what these portrayals have in common is that the source of sexual uncertainty is ultimately Europe, the Arab world, or America. The struggle to remain or to become culturally and politically really African involved resisting that uncertainty, and by extension all else that appears to come from beyond Africa. This notion is forcefully expressed in *A Question of Power* by Bessie Head (1974). Head's coloured protagonist Elizabeth is plagued by a nightmare of "moffies" (coloured effeminate men), a "disease" so pathetic that they cause her vicarious shame or contamination simply because she belongs to their same apartheid racial category (45). Because Elizabeth (Head too?) assumes that Africans are utterly disgusted by homosexuals ("Dog, filth" she imagines them thinking), the moffies cause her to feel alienation from that side of her heritage. To expunge this vicarious contamination is thus to strengthen her character as a coloured woman and hence the antiapartheid struggle (Head 1974; discussed in Jolly 1996).[7]

The dueling machismos convention did not quickly die away in political fiction, notwithstanding sometimes withering feminist criticisms and profound shifts in psychiatric theory over the decades. Its durability is attested by, among others, Lewis Nkosi (1994 and 2006), one of the founding figures in black journalism in South Africa in the 1950s. In Nkosi's novel *Mandela's Ego* (2006) the heterosexual appetite of Nkosi's main character is directly linked to the state of the freedom struggle. He is at his most virile when Nelson Mandela is a political fugitive, then endures twenty-seven years of impotence that precisely coincides with Mandela's prison sentence.

On the other hand, many of the authors in the African Writers Series wrote about Africa from exile in the cosmopolitan centers of the dwindling empires. They were clearly attentive to the rapidly changing gender and sexual mores of the "swinging sixties" in London and Paris. In that context, it was not necessarily easy to sustain dogmatic confidence in the immutability of African sexuality or of direct connections between virility and political consciousness. Indeed, many of the novelists in the African Writers' Series appeared to have mined from their personal experiences and observations to explore in print new ideas about African identity and modernity. At the same time as the literary tradition of homophobic Africanness was gathering confidence, a dissident articulation of homophilia (in Vignal's terms) also began to emerge. While much less pronounced than the "queer antiimperialism" Jarrod Hayes perceives in fiction from Algeria, Tunisia, and Morocco, nonhomophobic characterizations of African sexuality did contribute to critiques of both Western imperialism and African neocolonial national culture in Africa south of the Sahara in the hands of several accomplished authors.

Yambo Ouologuem's controversial *Bound to Violence* (1971; first published in 1968 as *Le devoir de violence*) was unquestionably the boldest and most precocious such challenge to the dominant narrative of African heterosexuality. While the novel starts off in the pattern described above, with violent Arab "pederasts" preying on African victims, the second part of the novel features a loving homosexual relationship between the African protagonist and a European mentor. To be sure, Ouologuem reiterated the trope of an imbalance of power between the races. Moreover, by locating the affair in Paris, the imperial metropole, he also reiterated the imagery of homosexuality as exotic to Africa. Yet what is striking in these scenes is that the author did not condemn the relationship as exploitative or essentially alienating to the African character. On the contrary, Ouologuem elevated it to a high level of dignity and emotional fulfillment in relation to the many exploitative, degrading, and violent or sordid heterosexual relationships in the novel.

Ouologuem drew withering criticism for this aspect of the novel, including that he plagiarized the homosympathetic sections from African American literature (hence, by implication, it was not an authentic portrayal of an African character and was not plausible to an African audience).[8] Such doubts are difficult to sustain in the case of Tanzanian author D. N. Malinwa, who wrote soon afterward. Malinwa's short story "Everything under the Sun" was published in England in a collection aimed primarily at a non-African audience. But it features two African men in a situation that few Europeans would recognize. Meta and Welimo share a room in an unnamed city, probably Dar es Salaam. Through their bickering over money, religion, and sex it gradually becomes apparent that they are lovers. Remarkably, and probably jarringly for the main readership, they are presented without a hint of corrupting exotic influences or moral judgment, even as they make subtle reference to shame, to their irritation, affection, and need for each other, and to their continuing desire for women (Malinwa 1969, 269). The relationship is normalized as a de facto marriage between struggling working-class African men.

Several other African authors followed soon after with sometimes stereotyped but ultimately sympathetic portrayals of homegrown African homosexuals. Yulisa Amadu Maddy's *No Past, No Present, No Future* (1973), notably, follows three young men from their childhood in Sierra Leone to graduate school in England. One of the three, Joe Bengoh, becomes increasingly more homosexual as the novel progresses. Maddy first "explains" this in unconvincing, pop-psychological terms. He introduces Joe as more emotional than a real African boy should be. Joe then converts to homosexuality following the betrayal of his young heart by a sexually easy woman. Joe also experiences seduction (or prostitution? — it is not entirely clear) by a white priest. Thereafter,

Joe's attraction to men becomes ever clearer when he moves to England, with his effeminate, emotionally unstable characteristics. Strongly homophobic views intrude along the way ("perverse," "sick," "battyman," "hog boy," "a corrupt pervert, an Afro-queer"), not least of all in Joe's own descriptions of himself. Joe is driven to drugs, debt, and a suicide attempt by the alienation he feels from himself and his countrymen on account of his sexuality.

What ultimately sets the novel apart from the genre in this era is that Maddy has Joe recognize "moral honesty" in his homosexual relationships. This stands as a sharp critique of the exploitative and racist motives that are broadly drawn in the heterosexual relationships that Joe's two friends are involved in (one, for example, has conquest sex with white women to vent his anger at colonialism). Joe is also ultimately saved from his suicide attempt by a loving white man who restores Joe's faith in the decency of human nature even as his friends, the heterosexual cads, go down in disgrace.

No Past is noteworthy as well in that the author uses Joe's voice to criticize Western intellectuals who project an image of heterosexual purity onto Africans. Maddy makes this point when Joe's white female mentor at college says with surprise that he is the first African male she has ever known to admit he is homosexual. Joe responds testily, "Well, now that you know, I hope you will start seeing Africans with a different eye. We are like people of other continents" (Maddy 1973, 200).

One other significant dissident strand in African novelists' treatment of homosexual relationships in the pre–gay rights era is to carefully distinguish between the sex act and more important transgressions of the moral universe. Omotoso, for example, describes an attempted seduction by his naked white English teacher as a "nightmare." However, he specifies that it was the offense against respect for social rank and age that was the really scary aspect of the seduction. "Frightened more by the thought of holding my English teacher tight, the representative, the Son of God, tight [sic] rather than the thought of sex, I rushed out of the house confused and screaming" (1971, 39). Zimbabwean Stanley Nyamfukudza also clarifies the source of his discomfort in a short story that has the narrator witness his fellow prison inmates having sex. It was not the sex itself, but rather the secrecy, denial, and hypocrisy around it that drives the narrator to distraction. "He didn't give a damn about it. He didn't even dislike the fact that they fucked each other's bums. He just wished they were more open about it. So he talked about it, asked them why didn't they hold hands or kiss. Were they really in love? He angered them because they much preferred to talk about the females in their photographs" (Nyamfukudza 1991, 85).

In all the cases cited above, homosexuality exists outside ostensibly real Africa. It happened to African men in the cities, in Europe, in prisons, and at the hands of slave traders or their descendents. Women as sexual dissidents or deviants are noticeably absent. But by the 1970s, many African intellectuals had begun to express weariness with blaming Europeans or Arabs for all of Africa's postcolonial ills, and for romanticizing the precolonial and unwaveringly heterosexual past. African women also began for the first time to contribute to the discussion in a significant (internationally published) way. Hesitant homophilia took on a new dimension as a result.

A small indicator of this change can be found in African novels that hint at homosexual relationships in rural and traditional settings rather than being the fault of outsiders. The earliest instances of this were sometimes so deeply couched in euphemism and metaphysical imagery that they could easily escape the eye of the unacquainted reader. Nigerian novelist Onuora Nzekwu's *Blade among the Boys* (1972), for example, has as its central conflict the struggle between European and African paths to proper religiosity and sexuality. The protagonist is Patrick-Okonkwo, a boy, then young man, who wants to become a Catholic priest. Patrick-Okonkwo aspires to celibacy out of his own innate desire and admiration for the European way, much to the horror of his family members. They and potential brides spend the novel scheming to bring him back to the heterosexual fold and are eventually successful in that goal through the secret use of a love potion and entrapment. In one scene, however, the author alludes to an indigenous awareness of another type of exception to the heterosexual rule of traditional society. That passage is worth quoting at length, both for the allusion itself and for the subtlety by which the author makes it.

The scene unfolds when the seminarian-to-be comes upon a traditional healer who has been trying to cure a girl of a mysterious ailment. Onlookers explain to him the she had apparently made a promise to join "a group of gambolling souls" before she was even born. "Such people are very bad people," Patrick-Okonkwo learns. "They cause their parents much sorrow and make them spend a fortune trying to cure them when they are ill." What exactly was the illness? Another boy's comments on what she will be like when cured makes it clear: "By removing these evidences of her promise," he explained, "she has severed connection with those gamboling souls. She will soon recover from her illness, grow up and become an additional Eve to tempt men" (Nzekwu 1972, 47). In short, she will be cured of her lack of interest in normal courtship and marriage. The scene is a deft acknowledgment of how traditional idioms have displaced blame from the girl as an individual while averting the stigma of homosexuality or unmarriageability.

"The Hill" by Zakes Mda (1990) also marked an important departure from the schema of blaming Europeans or Arabs. First performed in Cape Town in

1980, its action takes place in a cave in the hills above Maseru, the capital of politically independent but economically destitute Lesotho. Here men gather to await recruitment to the mines of South Africa. In among the ribald humor with some passing female prostitutes and the rhetorical dueling between a grizzled veteran, a mature man, and a young man who has yet to make the journey, there are several explicit references to sex among African men on the mines. The play is undoubtedly an attack on the overarching brutality of the migrant labor system and apartheid (Mda was a member of the banned Pan Africanist Congress who had emigrated from South Africa to Lesotho). But what sets the play apart from previous schematic treatments of mine marriage is both its frank admission of African agency and its straightforward language—for example: "We live in hostels where we fuck each other when the desire comes upon us" (96), "There is a man in my hostel whom I use as a wife" (100), and "You look soft and beautiful. When you get to the compounds of the mines they might make you a woman, and sleep with you. But that is not important now" (93).

Subtle recognition of African agency and sexual innovation also came through when female African authors started to treat lesbian themes in their novels. The idea of an African woman choosing to get her sexual satisfaction with another woman rather than a man was in many ways far more threatening to hegemonic African masculinity than acknowledging situational male-male sex. To raise the possibility of lesbianism for African women, even to condemn it, was thus a bold literary initiative. The first to do so understandably hedged their bets somewhat. They created encounters that at first glance seemed to conform to the trope of African naïveté or victimization. Aidoo (1974), for instance, set her novel *Our Sister Killjoy* in Europe and has a German woman, Marija, attempt to seduce the African narrator, Sissie. Sissie, as a good, real African woman, rejects Marija while reflecting on her Africanness. Rebeka Njau's *Ripples in the Pool* (1978) is also noteworthy as the first African novel to depict a lesbianlike relationship between a mature African woman and an African girl. But here too, the authenticity of Africanness of the active, lesbianlike partner is put in question. Selina lightens her skin and is proud to be nicknamed the European. Although married, she develops an intimate relationship with her niece that others characterize as "mad," "something shameful to talk about," "sickening," and "strange for human beings." Inappropriate sexual desire is what seems to finally drive Salina insane.

And yet, an element of subtle subversion can also be discerned in these pre–gay rights descriptions of lesbianlike encounters. The passivity and victimhood of Selina's niece, for example, is somewhat called into question by her apparent comfort with being the giver of enthusiastic back and breast rubs to

Selina (Njau 1978, 60). Similarly, Aidoo balances Sissie's assertion of proper African female sexuality with another scene that immediately casts doubt on it. In that scene, Sissie recalls a European missionary woman at her school in Nigeria who was enraged after discovering two "naughty African girls" not only in bed together but shamelessly defiant about it. The African characters, in other words, chastised the Europeans not for importing homosexuality but for attempting to repress its organic emergence among African girls in the new context.

TOWARD AN AFRICAN QUEER AESTHETIC

Some of the literature discussed above was clearly sympathetic to the principle of gay rights, however uncertain about its applicability to Africa. The liberation of Zimbabwe in 1980, however, followed soon after by the emergence of an antiracist gay rights movement in South Africa, inspired a new generation of African authors to tackle homosexual characters and themes in explicitly counterstereotypical ways. The liberation of Zimbabwe had not only ended decades of the repressive Christian rhetoric that had been central to the national identity of white settlers. It also took some of the pressure off black revolutionary countermachismo. A brief period ensued after the end of the bush war and through the early years of democratic government (roughly 1979 to 1983) where not only interracial but also homosexual sexuality flourished in relative openness. Dambudzo Marechera's *Black Sunlight* (1980) was pathbreaking for recognizing the shift. Marechera had earlier distinguished himself with a searing portrayal of sexual dysfunction and gender violence in the African townships of Rhodesia. In *Black Sunlight* he also boldly tackled African nationalist myths about virile and fecund sexuality. The novel opens with a naked, savage chief, "as black as human beginnings," who first gets an erection just thinking about a white woman reported to be approaching the village and then brusquely demands oral sex from his counselor, the narrator. A profound irony in this depiction is that the narrator, modern and Westernized, has to coach the traditional character on appropriate heterosexual love objects for big African chiefs.

Marechera also broke new ground in the representation of lesbianism in *Mindblast* (1984, 70). There he includes a brief but strikingly positive sex scene between a Shona woman and an American lesbian. That scene, a one-night stand, is not employed to hammer the theme of Western exploitation of Africa but rather establishes the African partner as a cosmopolitan, open-minded person.[9] Tsitsi Dangarembga's *Nervous Conditions* (1989) is subtler, but it too hints at female-female sexual intimacy among African girls as a socially positive thing. The girls in the novel struggle with their sense of individual identity in a world proximately dominated by African men who were—echoes of Fanon—deeply psychosexually damaged by colonialism (Dangarembga 1989; see also Wilkinson 1992; Boehmer 2005).

South Africa under apartheid lagged behind Zimbabwe in achieving a similar liberation from sexually repressive settler nationalism. A small, white, and politically ineffective gay rights movement had been in existence there from the 1960s, and the first gay newspaper, *Exit*, hit the stands in 1982. It was not until the mid-1980s, however, that a small number of white gays and lesbians conceded to racism in the movement as it existed and committed themselves to the antiapartheid struggle. Around the same time, Simon Nkoli and Alfred Machela came out as the first black antiapartheid activists. Nkoli in particular made a very public statement about his rights and his identity during the Delmas treason trial of 1986. Gay rights activists around the world, many of whom had been radicalized by the struggles against homophobia in the early days of the HIV/AIDS pandemic, took up the cause. Indeed it was a transplanted Australian, Peter Tatchell, who elicited the first public acknowledgement of gay rights by an African liberation movement. Tatchell, founder of the direct action group OutRage! invited Thabo Mbeki, then director of information for the African National Congress in exile, to comment on homophobic remarks that had been made by a colleague in the struggle. Mbeki responded in November 1987 with a promise that the ANC was firmly committed to combating homophobia along with all other forms of discrimination in a democratic South Africa (Tatchell 2005).

That commitment did not at first prompt a wave of nondidactic portrayals of black gays and lesbians by black authors. *The Invisible Ghetto* (Krouse 1993), the first book wholly devoted to gay and lesbian writing in Africa, had no fiction or poetry by black authors. Their contributions to the book came primarily in the form of memoirs and interviews of activists. Moreover, the stories as a whole still reflected the dominance of whites in the gay movement of the time, and the rarity or difficulties of forging interracial relationships. Nonwhite characters feature in only three of the stories, including the fanciful "Pathway to the Moon" by Mikki van Zyl (which imagines Great Zimbabwe being built by two lesbians as a cover for their illicit love). Aside from this whimsy, blacks tend to be depicted as victims and to be drawn instrumentally. The African, a nameless character in Adrian van den Berg's "Wild Trade" (1993), for example, serves as an object of sexual fantasy who facilitates the white protagonist's rebellion against his overbearingly macho father (which is the central conflict of the story).

Black characters are similarly underdrawn or instrumental in some of the key gay-positive novels published in this period of political change. It was not until 1988 that the first gay-identified author, Stephen Gray, even included a significant black character in a male-male sexual relationship. Gray's *Time of Our Darkness* depicts an affair between a gay white teacher and one of his black pupils. It suggests that the oppression or alienation of one group (white homosexuals) amplifies the oppression of another (Africans under apartheid — the novel ends pointedly with the death of the black boy; S. Gray 1988, analyzed in R. Gray 1999). Similarly, Damon Galgut in *The Beautiful Screaming of Pigs* (1991) depicts spontaneous male-male sexual passion between two white soldiers following the trauma of battle against Namibian freedom fighters. In Mark Behr's novel *The Smell of Apples* (1997), a white boy's trust is betrayed by his father against a background of Calvinist righteousness, middle-class propriety, and secret military operations against African nationalists in the 1970s. The moral in these stories is hard to miss: forced conformity for white boys and men to a narrow, repressive, and internally violent masculinity eventually must boil over into outward rage, racism, or homophobic self-hatred. Little was said about the sensibilities of Africans.

In this literary context the work of Tatamkhulu Ismail Afrika represented a decided break and an often discomfiting challenge to colonial and apartheid constructions of masculine sexuality. Afrika grew up in Transvaal where he was classified under apartheid as a white person. His name at that time was Jozua François Joubert. Then in 1964 he converted to Islam, renounced his categorization as white, adopted a new name, and founded the militant group al-Jihaad (Dunton 2004). He began to publish poetry and short stories in the period of transition to democracy in the early 1990s. A recurrent conflict occurs in his work as the male characters wrestle with self-doubt about racial identity and sexual desire. A common construct involves men who violently deny feelings of homosexual attraction yet at the same time voyeuristically describe male physiques and genitals. In "The Quarry" (in Afrika 1996), for instance, the narrator starts off by explicitly refuting that he is gay but then spends the rest of the story obsessing about the love life of a younger, bisexual, coloured man (Buddy). It includes one startling scene where he gently probes the drunken sleeping Buddy's anus, ostensibly to soothe Buddy's aching hemorrhoids.

African characters play a significant, albeit ambivalent, role in Afrika's work. In "The Vortex" and its sequel, "The Treadmill" (1996), for example, the white protagonist Colin is victimized (or is he saved?) by blacks, whose characters are drawn with greater complexity and sympathy than the norm in gay-identified literature to this point. Colin's sexual uncertainty and growth through the stories begin with the experience of a vicious gang rape by black men in prison. But this is then followed by a long-running love affair between Colin and fellow inmate Jason. Jason, a black man, protects Colin in a husband role for fifteen years behind bars. Afrika draws Jason as possessing both an "insatiable and impetuous" libido and a tender, paternal side. After all those years of sodomizing Colin, for example, Jason counsels him on the necessity and possibility of reasserting his masculine dignity with women on the outside. This reassertion of approved white masculinity proves difficult for the confused Colin to achieve and ultimately it takes another black man, Mjozi, to help him gain clarity. In a long and difficult process of developing the interracial friendship between Colin and Mjozi, homoerotic desire is hinted at constantly (notably, shared showers, shared prostitutes). Colin determinedly suppresses his feelings while Mjozi seems oblivious. The tension finally breaks when Mjozi learns of Colin's prison past and probable homosexuality. He takes that knowledge as license to roughly sodomize Colin in an ambiguous explosion of anger and desire.

Outside Zimbabwe and South Africa, gay scenes were few and far between and for the most part closeted.[10] Nonetheless, the late 1980s and early 1990s witnessed a wave of political transitions away from one-party regimes and military dictatorships. According to some accounts (e.g., Hooper 1990, on post-Obote Uganda), political transition was accompanied by a wave of celebratory, freewheeling sexuality. Yet at the same time, across the continent structural adjustment policies and the hollowing out of the state exacerbated a pervasive economic malaise and undermined social safety nets. A host of old problems — prostitution, the sugar daddy phenomenon, a "crisis of masculinity" associated with unemployment, street children, and more — reemerged with a vengeance. The tired and implausible machismo of so much of the first generation of postcolonial writing was vulnerable to a queer deconstruction in this context. Senegalese author Ken Bugul (pseudonym for Mariétou Mbaye) notably includes scenes where a female Wolof character reflects on the traditional role of *gor-djigen* and female-female intimacy in her village, part of the "healthier approach to sexuality" there than she sees among the confused homosexual and bisexual relationships in Europe (Ken Bugul 1984; 1991, 50, 58, 84-85). Abdulrazak Gurnah, while writing from exile in England, also challenges stereotypes in two of his novels dating from the period. In *Paradise* (1994), casual homosexual lust among a range of self-identified Arab, Swahili, Somali, and other traders and porters occurs against the background of creeping German colonialism in the late nineteenth century, while in his *Admiring Silence* (1996), the crudity of the sexuality of Tanzania's revolutionary leadership is offered as a powerful indictment of so-called socialism in the 1970s and '80s.

Another important author writing in this vein came from a country with a relatively rich and radical literary tradition in the treatment of heterosexual secrets, Cameroun, which in the mid-1980s was experiencing both a wrenching adjustment program and repressive, corrupt government. Calixthe Beyala's *Your Name Shall Be Tanga* is a commentary on the grim circumstances for African girls, in particular in a crumbling urban setting. It also takes specific aim at three of the pillars of African nationalist mythology concerning gender and sexuality. The first, African men's supposed ability to conquer and control white women, is quickly debunked by a backstory of failure in the love relationships between two European women characters and the men who drew them to Africa. Beyala then goes after the trope of the heroic, long-suffering African mother: the main character, a young girl named Tanga, is raped by an African man with the connivance of her own utterly cynical mother. Tanga ends up in jail, where Beyala further confounds stereotypes. Not only does she portray Tanga as the active, masculine seducer in a lesbian encounter with a coprisoner, but she adds the twist of making the passive partner European. Tanga offers sex to the humiliated Anna-Claude as a way to comfort her (44–45). In another scene with another white woman, Tanga also extracts a level of intimacy and shared female companionship that stand out in stark contrast to the mostly abusive and degrading heterosexual relationships in the novel.[11]

The real inspiration for the emergence of a queer African aesthetic, however, was political. The president of Zimbabwe, Robert Mugabe, began a series of demagogic denunciations of gays and lesbians in July 1995. He launched this rhetorical assault at the Zimbabwe International Book Fair, in front of the cream of the African literary scene, including Nobel laureates Wole Soyinka and Nadine Gordimer. In Zimbabwe itself this led to a number of gay-friendly interventions, such as *Sahwira* (GALZ 1995), a collection of autobiographical accounts and short stories written by Zimbabwean gays and lesbians. The highly respected author Charles Mungoshi entered the fray the next year with the short story "A Marriage of Convenience," which first appeared in the popular magazine *Horizon* (1996; republished in Mungoshi 1997). At a time when the state-controlled press and political and church leaders were all attempting to construe homosexuality as an alien threat to the nation, Mungoshi depicted all three of his main characters as indigenous Shona: Chasi was married to Shamiso but for no less than eighteen years had maintained an affair with his best male friend, Peter. In addition to depicting such a ménage as something that was not unknown in Shona society, the story portrayed the male-male relationship as closer and more emotionally fulfilling than the female-male marriage. It also vividly illustrated the power of denial by close family members and by Shamiso herself. Happily for her, although in such a contrived fashion that we have to suspect Mungoshi of pulling the reader's leg, Peter (the real homosexual) saves the day for the respectable status quo by killing himself.

The emergence of a small pan-African gay rights movement since the late 1990s helped pave the way for a burgeoning gay-friendly literature and visual arts. In part this was an indigenous response to the breaking of old public taboos, but it also benefited from external funding and support. In 1997, for example, the Rainbow Project in Namibia was established taking its inspiration and receiving direct mentorship from Gays and Lesbians of Zimbabwe, itself largely funded by a Dutch aid agency. Over the following years other sexual rights groups sprang up around the continent, including LEGABIBO (Botswana), Queer Somalia, Alliance Rights Nigeria, Gay Uganda, and And Ligueey ("Let's Work Together"; Senegal). While small and often harshly stigmatized, these groups contributed to a shift in popular discourse that has enabled antihomophobic opinion and research to enter mainstream media. South Africa has been especially fruitful in the production of gay-positive material, including anthologies of lgbti writing, magazines, and Web sites that promote a range of issues from gay tourism and shopping to dating, safer cruising, and safer sex.[12]

Probably more significant than these relatively obscure publications was the impetus that state-sponsored homophobia and its opposition in civil society gave to the production of gay-positive cinema. Two films from West Africa broke the mold in this regard. Mohamed Camara's feature film *Dakan* (1997) focused on a love affair between two young African men in Conakry, Guinea. *Dakan* is notable for its sensitive treatment of the theme as well as the first male-male erotic kiss ever to be shown in African cinema. But this is not a celebration of coming out in the Western sense. On the contrary, there is a strong affirmation of family in customary terms, including marriage and children. So, while it is true that the lovers Manga and Sori eventually leave their respective wife and girlfriend, presumably to live the gay life abroad, long scenes precede that establish how difficult that break from family can be. Manga is shown affectionately cradling his baby, for example. Manga's parents also somewhat frustrate Western audiences' expectations of African homophobia in that their opposition to the relationship appears to stem in part from the inferior social class of their son's lover, not from the homosexuality itself.[13]

Woubi chérie (Brooks and Bocahut 1998) was released soon after. It revolves around interviews with several variously trans-identified individuals in their struggles against homophobia and economic difficulties in modern Abidjan, Côte d'Ivoire. The focus is on efforts to create an association to protect their rights, culminating in a big party with expressions of big hopes for the future, including for political and social transformation to be achieved, in part, by proselytizing out gay lifestyles and identities in Africa.

Woubi chérie was the first of a series of documentaries that drew on new research by historians and anthropologists that questioned old orthodoxies about African heterosexuality by going directly to interviews or observation of African lgbti in day-to-day life. This cinema as a whole was often nakedly didactic: to prove the existence of homosexual desire among blacks in the African past (esp. Achmat and Lewis 1999), to show the leadership role of gays and lesbians in the antiapartheid and anti-HIV struggles (Schiller 1998; Tilley 2001; Ditsie and Newman n.d.), to demonstrate the humanity of African cultures in coping with exceptions to heterosexual norms (Alberton and Reid 2000; Njinge and Alberton 2002), to shed light on tensions and complexities within the gay rights movement (Lewis and Phungula 1998), and to encourage open debate about sexuality that might help in the struggles against HIV/AIDS (all of the above). Compelling interviews of the mother of a transgender man and of the female cowife of a transgender man in a polygynous marriage with a bisexual mine worker in *Dark and Lovely, Soft and Free* (Alberton and Reid 2000) underscore the continuities and compatibilities between traditional family values (*ubuntu*) and nonnormative sexuality. To give an example from another medium, the play *After Nines!* (Colman 1998) was based directly on oral history gathered in the black township of Soweto and aimed to undercut the notion that African societies are intrinsically homophobic. Here, upsetting one of the main conceits of modernization and progress, the ghosts of historical African lgbti characters return to advise the modern parents of lgbti children to show charity, love, and respect for their children. This, they suggest, is truer to the spirit of African humanistic traditions than dogmatic and coercive notions of heteronormativity.

The first generation of lgbti documentaries and plays was effective in part because they did not make it easy for the viewer by offering simplistic counter-imagery to the old pejorative stereotypes. *Dark and Lovely* touches on promiscuity and HIV, gender-based violence, poverty, and racism in the lives of black gay-identified or transgender men in small town South Africa. *Simon and I* (Ditsie and Newman, n.d.), told from the perspective of the pioneering black lesbian feminist Bev Ditsie, exposes misogyny and sexism among black gay men. And in *Sando to Samantha: A.k.a. the Art of Dikvel* (Lewis and Phungula 1998) we are at first encouraged to feel sympathy and admiration for the courage and humor of a gay conscript in the South African Defence Force. When he contracts HIV and is drummed out of the army, however, Sando/Samantha loses much of that sympathy by recklessly and knowingly endangering the lives of other men through unprotected sex.

The real milestone in the treatment of homosexuality in African cinema, however, came when it moved beyond documentary and polemics to entertainment, in effect normalizing same-sex relationships in the pursuit of titillation and profit. *Karmen Gei* (Ramaka 2001) distinguishes itself in that way. Not only is it the first feature film by an African director to feature an African woman who is completely, honestly, and voraciously bisexual in her desires, it is also remarkable for the explicit eroticism depicted on screen—tasteful and discreet by Western standards but daring by African cinematic traditions. *Karmen Gei* casts two stunningly beautiful women in the roles of the lovers. Angel is a light-skinned prison warden hopelessly bewitched by the radiantly black but scheming Karmen. Karmen uses Angel sexually to escape from prison, and then dumps her in favor of a succession of men. When the brokenhearted Angel kills herself, however, there is no doubt that Karmen feels a deeper emotion than anything she displays for her male lovers.

Homegrown lesbianism is also treated with ambiguity in a Nollywood film set in contemporary urban Nigeria but marketed throughout the continent and diaspora. The Nigerian film industry is characterized by its cheaply produced and heavily moralistic melodramas that set idealized traditional, patriarchal, family-oriented values against modern, sexually loose, money-oriented values. *Emotional Crack* (Imasuen 2003) appears to be the first to use female-female sexuality as representative of the latter and as a hook to draw in audiences. The film centers on a sexual triangle between an abusive and philandering husband, his unhappy wife, and her bisexual seducer (also his lover). The title forewarns of both a calamitous break and an uncontrollable addiction. Indeed, the husband's family is horrified to learn of his wife's lesbian affair and intervene to stop it, eventually leading to the wife's suicide. On the surface, heteropatriarchal norms are reestablished. "Nonetheless," according to one Nigerian film critic, "the depiction of Camilla and Crystal's affair tends to imply the possibility and potential of same-sex love, even when society disapproves so strongly" (Oloruntoba-Oju 2007). Further, the soundtrack refuses to pull homophobic strings. It is either neutral about the different types of love affair or suggestive that love can conquer everything.

Karmen Gei was banned in the home country of its director (Senegal) and is unlikely to have been seen by many Africans in Africa or even outside the college and alternative cinema circuits in North America and Western Europe (Diop 2004). The cultural impact of *Emotional Crack*, like most Nollywood ephemera and like most of the documentaries discussed above, would also be easy to overstate. Yet their mere existence indicates that an audience has emerged in Africa for a relatively sophisticated treatment of same-sex issues and even gay- and bi-positive portrayals of African characters. It would be a mistake to attribute too much of this to the successes of African gay rights groups. Often those groups have in reality been little more than a single determined individual, which, in some cases, evaporated the moment the founder emigrated to greener or safer pastures in the West or in South Africa. Moreover, rather than winning wide public approval, the emergence of gay rights groups has more typically invited popular scapegoating and negative stereotyping, even in South Africa, where they enjoy constitutional protections. The changing receptivity to gay-themed art thus likely reflects a more complex combination of factors. These include Africans' increased exposure to the small but perceptibly growing amount of gay-positive, or homonormative, imagery in globalizing Western and South African media, as well as direct experience in multicultural and "metrosexual" cities in the West. It is no longer just African elites who travel to live and work in such cities—migration has become a mass phenomenon. This is not to suggest an automatic acculturation to liberal values, and to the contrary, much in the Western media that is directed at black audiences is more explicitly and violently homophobic than anything produced in Africa (Crichlow 2004; Calixthe 2005). It does mean, however, that larger numbers of Africans have directly witnessed or participated in public debates about the diversity of human sexuality than ever before. For people who are not ideologically committed to a homophobic position, the relative openness and confidence of lgbti in the West can have a destabilizing affect on the hegemonic discourses of African sexuality and identity. Gays and lesbians of African descent are an especially powerful and thought-provoking presence in the pride marches of Toronto, Sydney, New York, and elsewhere.

This is also the first generation of Africans to have been born and come of age under the shadow of HIV/AIDS. While it is true that the disease has often been accompanied by a surge of stigmatizing attitudes like homophobia and xenophobia, and of morally conservative religious movements, it is also true that tolerance for sweeping generalizations about a monolithically heterosexual African sexuality has grown thinner for a significant swath of African society. Indeed, three of the first novels by African authors to deal substantively and sympathetically with gay themes suggest that a new generation of African authors has intuited an audience that appreciates art that resists state- or church-sponsored homophobia or other demagoguery surrounding sexuality. Sello Duiker's *The Quiet Violence of Dreams* (2001), Calixthe Beyala's *Femme nue, femme noire* (Naked Woman, Black Woman, 2003), and Jude Dibia's *Walking with Shadows* (2005) tell us much about the relationship between tradition and modernity, between sexuality and freedom, and between Africanness and homosexuality in the contemporary imagination.

The Quiet Violence of Dreams is set in postapartheid Cape Town, where a group of young people are testing the limits of interracial love and sex, drug use, fashion, and rapidly changing gender roles and identities. Duiker's two main characters are a university-educated Xhosa man and woman, Tshepo and Mmabatho. Tshepo, we learn, was anally raped at age seventeen during a horrific act of gang violence that also resulted in the rape and murder of his mother. His abusive and homophobic father was complicit in the crimes. Tshepo remains deeply troubled about both his relationship with his father and his sexuality, relying heavily on Mmabatho for emotional support. The strain, and frequent drug use, almost drive him insane. Healing is complicated when he begins an infatuation with his coloured roommate, Chris. Neither he nor Chris identify as gay, although Chris does like to peek through the key-hole to try to catch a glimpse of Tshepo masturbating. In fact, we soon learn that Chris is a volcanic stew of misogyny, homophobia, and class rage. Eventually, he and two of his friends anally rape Tshepo, in the process coming out as 28s—members of the violent homosexual gang that has been notorious among black South Africans for nearly a century.

Up to this point, not much in the novel distinguishes it from the old associations of homosexuality with coloureds, foreigners, criminality, or insanity (or all), and the commonplace portrayal of Africans as victims of homosexual rape or exploitation. In a remarkable transition, however, the just-raped Tshepo takes up a job as a "stallion," the local term for a black male sex-worker at an elite massage parlor. Through the process of learning the trade, he listens and learns about the meaning of masculinity from his diverse clients and fellow sex workers. There are loving, erotic scenes between many of the characters, as well as frankly commercial exchanges that the author presents nonjudgmentally. Some of this may strike readers as overly romanticized or potted in its Freudian analysis and symbolism. In suspiciously close parallel with Tshepo becoming more and more aware of his homosexual orientation, for example, he also becomes emotionally liberated and stable. The first time he allows a client to penetrate him anally is a turning point, allowing Tshepo to mentally break from his family and the oppressive expectations of men in African culture. Elsewhere, Duiker states almost explicitly that the violence inherent in hegemonic masculinity today is the result of men repressing the full range of the sexuality. If they could let themselves be free to enjoy their sexuality as feels natural and good rather than as society expects, then a new, nonviolent, and implicitly woman-friendly culture of masculinity would emerge.

Reminiscent of Maddy in *No Past, No Present, No Future*, Duiker also uses some of these male-male sexual encounters to defend Africa against the accusation or assumption by Westerners of being home to an atavistic, essential homophobia. For example, one of the sex workers extols the absence of homophobia in rural, customary Xhosa society and blames the European missionaries for introducing intolerance. In another scene, Tshepo pointedly chastises an African American who condescendingly worries about "the whole tribe thing" (which he incorrectly presumes makes it hard to be black and gay at the same time). Yet Tshepo also laments at how angry modern black men seem to be just because they are attracted to men sexually. They are "schizophrenic dancing queens by night who are rigid grey suits by day. Everything about their lives is secretive" (Duiker 2001, 331).

Far from the kind of tragic end that sexually transgressive characters have tended to meet in African novels, Tshepo eventually experiences an epiphany that leads to a better life and the fulfillment of African humanist ideals. Significantly, this epiphany occurs while being penetrated by a gangster character who had picked him up wandering the streets of Nyanga, an impoverished black township. Tshepo decides to leave his life on the fringes of the mostly white and often racist Cape Town elite and to move to Johannesburg. There he takes up residence in the inner-city district of Hillbrow. Duiker's choice of locale for this conclusion is surely no accident. Hillbrow is both the symbolic and historical center of black gay life in South Africa and the overcrowded slum that today provides refuge for economic migrants from all over the continent. Tshepo finds a sense of happiness and self-esteem as an African homosexual doing social work among poor, despised migrants from the rest of Africa.

Femme nue, femme noire offers a much bleaker, almost Sadean vision of African sexualities. The absurdist plot is little more than a vehicle to set up a series of more and more outlandish sexual adventures. Beyala's clear intention is to shock and titillate the reader and hence to tear at the stereotype of African women's passivity and subservience to men's needs. *Femme nue* pushes that theme much farther and more boldly than her earlier *Tanga*. The female characters in this one both enjoy and actively seek out clitoral orgasms, frequently independently of men, and by a wide variety of techniques described in frank, erotic, and quirky detail. The young narrator, Irene, is meanwhile drawn with both an aggressive, "masculine" sexuality and a deep maternal instinct. This seeming contradiction allows Irene (and us) to reflect on oppressive gender roles and hypocrisies in African and Islamic culture as they exist (indeed are exacerbated) under contemporary neocolonial conditions. Whites appear only by allusion, not for their homosexual decadence or exploitation of African sexuality but for their role as the foreign experts who pushed structural adjustment on Africa. It is the consequent poverty and corruption that fuels the crises of sexuality and family dynamics that Beyala satirically deplores.

Much of the eroticism in the novel is lesbian or bisexual, including tender encounters between Irene and her elder cowife. But Beyala also includes one startling scene that portrays a male-male sex act in a somewhat positive light. A man who had once been a boy-wife to a career soldier, but who is now married in proper fashion to a very beautiful woman, deeply regrets that he is unable to make his wife pregnant. After many years of impotence, however, his virility is restored when he is anally penetrated by another man. The main male character, Ousmane, also recalls that boredom and frustration with his sex life within marriage was cured after discovering "the pleasures of sodomy," among other unleashed passions.

Irene watches, listens, and to some extent inspires the various activities and unexpected confessions of the other characters. They, in turn, regard her as insane or perhaps possessed by a powerful spirit, and perhaps she is. In any case, it ends badly for her. Beyala seems to be saying that the real insanity in the context is not defying sexual norms. Rather, it lies in Irene's ability to reflect honestly on the meaning of desire and not to impose moral judgments on others. The achievement of pleasure and sexual self-knowledge, by whatever partners or orifices, is a radical and necessary political act in the insane and immoral context of postcolonial, AIDS-ravaged Africa.

Finally, Jude Dibia's *Walking with Shadows* is Nigeria's first gay-themed and gay-friendly novel. Dibia wrote it at a moment when Nigeria was starting to supersede Zimbabwe and Namibia as the source of the harshest homophobic political rhetoric on the continent. Indeed, while the film *Emotional Crack* noted above raised a tentative element of doubt about heteropatriarchal certainties, the dominant discourse in Nigeria since the late 1990s had swung dramatically in the opposite direction. Competing Christian and Islamic fundamentalisms were not only demanding a return to imagined moral rectitude but represented a terrifying danger of civil war. Politicians scrambled to co-opt or to appease those fundamentalisms in part by scapegoating homosexuality (Anele 2006). In the context, with different levels of government proposing draconian crackdowns on both homosexual acts and public speech that advocates gay rights, Dibia's novel is a bold, ambitious attack on many of the staples of homophobic politics and culture in Africa generally.

Walking with Shadows keeps close to novelistic conventions of realism, making its almost systematic overturning of "common sense" all the more powerful. The narrative follows the journey of Ebele Adrian Njoko from an effeminate, confused, and persecuted boy to a man who, through tragedy, comes to understand and accept his adult sexuality. As a young man, Adrian first discovers his capacity to love (and be hurt by) men. He then tries to hide and repress his desires within a normal-seeming marriage to Ada. He is successful to the extent of maintaining his fidelity to Ada for eight years and in fathering a child with her. A vengeful coworker, however, plunges everything into turmoil by outing his secret from years ago. Much emotional pain ensues, but Adrian ultimately brings himself and his wife to a mature acceptance of the fact of sexual difference. True, he and Ada will still be getting divorced, but they promise to remain friends and to discuss the issue honestly with their one child together. It would be a triumph, except that such honesty and homosexuality are not compatible in contemporary Nigeria. The novel ends with Adrian pondering whether to emigrate to England so that he can be true to himself as a person.

Walking with Shadows is full of dramatic inversions and ironies. For example, rather than simply looking admiringly to international gay rights, Dibia casts the main European character as a betrayer who is irrationally, recklessly, and self-destructively promiscuous. Rather than portraying Africa as an angry victim of foreign sexual intrigues, Dibia portrays a variety of African homosexuals and bisexuals comfortably at ease with themselves. This includes Abdul, a Muslim man in a mutual loving relationship with another man, Femi, plus several men who have sex with men but publicly claim to be heterosexual. Their wives either do not know or are not really bothered by it. The only significant foreign influence is Christianity, which, through the character of a Pentecostal minister and his followers, is portrayed as introducing a brutal homophobia (they attempt to beat the effeminacy out of Adrian). Even in conceding that many Nigerian homosexuals are promiscuous, Dibia pushes his presumably heterosexual audience to reflect on their role as the dominant culture in creating that situation. Because homophobia in the dominant culture makes it almost impossible for homosexuals to share an enduring emotional attachment, they turn to multiple partners as an "emotional trump" against expected disappointment.

Adrian, the African homosexual, emerges in this way as an advocate for sexual monogamy and emotional stability, and as a powerful voice against the hypocrisies and intolerance of the dominant heteropatriarchal cultures.

↪

Opponents of gay rights will probably never be convinced that any of the above represents an authentic African voice. Those African novels that treated same-sex sexuality with sympathy were for the most part published or produced in the West or (for many Africans, the same thing) South Africa. The films were frequently bankrolled by Western donors and are often set in highly Westernized milieus. In both genres, both the characters and the authors or directors themselves were culturally liminal. Beyala, for example, was mostly educated in Spain and France, where she now lives, while Dibia at the time of writing was an airline steward who spent much of his time in Germany. And in *Woubi chéri*, while lgbti are depicted as out, fun-loving, and African through and through, this point is somewhat offset by one of the most memorable images in the video: a stylish young man speeding along an open highway in an expensive imported convertible with the gleaming skyline of Abidjan in the background (Brooks and Bocahut 1998).

Historians and social scientists, meanwhile, tend to be leery about fiction as a source, and indeed the works discussed in this chapter are all products of creative imagination and embellishment. They may or may not be even loosely accurate in their depictions of specific historical situations. The bottom line, however, is that African artists who were once coy about portraying same-sex desire in positive light, now do so with considerable verve and artistic merit. Monica Arac de Nyeko's story of a lesbian relationship between two young Ugandan women won the highest prize accorded to a short story by an African author in 2006 (the Caine prize, adjudicated by African and international authors). Considered collectively, works such as these allow us to make several important observations about the history of African sexuality.

The first point is the fact that same-sex sexuality has been raised in African literature, film, and theater by an extremely diverse group of people over more than five decades. The creators of the characters in question span a range from the respectable and established (Mungoshi, Soyinka) to young and iconoclastic (Duiker, Dibia, Arac de Nyeko), from chiefs (Mopeli-Paulus) to Western-educated feminists (Beyala). They include self-identified heterosexuals (Camara 2005), closeted homosexuals or bisexuals (Afrika? Marechera?) and proudly out gays (Nkoli) and lesbians (Ditsie). The lgbti, msm, and wsw characters they created range from peasants to urban sophisticates, working-class heroes, young girls, and doddering men. They include traditional healers, chiefs, Muslims, Christians, and thoroughly modern secularists.

This very diversity of authorship, origin, setting, and characterization, plus the fact that so many of the images and relationships described can be roughly corroborated by ethnographic and more recent queer research, suggests that the creative imagination behind the fiction is speaking to important common truths. Above all, differing treatments of same-sex sexuality in African writing and filmmaking contradicts the notion that there is an essentially heterosexual African sexuality that transcends the ages and different cultures.

Second, while homophobia and xenophobia are fairly common in depictions of same-sex sexuality in Africa, they are not unrelenting. On the contrary, for every didactic portrayal of homosexuality as a destabilizing force that threatens authentic Africanness, and for every implausible or stereotyped rationalization of Africans who engage in same-sex practices, there are ambiguous and even sympathetic portrayals of indigenous gay characters. Even authors who express or imply disapproval of same-sex sexuality are in many cases subtly equivocal about it. Is it the sex/love object that is disapproved in and of itself, or is it the transgression of age, rank, and family duty?

Third, the frequency and stridency of homophobic depictions of same-sex sexuality have declined noticeably, even since Vignal (1983) and Dunton (1989) first raised the issue. The change in tenor reflects the profound shifts that have occurred in Africa since the 1980s, including the spread of HIV/AIDS with all its attendant implications for hegemonic gender and sexual cultures, as well as Africans' increased exposure to globalized culture industries. The fading of the pall of colonialism has also freed up African imaginations to move beyond anticolonial conventions in the literature. Uzor Maxim Uzoatu puts this development succinctly in his foreword to Dibia's *Walking with Shadows*. Summarizing three generations of Nigerian literature in its engagement with Eurocentric constructions of African sexuality, he writes, "The grandfather [Achebe?] may have won his plaudits for his holy celibacy only for his son [Nzekwu?] to earn his mark as a libertine of the heterosexual mode; then comes the grandson [Dibia] who sees no greater gain than homosexual love" (Dibia 2005, preface). For the character Adrian Njoko, the gain is clear understanding and reproof of both homophobia in contemporary Nigerian society and of self-indulgence and recklessness in Western gay identity.

Fourth, the African artists reviewed here do not on the whole portray same-sex desire as incompatible with conjugal and extended family obligations. On the contrary, the majority of African so-called homosexual characters are in fact closer to what was formerly called bisexual or more commonly in the present, msm and wsw. Most of the African men who have sex with men and women with women do so while maintaining heterosexual relationships, including marriage. They desire children and, significantly, do not always rupture from parents, children, friends, or even wives and husbands on account of their same-sex preference. Some of the most sympathetically drawn gays and lesbians are also strongly family and child oriented. In some cases (esp. Beyala, Duiker, and Dibia) they are seeking to recover from abusive and violent upbringings in heterosexual families by building healthy, loving families of their own or through surrogates.

African artists, in short, at least in their principal English- and French-language publications and films, did not uniformly share the view that homosexuality and bisexuality are nonexistent, insignificant, or always stigmatized in Africa south of the Sahara. Nor did they agree that homosexuality is an unalloyed threat either to the African family or to African dignity. For a small but a growing number of courageous artists, diverse homosexualities and homosexual characters wield a powerful critique of contemporary African society and of Western prescriptions for Africa in line with Boehmer's notion of a "restorative queer aesthetic" (2005).

Conclusion

I HAVE SHOWN KEY WAYS by which the idea of a uniformly heterosexual African identity came into being, was debated and, while somewhat changed over time, still persists in major venues in the face of strong evidence against it. Originally it was European authors who sought to lump all of Africa together according to perceived or preconceived sexual practices and mores. They did so in often blatant language of racial prejudice, fear, or titillation — unspeakable tribal rituals, Black Peril, non-Sotadic zone, adult suckling, voodoo eros, and more. Often the sweeping generalizations were confidently asserted without the author ever having visited Africa, learning a language, or talking to more than a (male) missionary or colonial official or two. Indeed, they quite commonly *were* male missionaries and colonial officials and their intent was frequently hostile or proudly colonizing. The "African sexuality" that they asserted was central to their construction of an African, Native, or Bantu identity that justified a host of discriminatory laws, restrictions on mobility especially for African women, and racially segregated urban development. This African sexuality stood in stark contrast to and so helped define "European," "white," "modern," "civilized," "respectable," "*assimilé*," "*evolué*," and many of the other identities that colonial rule and apartheid privileged. Exceptions or eccentricities when noted at all were commonly explained by reference to other Others, such as the Arabs, further justifying supposedly paternalistic colonial protection.

Despite such origins, elements of the idea of an African sexuality were picked up and adapted by people who were clearly sympathetic to African struggles against racism and colonialism. Henri Alexandre Junod, Max

Gluckman, and Wulf Sachs, for example, put in significant effort and personal, lifelong commitments to understanding the subtleties of African cultures, histories, and the social stresses in rapidly changing environments. Such men were joined from the 1920s by African intellectuals such as S. M. Molema, Alfred Nzula, and Jomo Kenyatta. Over the decades of struggle for political independence, many other prominent African authors in professional fields and literature promulgated their own visions of an African sexuality as a counterweight to the old racist ones. From Communists to Presbyterians and from chiefs to womanists, the common denominator was the elevation of heterosexuality to a defining characteristic of Africanness, often exemplified in terms of virility, fecundity, and an organic confidence in the naturalness of sharply distinct yet smoothly complementary gender identities and sexual roles. Sometimes this African sexuality was framed in "respectable" terms of Christian monogamy. Often, however, particularly in literary representations through the 1960s and '70s, it asserted African men's ostensible right or even obligation to multiple partners as a marker of mature masculinity. Homosexuality—rarely defined with any precision—emerged in the process as an insidious, corrupting antithesis of African identity, dignity, and independence.

Claims about so-called African sexuality swelled in volume after a flurry of overstated interventions by Western scientists, demographers, and activists in the first flush of anxiety at the onset of HIV/AIDS in the mid-1980s. These interventions rarely questioned the consensus on homosexuality. However, they did stir controversy by pathologizing the multiple-partner aspect of African sexuality in ways that were strongly reminiscent of the old colonial discourse. This in turn produced a defensive reaction by many African leaders and intellectuals. With some notable and largely discredited exceptions (J. Caldwell, Rushton), the most vocal proponents of a distinctive African sexuality from the mid-1990s are now African politicians and theologians who emphasize what they regard as its positive or moral elements in comparison to corrupting Western influences. Prominent among these positives is the supposed absence of homosexuality. As most dramatically illustrated in the case of threatened schism of the African Anglican churches from the world Anglican congregation, and in Nigeria's 2006 prohibition of same-sex marriage bill, the issue has revealed a striking harmony of opinion between secular, traditionalist, Christian, and Islamic leaders. Defense of this idea has also resulted in some extraordinarily strange intellectual bedfellows. Supporters of the same-sex marriage prohibition bill reached as far back as Edward Gibbon, Richard Burton, and Jacobus X to justify their position, even as they excoriated the supposedly neocolonialist mentality of African intellectuals who favor human rights for sexual minorities.[1]

How could an idea that had its origins in racist, sexist, and homophobic understandings of human sexuality survive for two hundred years and across such radically different political and religious perspectives? The usual answer is that the absence of homosexuality in African societies is such a fundamental truth that not even racists, sexists, homophobes, and foreigners could get it wrong. African societies were and remain powerfully heteronormative, with little public social space or unambiguous vocabularies for people who openly did not conform to the virile and fecund marital ideals. "The sodomite," "the lesbian," "the homosexual," "the bisexual," or any other equivalently and self-consciously identified individuals did not exist among Africans until very recent times. To the extent that they exist today, their coming out has been self-evidently in response to debates and fashions largely originating in the West.

I have not significantly disputed this argument, nor that broad commonalities can be observed in respect to gender and sexuality ideals across the continent. Those commonalities were often deepened as common political and economic structures emerged over vast areas and across historical borders in the period of colonial rule (male migrant labor, for example, demographically skewed urbanization, and the spread of "respectable" values for men and women associated with progress or modernization). But we now know that heteronormativity and "African family values" are not the whole story. Subtle or unacknowledged spaces and vocabularies did exist for individual variation from the ideals, including for msm and wsw. These changed over time in response to many factors, including debates and fashions coming from the West but also, indisputably, from African men and women who for their own diverse reasons constantly pushed the limits of the meanings of tradition and normal. Very few people acknowledged the practices as homosexuality or bisexuality although, in physical and emotional terms, they involved activities that could often very reasonably be described in those terms.

Commonalities regarding heteronormativity in African societies are thus neither so different from other parts of the world nor have they have remained sufficiently constant and coherent over time to warrant loyalty to even an implicit African sexuality. The fact that this complicating knowledge is still not incorporated into so much of the scholarship and education about HIV/AIDS and gender in Africa thus represents a remarkable ongoing intellectual achievement.

How then to explain the durability of the no-homosexuality stereotype? I have argued that it was overdetermined, and that actually existing homosexualities and bisexualities were "invisibilized" by a wide range of overlapping factors and by diverse authors with disparate agendas over many decades. This invisibilization may in some cases have been the outcome of straightforwardly masculinist or even racist sentiments by its proponents such as those influentially articulated by Sir Richard Burton. In other cases, including some of the more outlandish claims of African politicians and church leaders in recent years, denial was the intention of unambiguously homophobic rhetoric. Yet in most cases, I have argued, this invisibility reflected a profound blind spot or cultural intimacy that was much more nuanced. For example, since the early days of crudely racist imagery, there has been an incremental shift in the dominant discourse over time—a move from explicit to implicit language in which the central organizing concept was so taken for granted that it did not need to be said. Bald and easily refutable generalizations couched in moralistic or normative language gave way to more subtle euphemisms ("the African mind," "culture," "African values," and so forth). These often employed scientific terminology that created an appearance of intellectual sophistication, discipline, progress, and change—even revolutionary change. Key elements of stereotyping or essentialism in the analysis went unnoticed and unchallenged in this process.

Over the course of the twentieth century there was also a move away from the kind of anecdote and presumption that were the staples of the early writing to far more rigorous research methodologies and theorized analyses. The new approaches pointedly recognized and often celebrated Africa's hugeness and cultural diversity. They denied singularity and called attention to the importance of specific historical experiences in shaping ideas and practices regarding sexuality and gender relations. Some early, high-profile publications aside, this quickly became the norm in the bulk of the scholarship on HIV/AIDS. Mainstream discourse about the disease has by now for the most part strongly repudiated the initial notion of "African AIDS," in distinction to elsewhere in the world. Yet at the same time, the newer and more sophisticated discourse has tended to quietly reiterate the same old homogenizing theme as a hidden subtext: real Africans can be known by the absence of homosexualities in their traditional cultures and by their disinclination or intolerance toward homosexualities in contemporary settings. Akin to the "race-evasive" or "power-evasive" language that Frankenberg (1993) and Carter (2007) described as central to the construction of hegemonic American whiteness, "homosexuality-evasive" discourse in Africa helped reinvent the hegemonic ideology of Africanness over the decades.

In retrospect there are obvious fundamental methodological errors in even the more sophisticated research that established and clings to this aspect of a singular African sexuality. How could men who could not even agree among themselves what sodomy, bisexuality, or even sex meant have expected consistent responses from their African informants and translators on questions pertaining to those activities, particularly as those activities were for the most part illegal or held in severe disdain under the colonial dispensation? Indeed, profound, unrecognized cultural dissonances over the meaning of sex and its relationship to individual identity clearly skewed the research. Of course it would not be fair to judge the Burtons, Cureaus, and Kenyattas by today's standards of critical enquiry. It is fair, however, to note that as early as the 1970s Africanist scholars already had doubts about their methodology and their bigger claims by the standards of professionalism that they expected of themselves. The failure of researchers to investigate hidden same-sex practices or subcultures with due rigor in the 1980s thus comprised a major lapse when judged by the reasonable expectations of good social science research current at that time. This failure translated into the development of self-described comprehensive HIV/AIDS strategies that somehow neglected to address msm even in glaringly obvious contained spaces like prisons. That lapse continues, often unthinkingly, even in countries like South Africa, with its highly re-spected and well-funded research tradition and where African lgbti are visible and vocal.

If this sounds like a pan-African conspiracy of thousands of people over many decades and different contexts, it is not. The people who first actively propagated these ideas in the colonial and early apartheid eras were rela-tively few, had often been to university together or knew each other socially, and moved around the continent to apply the same analysis to different peo-ples. Hence, while there were huge differences in types of colonial ad-ministration and dissenting voices within the different professional disci-plines, on this topic the sharing of knowledge (or rather, prejudice and assumption) was profound. That prejudice accorded with what most people believed from elsewhere, what they wanted to believe about Africa, and what they were flattered to believe about themselves in Africa, and so it grew stronger. It included the notion that homosexuality was a sign of decadence that could be controlled by strength of will or moral character, that Africans were primitive (hence had no "civilized vice"), and that colonial rule and Christianity as conceived by northern Europeans were particularly well suited to protecting Africans from moral decay. The majority of Africans (and Europeans with a close ear to the ground) who knew or suspected that the truth was more complicated had little incentive to speak out against the emerging consensus and in fact had many positive incentives to keep their mouths shut and pens still. Exceptions like Henri Junod, Günther Tessman, Monica Wilson, and Pierre Hanry were easily overlooked. This became particularly true as a new generation of African novelists and rhetoricians in the late colonial and early postcolonial eras promoted a powerful anticolonial African identity, sometimes with explicitly homophobic and xeno-phobic undertones.

Yet a small number of African artists began to raise doubts about the uniformity of African heterosexuality from at least the 1950s in works published in English (e.g., Mopeli-Paulus). The challenge gathered self-confidence in the 1960s and '70s with works by Malinwa, Aidoo, Njau, Ouologuem, and Maddy, among others. Around this time Western researchers influenced by feminist and queer critiques of language and the production of knowledge about Africa also began to question silences concerning same-sex sexuality. The emergence of African lgbti groups in the 1980s and '90s, plus the urgent pressures to deal with the HIV/AIDS pandemic, raised interest even further. Long-standing secrets began to come out through the efforts of Moodie with Ndatshe, Harries, Nkoli, Gevisser and Cameron, GALZ, Brooks and Bocahut, Colman, Murray and Roscoe, and many others. By the late 1990s it had grown increasingly difficult simply to ignore the existence of lgbti, msm, and wsw in Africa, or the pertinence of homophobia and heterosexism to understanding the social context of sexually transmitted infection and gender-based violence. Sensitive readings of the latest generation of antihomophobic and antipatriarchal novels such as by Dangarembga, Duiker, Beyala, and Dibia can only cause presumptions about a timeless and uniform African sexuality to founder.

Opponents of the existence of homosexualities in Africa reacted to the gathering visibility of African lgbti, msm, and wsw in different ways. Many of these upset by public gay personas turned to strident denial and coercive strategies to make them go away or get back to the closet. This included a number of high-profile African scholars who sought to browbeat or shame Western researchers and activists away from the topic (Ifi Amadiume, notably, but from my personal experience I could name at least two white Zimbabwean historians as well). The browbeating was somewhat effective in stalling new research, given the political sensitivity of white, foreign, gay, or otherwise "outsider" authors presuming to challenge the right of "insiders" to set the research agenda. Nonetheless, antihomophobia scholarship progressively gained credibility and assertiveness over the 1990s. It did so in part by employing relatively conservative methodologies and uncontroversial sources (ethnographic research with traditional healers, government enquiries, court documents, and oral history, for example). A small number of African intellectuals also sometimes used tried-and-true methods and logic judiciously borrowed from the civil rights movement in the West in order to promote nonideological research into sexuality. Nigerian philosophers Douglas Anele (2006) and Leo Igwe (2006), for example, made hard-hitting attacks on the enemies of homosexuality and other "hypocrites" by employing arguments ranging all the way from genetic science to the Marquis de Sade. Kwame Anthony Appiah (2006) made a gentler appeal for tolerance with reference to a wide range of both Western intellectuals and Asante traditions.

Foucault has been important to this project, as he was in the West, but often only indirectly. Far more commonly, scholars and activists in Africa have turned to the ethnography to buttress the argument against African sexuality. Unfortunately, the ethnography has not always been a reliable ally. On the contrary, one of the lessons of this book is that there are clear dangers in turning to the ethnography and other purportedly scientific research for material that actually helps in the struggle against homophobia. Digging out select indigenous African words for "homosexuality" that purportedly predate European colonialism, notably, has been a deeply problematic project from the beginning for several reasons. The terms, where they exist at all, are often quite specific to an ethnic group or region. Invoking them stands to evoke ethnic or sectarian tension (Nigeria and Kenya are prime examples). The highly uneven distribution of ethnographic studies of same-sex sexuality can also create a wrong impression with consequences for ethnic stereotyping, at least for readers who are unfamiliar with local histories and historiographies. The relative wealth of research on the topic from Lesotho (Chevrier, Gay, Kendall, Coplan, Epprecht), for instance, almost certainly has more to do with that country's agreeable climate for North American researchers than radically different or queer notions about sexual propriety among the Basotho. Moreover, the behaviors and roles that indigenous terms described in their original cultural context are often very far from those that gay rights and human rights activists today could ethically support. In many cases they border on what a modern eye would more likely see as child abuse, rape, or prostitution rather than an innate gay or lesbian sexual orientation or consenting adult decision.

Antihomophobia scholarship was also not immune to the same homogenizing (or dichotomizing: either/or) tendencies as its main target. Early attempts to challenge the dominant narrative often clutched at straws of highly dubious evidence from disparate corners of the continent to make huge, ahistorical claims. The intention may have been honorable, if not perfectly in keeping with African governments' own stated goals of expanding the protection of human rights and challenging oppressive customs and gender roles. However the means (words) sometimes unintentionally contradicted the ends. As Vangroenweghe put it about "homosexuals": "Il y a encore un long chemin a parcourir afin de modifier la mentalité des Africains a l'égard de ce groupe" (2000, 408). *The* attitude? *All* Africans? This group of homosexuals as defined by whom?

The situation is in fact far more complex and fluid than acknowledged in such statements. Not all African religious leaders, for example, have aligned themselves with the homophobic extreme and, on the contrary, have taken big risks to denounce that extreme in unambiguous language (Desmond Tutu, Allan Boesak, and Njongonkulu Ngungane, for example, along with a scattering of gay-friendly local churches around the continent). During the height of state homophobic rhetoric in Zimbabwe in the mid-1990s, meanwhile, GALZ continued to hold its annual Jacaranda Queen Drag Pageant, open to the public, and steadily to expand its membership in the historically black townships and small cities outside the capital. Even more confusingly, traditional and modern have by now become so jumbled that appeals to one or the other easily wander from the empirical path. A leading African medical scientist, for instance, has suggested that male-male sexuality among Africans is likely underestimated in the literature and needs to be a research and education priority. Malegapuru William Makgoba, former president of the Medical Research Council of South Africa, is absolutely correct in this view. But the proof he offers—"the ancient sePedi word matanyola"—is neither originally sePedi nor even all that old. It can be positively traced back to Malawian migrant laborers in Zimbabwe during the 1920s, whence it migrated to South Africa to be picked up by the Pedi (as well as the Tswana and Basotho and Zulu . . .). The meaning of the word has meanwhile changed radically over the decades from being absolutely pejorative (with ethnic connotations) to contested respectability (Epprecht 2004, 160).[2]

The implications of such semantic fineries may not at first be apparent or seem relevant to the burning development problems of the day in so much of Africa—water shortages, economic disparities, war, pollution, and such. My conviction, however, is that carefully unraveling some of the strands in the history of ideas about same-sex sexuality can help us move forward from an obvious impasse on very important issues, namely, sexual health, human rights, and the empowerment of women and youth. Much more is at stake than to score debating points about the meaning of obscure texts or the unity of the world Anglican community. Indeed, if African sexuality is a misleading concept, it is also a deeply harmful concept. The harm is not just to those individuals whose existence is directly denied. It extends to the majority of African citizens and, I would argue, to people in the West as well. That is, the concept of an African sexuality—even when deployed to argue against colonial stereotypes and even when qualified by nods toward the diversity of African cultures—denies real diversity, nuance, imagination, creativity, and change over time. It fosters complacency and condescension in the West about Africa and, by extension, people of African descent. It tacitly condones or actively demands denial and stigma against anomalies from the ideal such as same-sex sexuality and sensual desire. Denial and stigma in turn tend to reinforce gender inequality, injustice, and violence including, importantly, violence done by people to themselves and their personal integrity through internalized homophobia and internalized misogyny.

Denial and stigma are to HIV/AIDS as oxygen is to flame. I want to conclude the book, therefore, by making a case for further efforts both to reveal and to contest not just overt expressions of homophobia but also the subtle or unintentional reiterations of an exclusively heterosexual African sexuality such as commonly found in material that glosses over the possibility or relevance of lgbti, msm, and wsw in the fight against HIV/AIDS in Africa.

Let me put it this way. Same-sex sexuality matters in Africa.

Same-sex sexuality matters, in fact, in two ways. Same-sex sexuality matters (the noun) means those wide-ranging issues, personalities, practices, discourses, and anything else that stands as testament against the assumption or claim that Africans are preternaturally and exclusively heterosexual. Same-sex sexuality matters cover a far wider swathe than the (so far) tiny numbers of out, self-identified African queers suggests. Figures don't lie, they say, but liars figure, and I am therefore wary of bringing numbers into the debate. At this point, however, it is sobering to recall that at the time of writing there are an estimated 27 million Africans with HIV or AIDS. Taking the lowest reasonable estimations of male-male transmission of HIV, and disregarding all the indirect effects of homophobia or male-male transmission of other sexually transmitted infections or issues arising from female-female sexual relationships, this still means the blind spot toward same-sex sexuality in Africa is costing a lot of lives. Even if only 2 percent of infections can in any way be attributed to msm, that translates into over a half a million people who are already sick and dying from an easily preventable disease. That number is roughly the same as the entire number of people living with HIV and AIDS in Western Europe. Why is one population of that size accorded significance yet not the other?

From the evidence of cross-cultural research gaffes or purposeful self-censorship in the ethnography that understated msm, moreover, and from recent studies that are sensitive to the question, there is good reason to suspect that the percentage, and the lives at risk, is significantly higher than 2 percent. The discrepancy in concern, let alone public acknowledgment, is that much more disturbing.

But same-sex sexuality matters that invite investigation and action also extend to the close critical evaluation of how the hegemonic culture of heteronormativity actually works and sustains itself, including:

- how African cultures explained, "cured," honored, harnessed, stigmatized, or averted their eyes from nonnormative sexuality

- how exogenous philosophies such as evangelical Christianity and, to some extent, Islam challenged (or not) those normative traditions

- how colonialism and capitalist enterprise introduced new institutions, laws, and labor regimes that sought to define, control, and channel African sexualities so as to maximize their ability to exploit African labor

- how professional scholarly discourses reinforced homophobic and hetero-sexist preconceptions about African sexualities

- how African intellectuals and political leaders adapted and deployed those discourses to advance their own distinct agendas

- how African artists subtly queried or challenged the cultural intimacy so created

- how African lgbti are coming out and expressing their sense of selfhood and political activism in new ways in alliance with (and in the process "queering") other civil society groups

- how the majority population is denied safer-sex education because of misguided homophobic fears or heterosexist blindness

Each country, "tribe," or city in Africa could benefit from close empirical studies of each these same-sex sexuality matters. The last point, however, cries out for immediate attention. For example, we now know that HIV is extremely inefficient in comparison to other infectious agents, and that men may have high-risk sex with men and not get infected with HIV. But men who have sex with men can fairly easily pick up other sexually transmitted infections. By passing them on to their female partners, msm then hugely increase the female partners' susceptibility to HIV infection. Indeed, female sex workers with syphilis have been shown to be many times as vulnerable to HIV as uninfected women. In other words, even if we accept that direct male-male transmission of HIV is insignificant, the indirect consequences of unsafe sex among msm who also have sex with women could be much greater.

The hidden risks, it must be stressed, are taking place in the context of de-teriorating social safety nets over the past two or more decades. Notably, while the number of male street children in Africa is unknown, it is certainly in the millions and guaranteed to grow as the pandemic progresses. We know that mutual, albeit sometimes violent, same-sex relations take place among these children. There is also an element of male prostitution for survival sex by street children (and other young men) that needs investigation and targeting. These children and sex workers, like the hundreds of thousands of African men in prison, are not only at heightened risk of violent and unprotected sex; the fact that most will go on to marry or have girlfriends makes them a potentially significant bridge for disease from men to women. Women's vulnerability in the context of economic structural adjustment makes it unlikely for the foreseeable future that they will generally feel empowered to ask their male partners about high-risk male-male sex.

The costs of hidden emotional trauma in some of these relationships can only be imagined. From studies in Tanzania, South Africa, and elsewhere in the world, however, we know that intense homophobia is a common result of male-male rape. There are as well significant distinct forms of violence perpetrated against lesbians or suspected lesbians, and in wsw relationships in prisons and other female-only institutions, which can have a similar traumatizing impact or feed into internalized homophobia. Internalized homophobia in turn ramifies throughout society, imbuing with violence a whole range of other discriminatory attitudes, including xenophobia and misogyny. These feed back once again to the disempowerment of minorities and women that fuels the HIV/AIDS pandemic.

Homophobia, heterosexism, and other related stigmatizing attitudes are thus not just the narrow concern of direct victims of hate crime and speech. They have a rippling effect that endangers the majority population.

Homosexuality, homophobia, heterosexism, and other related stigmatizing attitudes, in short, comprise a critical missing piece to the puzzle of HIV/AIDS in Africa south of the Sahara. To repeat, it is not that there are that many people who identify as gay, lesbian, bisexual, transgender, intersex, or queer. Nor does transmission of HIV through male-male sexual intercourse or female-female genital contact even remotely approach its transmission through male-female sexual intercourse. The presence of msm and wsw is large enough, however, to warrant more attention than it has earned so far. The fact that lgbti, msm, and wsw are largely written out of even scientific scholarship even after more than a decade of serious social scientific and humanities research on the issue is therefore highly significant. In Oliver Phillips's memorable phrase, "the invisible presence of homosexuality" in mainstream HIV/AIDS discourse in and about Africa is an integral part of an arguably racist construction of African AIDS that increases risks for the entire population.

Same-sex sexuality *matters* (verb), therefore, in the sense that research into seemingly marginal issues can shed light on and hence contribute constructively to addressing the broader issues, struggles, and other same-sex sexuality matters (noun) just noted. Queer theory may be helpful in this, but can equally contribute to the problem. Queer theory arose out of the gay rights movement in the West and the main reference points in the scholarship, in style, and in sense of priorities in the literature still reflect predominantly Western concerns. As such, queer theory could unwittingly deny or submerge African perspectives within a falsely homogenizing or "homonormative" paradigm, and indeed, in practice it has resulted in some decidedly weak scholarship. As such, queer theory awaits a rigorously theorized indigenous term or terms grounded in African culture and contemporary struggles, sensitive to lessons learned through decades of Marxist, feminist, and postcolonial critiques of power and the sociology of science. Same-sex sexuality research so informed would be, I argue, completely compatible with pan-African resistance to or reimagining of the dominant globalization paradigm.

At the moment, outside of South Africa, the political landscape may not seem very promising for indigenizing queer theory. That may change, however, and in fact even now the situation is not as dismal as many people suppose. Close histories of the tangle of secrets and speculations about same-sex sexuality have begun to appear from around the continent. They make it clearer than ever how lgbti, msm, and wsw are not as new and exotic to Africa as commonly assumed, and are decidedly not the invention of Western "gay imperialists." Such histories might help calm populist fears that demanding attention to lgbti rights will somehow destabilize civilization or nature as we know it. History may also help forge stronger coalitions between scholars, civil society groups, and nonliteralist religious leaders. Such coalitions have already begun to form. African activists and scholars are picking up these themes in their work, even in places where civil war, economic crisis, and crudely homophobic politics would seem to make it impossible (Somalia, Uganda, Sierra Leone, Nigeria, Cameroun, and more). Such coalitions have begun to have an impact on human and sexual rights discourse, as witnessed by the wide respect and success garnered by the Treatment Action Campaign, by the African Union's Commission on Human Rights' acceptance in principle of sexual orientation as a category worthy of protection, and by the involvement of nongay activists in the opposition to Nigeria's same-sex marriage prohibition act in 2007.

The obvious good news in all this is that if a harmful construction of African sexuality were made in the first place, then it can be unmade in the second. This is definitely not to promote queer theory as the only way to do so. On the contrary, I have disassociated the present study from a strand of obtuse and unwittingly colonial queer practice that queer theory seems incapable of expunging and that brings the term into discredit. I nevertheless acknowledge a rich body of scholarship, art, and activist writing in Africa that uses (or tacitly borrows or intuits) queer theory to destabilize an oppressive and stigmatizing ideology. Recalling the African Union's protocol on the rights of women (July 2003), Article 2 is an apposite way to conclude in that respect. Without mentioning homosexuality, this document opens the door to the requisite research, activism, and reformulation of laws and policies that deny the diversity of human sexuality in Africa:

> States Parties shall commit themselves to modify the social and cultural patterns of conduct of women and men through public education, information, education and communication strategies, *with a view to achieving the elimination of harmful cultural and traditional practices and all other practices which are based on the idea of the inferiority or the superiority of either of the sexes, or on stereotyped roles for women and men.*[3]

I hope this book has been a contribution to that goal.

Notes

CHAPTER 1: A PUZZLING BLINDSPOT

1. For wide-ranging discussions of the history of HIV/AIDS in Africa, see Vangroenweghe (2000) and Iliffe (2006), plus the compelling firsthand accounts of the emerging epidemic in Uganda and Burundi by Edward Hooper (1990) and Paul Kocheloff (2006), respectively. I will return to this topic in chapter 4, together with attention to some of the key scholarship in French.

2. See Mbeki's accusations or innuendo of racism against white activists and politicians on this issue, for example, Mbeki, "When Is Good News Bad News?" *ANC Today* 4, 39 (October 1—7, 2004), www.anc.org.za/ancdocs/anctoday/2004/at39.htm. Sabatier (1988), Chirimuuta and Chirimuuta (1989), and Bibeau (1991) remain powerful polemics that challenge racist assumptions in the early HIV science, while Robins (2004), Fassin (2004), Posel (2005), Hoad (2005, 2007), and Nattrass (2007) have all written cogent analyses of the fraught politics of sexuality, HIV, and race in South Africa. Ward (2002) and Hoad (2004) discuss struggles on these issues within the Anglican church.

3. For one of many examples (to be discussed further below), see Essex et al. (2002).

4. Histories and memoirs of the early days of struggle against HIV/AIDS in the West often only tangentially refer to Africa other than to make this point. Landmark studies include Shilts (1987), Fee and Fox (1988), Grmek (1990), and Patton (1999).

5. Pointed critiques include Ahlberg (1994), Heald (1995), Patton (1999), Stillwaggon (2003), and Lyons and Lyons (2004). A controversial intervention that claims sexuality was overstated in the research while unhygienic needles were understated as a cause of infection is not given much credence in the literature. Nonetheless, Gisselquist et al. (2003) make some important points about assumptions and hasty or overconfident conclusions in the early science on HIV/AIDS in Africa.

6. See, for example, Kalipeni et al. (2004) and Irwin et al. (2003), as well as the main voice of authority on this issue, UNAIDS (http://www.unaids.org/en/Regions _Countries/Regions/SubSaharanAfrica.asp), and the UN's special envoy on AIDS in Africa, Stephen Lewis (Lewis 2005).

7. See also the frank reflections by the women in Morgan and Wieringa (2005).

8. The terms employed here are borrowed from Gueboguo (2006c).

9. The issue of narrowly defining "real sex" in part to protect oneself against suspicion of homosexuality is the subject of several astute analyses, including Jeay (1991), Kendall (1999), Teunis (2001), and Lockhart (2002). Sedgwick (1990) remains a key theoretical formulation of this point, which I will be discussing at length in chapter 4.

10. The international literature on the history of sexuality is by now truly vast and can be accessed through many of the Africanist interpreters to be discussed below. Global queer theory (with critiques and comparative empirical evidence) will also be discussed below. Here, let me simply acknowledge the insights arising from Foucault (1978), as well as influential and still compelling works by Said (1978) and Gramsci (1971) toward the formulation of key theoretical concepts in these fields. Also pertinent are the astute analyses of the construction of racial whiteness and the heterosexual norm in hegemonic U.S. culture by Frankenberg (1993) and Carter (2007).

11. See, for example, Murray and Roscoe (1997) and Najmabadi (2005).

12. The flawed studies just mentioned are, respectively, UNAIDS 2006; "Zambia: Supporting Prisons in the Response to HIV," http://data.unaids.org/pub/InformationNote/2006/20060730_Project_page_Zambia_prisons_en.pdf. accessed November 23, 2006; UNICEF 2001; "BTW: The Sexual Behavior of Young People in Botswana" http://www.unicef.org/evaldatabase/index_15342.html. accessed November 23, 2006; and Abdool Karim and Abdool Karim (2005). Other examples of heterosexist scholarship are discussed below and in Johnson (2007). Heterosexist blindspots in the popular media are discussed in McKenna (1999) and ARSRC (2005a), and demonstrated in the otherwise sensitive, award-winning journalism of Stephanie Nolen (2007). A great deal has meanwhile been written about homophobia and AIDS in the West (notably Mann 1995, whose leadership guided the World Health Organization through the critical first decade of the pandemic). For a succinct summary of how it is pertinent to Africa as a development issue, see ICAD (no date), Attipoe (2004), Lwabaayi (2004), a point I will be following up in my concluding chapter.

13. Compare Tamale (2003), Arac de Nyeko (2007), and Arac de Nyeko's interview in Attah (2007).

14. See, for example, Hennessy (1995, 2000, 2005), S. Jolly (2000), Cover (2004), Barnard (2004), and Hoad (2007).

15. See, for example, Reddy (2001), Crichlow (2004), Calixthe (2005), Potgeiter (2006), and Boellstorff (2007). Another acknowledgment of queer as a category pertinent to Africa comes in Ifi Amadiume's call for reconceptualizing African sexualities (2006, 28). I read this acknowledgment as significant both because of Amadiume's high profile in African feminist scholarship and for her earlier reputation for hostility to Western lesbian appropriation of African evidence. See below, chapter 2.

16. www.mask.org.za/SECTIONS/YAQ/features/features_004.htm.

17. Zinanga (1996), Mutongi (2000), Dlamini (2006), Igwe (2006), Salo and Gqola (2006), Eboussi Boulaga (2007), and Azodo and Eke (2007), for example. Skepticism toward queer theory is explicitly called for by Stephen O. Murray, one of the pioneers of global and African homosexualities studies (Murray 1997 and 2000, for example).

18. Behind the Mask, "Nigeria Broadens Anti-gay Bill," April 18, 2006; emphasis mine; "Rising Homosexuality Dangerous," July 11, 2006, both at www .mask.org.za. State-sponsored homophobia throughout the continent is monitored on this Web site.

19. For examples of the work of African feminists who have postulated links between homophobia and women's oppression generally, see, among others, McFadden (1992), Zinanga (1996), Potgeiter (2006), and Reid and Dirsuweit (2001).

20. www.unaids.org/en/default.asp#.

21. The Canadian International Development Agency's official, public discretion on this topic, for instance, contrasts with CIDA's quiet funding of the production of an explicit booklet on counseling msm (SAT 2004), as did USAID on msm in Senegal (Niang et al. 2002). Similarly, the World Bank indirectly supported a sexual health resource that normalizes same-sex issues (*Dear Auntie Stella*, Zimbabwe, www.tarsc.org/auntstella/index.html). See also ARSRC (2005b) on bold new research coming out of Nigeria.

22. A. Muula, quoted in Senior (2006, 10).

23. For personal reflections on this demoralizing experience, see Kaler (2007).

24. "African LGBTI Human Rights Defenders Warn Public against Participation in Campaigns Concerning LGBTI Issues in Africa Led by Peter Tatchell and Outrage!" African Solidarity 2006, press release, January 31, 2007. Hoad (2007, 69) adds an even further caution against transnational careerism by queer researchers that exploits stereotypes of African victimhood.

25. Wendy Landau, "LGBTI Rights Enter the African Human Rights Discourse for the First Time," May 11, 2006, www.mask.org.za. For discussions of how Western rights discourses around sexuality and identify pertain in Africa, see Stychin (1998) and Englund and Nyamnjoh (2004).

26. www.africa-union.org/home/Welcome.htm; emphasis mine.

27. www.africa-union.org/root/au/Documents/Treaties/Text/African_Youth _Charter.pdf.

28. Ibid.; emphasis mine.

29. Niang et al. (2002) and IRIN, "SENEGAL: HIV-Positive Gays Face Double Stigma," http://www.plusnews.org/Report.aspx?ReportId=39349, December 6, 2006, accessed May 4, 2007. Changes and uncertainty about terminology can be followed in publications by lgbti associations. Compare, for example, GALZ 1995, 2005 and 2007.

30. See Dirsuweit (2006) on the power of the market to define and disempower certain lgbti in contemporary South Africa. The cover image of Hoad et al. (2005) seems to confirm her argument as it features a nearly naked white man front and center with normally dressed and bemused black men looking on.

31. For example, see the Web site Behind the Mask and Dirsuweit (2006).

32. On global disability rights, see Shuttleworth (2007). For other pertinent debates, see Teunis and Herdt (2007). Ouzgane and Morrell (2005) provide a concise rationalization of the continental approach to gendered writing on men, in their case including Africa, both north and south of the Sahara. For an argument for a global culture of kindness to strangers, including homosexuals, see *Cosmopolitanism* by Ghanaian-born philosopher Kwame Anthony Appiah (2006).

33. For a strong critique of such moralism in relation to female genital cutting, see Nnaemeka (2005); on the "intransigent" attitude of male African intellectuals toward gender sensitive research, see Mama (2005).

34. IGLHRC, "International Human Rights Group Demands Accountability from US HIV/AIDS Fund: Is the U.S. Financing Homophobia in Africa?" press release October 7, 2007.

35. Keith Goddard, interview, http://www.outinkingston.org/galz.php. See also interview with Sierra Leonean Canadian Notisha Massaquoi, by Selly Thiam, broadcast on National Public Radio, http://www.chicagopublicradio.org/worldview/series/diaspora.asp, accessed May 4, 2007.

CHAPTER 2: THE ETHNOGRAPHY OF AFRICAN STRAIGHTNESS

1. For a study of one particularly avid pro-colonial anthropologist, S. F. Nadel, whose work is discussed below, see Faris (1973). Moore and Vaughan (1994), Ferguson (1999), and Schumaker (2001) provide important analyses of some of the many unexamined assumptions, undisclosed methodological difficulties, and behind-the-publications tensions at the influential Rhodes-Livingstone Institute. Colonial efforts to restructure African gender relations and sexuality along the lines just described (and African responses or initiatives under colonial rule) are the focus of a large body of scholarship. Overviews with select case studies of women, gender, and colonialism that I have drawn on include Obbo (1980), Cornwall (2005), Allman, Geiger, and Musisi (2002), and Coquery-Vidrovitch (1997). Ouzgane and Morrell (2005) and Lindsay and Miescher (2003) assess African masculinities in comparative colonial contexts.

2. I will be elaborating on this point below and in chapter 5, but a starting point for the critique of homophobia and heterosexism in African anthropologies should include Murray and Roscoe (1998), Pincheon (2000), and Morgan and Wieringa (2005).

3. For a suggestive challenge to African constructions of silence on homosexuality, see also Jeay (1991); for a comparative overview with the ethnography of American native societies, see Baum (1995).

4. Ibn Battuta (1983), Elbl (1996), and Theal (1896), among hundreds of other accounts in many different languages, are ably analyzed in comparative perspective in Bleys (1995).

5. A truly vast literature exists that makes these points, much of it accessible through the histories of women and gender mentioned in note 1 of this chapter. Other important interpretations include Amadiume (1997), Kaplan (1997), and Davison (1997). An important, sympathetic yet trenchant critique of African feminist writing on sexuality can be found in Arnfred (2004a).

6. Vangroenweghe (2000, 193) provides several other references in other European languages to the *chibados* or *quimbandas* of Angola in the sixteenth and seventeenth centuries. See also Thornton (1991) on the case of the cross-dressing and possibly transgender court of Anna Nzinga of Matamba, and Sweet (1996, 2003) and Matory (2005) on same-sex practices among Africans reputedly transferred across the Atlantic during the slave trade.

7. For sources on male-male sexuality specifically as medicine, see Estermann (1976), Niehaus (2002), and Matory (2004). Estermann (1976, 196–97) is also noteworthy for his discussion of "lesbians" among the Kwanyama, who, pointedly, did not claim spirit possession or ritual to explain their sexuality (hence leaving the reader to infer that the female-female relationship was based on sensual and emotional attraction).

8. For interpretations of Foucault in the construction of race, class, and sexuality in different historical and developing world contexts, see esp. Bleys (1995), Bederman (1995), Young (1995), Stoler (2002), Sigal (2003), and Carter (2007). Aldrich (2003) applies these concepts in his discussion of the role of homosexuality (and repressed homosexuality) among white men during the colonial conquest of Africa.

9. David and Charles Livingstone (1865, 284) make an allusion to self-censorship or deliberate averting of eyes on unspecified issues of "immorality" that could have included same-sex relations. Reid (2002, 193) is also worth noting here for his allusion to even more aggressive silencing, in this case involving university archivists who embargoed or actually destroyed inciminating documents written by a prominent South African minister.

10. See Jeater (2007) on how European experts on African languages supplanted African informants on cultural matters in the early twentieth century, imposing both moral judgments and epistemic values in the process.

11. As an aside, Roger Casement, whose exposé on atrocities in the Congo Free State helped bring an end to that regime, implicated himself (and by association, Catholic Irish), through his lustful thoughts on men in his published diaries. The diaries are now widely thought to be forgeries used by Casement's enemies to discredit Irish nationalism. Nonetheless, the discrepancy between the South American and African sections provides a small affirmation of my argument. Unlike the desire he articulated for Indian men in Brazil, Casement's homosexuality was never consummated and scarcely even admitted during his time in Congo. Either he or his forger appeared to accept that Africans could not conceivably be the

object of homosexual desire (Singleton-Gates and Girodias 1959, 183; Aldrich 2003, 193).

12. S. F. Nadel (1942, 152), for example, found only Arabic words for rumored behavior in the royal harems of Nupe. On Islamic influence on the Swahili coast, see also Shepherd (1987), Murray and Roscoe (1997), and Amory (1998).

13. For discussions of Burton's work, his racism against blacks, and the context of his times, see Lyons and Lyons (2004), R. Phillips (2006), and Appiah (2006). Burton's certainty about the whole of "Negro Africa," largely based on his Dahomey experience, can be set against Herskovits (1932), who found a high level of tolerance in Dahomey toward adolescent homosexuality, understood by informants as sometimes extending into adult years.

14. On an investigation into male-male sex in a Durban prison, for example, see Epprecht (2004, 91).

15. Karsch-Haack (1911, 130), translated and cited in Wieringa (2001, 13).

16. See, for example, Cureau (1915), Weeks (1909), H. A. Junod (1911, 1962 [1916]), and South Africa (1913).

17. On this particular scandal, See Richardson (1982) and Harris (2004).

18. See Moodie with Ndatshe (1994) and Harries (1994). Research into private mission archives on this issue remains to be done. But note, for an example, the striking contrast between Junod's early polemics and the silence of his fellow Swiss Protestant missionaries and their Basotho evangelists on the Witwatersrand in the 1930s through the 1950s (esp. Khouthu 1939). Nothing yet has been published on homosexual scandal among the Battalion d'Afrique or the *Tirailleurs Sénégalais*, conscripts who served and moved around French colonial Africa, but we can reasonably surmise a similar and perhaps even more politically urgent hushing.

19. On the former claim, see Corre (1894, 80 n1), Bâ (1984, 70), Gorer (1962 [1935], 36), and Ken Bugul (1991, 58), and for the latter, Crowder (1959, 68), Hanry (1970, 86), and Davidson (1988, 165).

20. On the nature of social interactions between European anthropologists and their African assistants at the prestigious and productive Rhodes-Livingstone Institute in the 1950s and 1960s, see Schumaker (2001). In more general terms, much has been written on the African petty bourgeoisie, or Christianized middle classes, and their role in shaping colonial knowledge and gender ideology. Select studies that inform my understanding come from Ghana, Nigeria, Zimbabwe, and South Africa, including K. Mann (1985), Burke (1996), Zachernuk (2000), Hawkins (2002), and West (2002). A poignant example of African evangelists advocating sexual repression as a means to win the approval of whites can be found in Bokwe, Mbali, and Jolobe (1945; available in translation from Xhosa into English in the South African Archives, Pretoria, file number 1460a/60/38). In this case, the custom to be repressed was adolescent heterosexual sex play (thigh sex, or *ukumetsha*). The hyperbolic language is evocative: "All the lovers of our race must, therefore, rise up against it, abhor it and rid the race of its contamination. That practice is out to destroy our race." Repression of ukumetsha was urgent in part

because the practice provided fodder for European racists to sneer at African sexuality and hence to block middle-class African aspirations. Salamone (2005, 84) alludes to a similar competitive respectability among the Hausa in a reference to the declaration of *tsarance* (thigh sex) as un-Islamic in the 1950s.

21. This case involving mutually reinforcing homophobic claims is discussed in Matory (2004, 2005), to which I return below. Vance maintains that academic conformism and lack of courage persisted into the 1980s and that "Most advisors actively discourage graduate students from fieldwork or dissertations on sexuality for fear that the topic will prove a career liability" (1991, 875), a view also attested from personal experience by Weston (1998). This may be overstated, but the resurgence of Cold War tensions and a political reaction against sexual liberation under Ronald Reagan likely affected many research institutions in the United States, as alluded to, for example, in Shilts (1987).

22. When I tested this Zulu phrase out on native speakers in Pietermaritzburg, it first elicited straight bafflement. Only after prompting could I get a reluctant, smiling concession that the words could indeed potentially mean homosexuality (e.g., Monica Zondi, pers. comm., June 10, 2006).

23. Another, even more eccentric source in this respect is Fischer (1985), which contains convoluted translations for *homosexuality, homosexualist, lesbian, sodomy, pederasty*, and *pederast*, all for the first time ever in Xhosa.

24. The word *ngochani* does not appear in the *Standard Shona Dictionary* (Hannan 1984 [1959]), although it is on record as being in use among Shona speakers from at least 1907 (Epprecht 2004).

25. What is probably even more significant to us is that Turnbull and Towles did not report, or even discuss among themselves, any significant homophobia in Uganda, either on account of their relationship or other extracurricular activities while in the field. Towles's diary from Kampala in the early 1970s in fact points to a very active sex life with Ugandan men, including with at least one married man and "a real queen" who managed the best restaurant in town (Grinker 2000, 203–4).

26. See Aken'ova (2002) on Nigeria, for example, or (Goddard 2004) on Zimbabwe—both referring to the 1980s.

27. In addition to "canonical" coming-out works cited in the introduction, local studies of modern forms of homophobia and gay rights struggles can be found in Reid and Dirsuweit (2001), Niang et al. (2002, 2003), Tamale (2003), Swarr (2004), Bloch and Martin (2005), Hoad et al. (2005), and Kuria (2005).

28. Vangroenweghe (2000) cites Ellis (1890, 183, 290), for example, to support the claim of "homosexual practice" among the Ewe, when in fact Ellis refers only to the "unexpected gallantry" of women recruited to fight in a desperate battle. See Amory (1997) and Pincheon (2000), among other sympathetic critics of overreach in the emerging queer anthropology. Less sympathetically, Christine Obbo (1999, 75) partially blames sloppy work by Northern researchers on this topic for the failure of African scholars to give it the serious attention it deserves.

CHAPTER 3: ETHNOPSYCHIATRY AND THE MAKING OF GAY SHAKA

1. Here I am summarizing a vast literature that admittedly indicates many local exceptions and enduring forms of highly dysfunctional colonialism and capitalism in Africa. While many historians would dispute my reading, I point to overviews such as Zeleza (1993) and Freund (1998) for support.

2. Almost no end exists to colonial, missionary, and African middle-class whining about African ingratitude, neopaganism, laziness, lustiness, and such. Two examples pertinent to the following discussion are Molema (1920) and Gordon (1934). Many of the studies to be discussed below visit these questions, but also see analyses of specific aspects of cultural change and dissonance by McCulloch (2000), Whithead (2001), and Achebe (2003), the latter in reference to an especially ambitious, polygynous female "king" in the interwar period in Igboland, Nigeria. Jeater (2007) provides an important, close case study of the intellectual underpinnings of the transition to paternalistic colonial containment of Africans through a discourse of development and scientific expertise. Neo-traditions around witchcraft subsequently became a focus of study in relation to HIV/AIDS, to be dealt with in chapter 4 below.

3. For overviews and case studies of the history of psychology in colonial Africa, all of which contain critiques of the Eurocentrism of its practitioners, see Wober (1975), Sow (1980), Mullings (1984), Nsamenang (1995), Vaughan (1991), Westley (1993), Dubow (1995), McCulloch (1995), Sadowsky (1997), and Parle (2007). The subdiscipline of sexology—whose pioneers in many cases echoed or even anticipated Freudian theory—is discussed in relation to anthropology in Lyons and Lyons (2004). Specific examples of attempts to blend anthropology and psychology in Africa will be discussed below, but one of the more substantive theoretical interventions from that era is Evans-Pritchard et al. (1934), which includes an important contribution by Marie Bonaparte. Jung did not directly contribute to the African debates but was indirectly highly influential through his theories of dream analysis. These were partially developed during a 1925 research expedition to Kenya, Uganda, and Sudan, vividly recalled in his memoirs (Jung 1963). Please note that for the purposes of this discussion, I will be conflating psychology, psychiatry, cross-cultural (or comparative) psychology, sexology, and other traditions of psychotherapy. The differences between them will probably be significant to future, more specialized investigations.

4. A powerful feminist critique of Freud can be found in Sprengnether (1990), while Bayer (1981) and Terry (1999) critically analyze the history of psychiatry and homosexuality in the United States. For an explication of Erik Erikson's model of psychological development with reference to (mostly white) South African homosexual men, see Isaacs and McKendrick (1992). Young (1995), albeit with little attention specifically to homosexuality, provides a helpful interpretation of Wilhelm Reich's critique of sexual desire under capitalism as it might pertain to colonial and racist contexts, while Herzog, in her overview of German sexuality

(2005), offers compelling insights into Reichian theory, as it influenced the political left.

5. Including in one of the leading textbooks directed at African audiences, virtually unchanged in its treatment of the topic between its 1975 and 1994 editions (Swift and Asuni 1975, and Asuni et al. 1994, pages 119 and 150, respectively).

6. Again, there is a huge scholarship on this topic, but I would point in particular to Sow (1980), Janzen (1982), and Feierman and Janzen (1992).

7. This is a common theme in the ethnography but see, for example, Dennett (1968 [1906]), a Christian missionary who was respectful of the high spirituality and sexual morality concurrent with "fetishism or Jujuism," or Krige on Africans' "natural and good" attitudes toward sexual intercourse even in the city (1956 [1937], 108). Kenyatta (1961 [1938]) and Gelfand (1968, 1979) are unusual for their explicitness in praising their subjects' no-homosexuality-therefore-mentally-healthy cultures, but the same opinion is implicit in many of the other studies noted above, right up to Asuni, Schoenberg, and Swift (1994, 150).

8. Polemics that make these points are legion, but, to bracket the time period under consideration here, see Cureau (1904) and Junod (1962 [1916]) for early articulations of this view from French and Portuguese colonies, respectively, and Turnbull (1972) for a controversial portrayal of cultural collapse dating back to British rule in Uganda. Among anthropologists who dabbled in psychological theory, see Schapera (1934, 46–48, 229) on Africans' "new outlook on sexuality" and "moral degradation" and Gordon (1934, 241) on the "alarming" "degradations," "sexual perversions," and "new growths in the wake of so-called civilisation." Ashforth (2005) makes the important point that from many Africans' point of view, it was not so much urbanization per se but attempts by colonial states to suppress witchcraft that exacerbated peoples' sense of injustice, which in turn may have fueled a willingness to flout cultural taboos.

9. The first provision for black female patients in colonial Natal, for example, included a six-foot-deep pit "into which difficult patients were dropped daily" (Mirde 1975, 324). See also Sivadon (1958) for descriptions of Bedlam-like conditions in different African colonies well into the twentieth century.

10. "In a hundred years from now, but maybe even sooner, the primitive peoples of the earth will either be eliminated or more or less tamed by our civilizations. Those who still remain are precious, fleeting witnesses of a time gone by." My translation.

11. See Dubow (1995) and McCulloch (1995, 2000) on this theme, also implicit in the work of influential French psychologist Octave Mannoni (1984 [1950]).

12. A virtual reprint of this book published in 1972 dropped even this obscure reference to the topic (Carothers 1972). Carothers, it should be noted, consolidated his reputation as an apologist for the colonial government of Kenya early in his career in an influential book that largely exonerated the British from the violent suppression of the Mau Mau revolt (Carothers 1954).

13. Freed to Dr. P. de Vos, December 19, 1950. Freed file at the William Cullen Library, University of the Witwatersrand, Johannesburg (A1212).

14. See Jacobs (1969), for example, and documentation of the aVersion Project at the Gay and Lesbian Archives of South Africa, www.mask.org.za/sections/AfricaPerCountry/southafrica/aversion.html. Lynette Jackson (1997, 293) also records at least one experimental lobotomy to cure homosexuality in Rhodesia in 1947, a rare instance of a white man being subjected to the same type of unethical medical experimentation that was commonly meted out to black women.

15. The literature about African sexuality written by Europeans or European settlers in Africa is beyond the scope of this study. The politically revolutionary potential of heterosexually liberated sexuality does reoccur, however, much in keeping with the fascination of the New Left in Europe with the theories of Reich (Herzog 2005). In Gordimer's *Sport of Nature* (1987), for example, shared hetero-sexual lustiness symbolically binds the preternaturally horny white girl to the cause of black revolution. Gay-identified authors who began to write in the same period brought similar insights. The moral in these stories is that forced conformity for white boys and men to a narrow, repressive, and internally violent masculinity eventually must boil over into outward rage, racism, or homophobic self-hatred. Indeed, the literature often portrays the characters who feel homoerotic desire as borderline psychotics who act out in a self-destructive or criminal way (e.g., Galgut 1982; Behr 1997). This theme in Afrikaner literature is explored in De Waul (1994) and Heyns (1998), while for a literary exploration of it in Portuguese (set in late-colonial Lourenço Marques, Mozambique) see Melo (1981).

16. Examples of a gay-positive Shaka can be found at the British gay rights Web site Schools Out (www.schools-out.org .uk/news/lgbthistory.htm), the U.S. travel site Gay 2Afrika (www.2afrika.com/safaris/programs/102_alt.asp) and many others.

17. For a summary of the new historiography, see Hamilton (1995, 1998) and Wylie (2000).

18. See esp. Golan (1994) and Schumaker (2001).

19. On an unpublished manuscript of Gluckman's, see Golan 1994 (115).

20. Somewhat to his credit, Mazrui did caution against "excessive virility and violence" in this embarrassing polemic, and he does not list it among his list of publications on his personal Web site. http://www.alimazrui.com.

21. For critical insights into the production and marketing of *Shaka Zulu*, see Mersham (1989), Golan (1994), and Hamilton (1998).

CHAPTER 4: SLIM DISEASE AND THE SCIENCE OF SILENCE

1. The scholarship on biomedical interventions in colonial Africa is rich and in many cases quite damning of the science and scientists involved. See, for exam-ple, Packard and Epstein (1991), Vaughan (1991), Comaroff (1993), Young (1995), and Echenberg (2002). More recent controversies—with strong allegations of ethi-cal breaches—can be found in the work of Hooper (1999) and his Web site http://www.aidsorigins.com. For a powerful critical assessment of sexism and homopho-

bia in the history of AIDS epidemiology in the West, see also Treichler (1988) and S. Epstein (1996).

2. "Terrible Twins," editorial, *Mail and Guardian*, April 7–12, 2006, 22. For early folk explanations of slim disease in Uganda, see Hooper (1990); for case studies of witchcraft explanations of AIDS, see Yamba (1997), Ashforth (2002, 2005), and Rödlach (2006). The denialist phenomenon in secular discourse is ably analyzed in Robins (2004) and Hoad (2007), for example, and passionately denounced in Cameron (2005). The issue can be contextualized in the proliferating scholarship in HIV/AIDS, including Webb (1997), Kalipeni and Oppong (2004), Iliffe (2006), and Abdool Karim and Abdool Karim (2005) (the latter with especially strong chapters interpreting the science for nonscientist readers).

3. A large historiography makes these points, including Cornwall (2005), Allman, Geiger and Musisi (2002), and Epprecht (2000), and specific to sexual health, Setel, Lewis, and Lyons (1999) and Jeeves (2001).

4. The scale of the error can be inferred from missionary claims of a rate of syphilis infection of 75 to 80 percent among Basotho and Ndebele men in 1906.

5. Van Onselen (1976, 1982) and Beinart (1987) were the first historians to make this case, subsequently developed (with reference to a series of discreet South African government commissions of enquiry from 1906 onward) by Moodie (1988, 1994), Harries (1990, 1994), and myself (Epprecht 2001, 2004).

6. The latter included covering up the scandal from public debate, as suggested by the hasty assurances given to Transkeian chiefs who had gotten wind of the practice of mine marriage in the 1920s. For more extensive consideration of this history, see Moodie (1994) and Epprecht (2004).

7. Freed to Dr. P. de Vos, December 19, 1950, citing research for his book (Freed 1949). See Freed's file at the William Cullen Library, University of Witwatersrand, Johannesburg, A1212.

8. That section of the interview of Nyerere by Hubert Fichte was cut from the published version in 1974. It exists only in an unpublished transcript, the details of which I am constrained from revealing. An imaginative re-creation of a similar interview between fictional characters can be found in Dunton (2008).

9. For a firsthand account of the outbreak and political reactions in Uganda, see Hooper (1990). An overarching, nonheterosexist synthesis of the many national or issue-specific histories of HIV/AIDS in Africa has yet to be written. However, for some of the key pieces of the puzzle, see Grmek (1990), Packard and Epstein (1992), Hooper (1999), Delius and Walker (2002), Kalipeni et al. (2004), Iliffe (2006), and Abdool Karim and Abdool Karim (2005). The following analysis draws on English-language publications, but a glance over key publications in French suggests that the same points can be made for the scholarship in that language. See esp. Caraël (1987), Becker et al. (1999), Fassin (2004), and Denis and Becker (2006). Attitudes within the medical profession at the front line of the disease in the United States are powerfully revealed in Fee and Fox (1988) and Bayer and Oppenheimer (2000).

10. On the later but even more devastating outbreak in KwaZulu-Natal, see Carton (2006).

11. On this point see esp. Clumeck et al. (1983), Clumeck et al. (1984), Van de Perre et al. (1984), Greenwood (1984), Piot et al. (1984), Kamradt, Niese, and Vogel (1985), and Hrdy (1987).

12. Estimates here are based on antenatal clinic attendees, a contentious means to measure prevalence. Recent revised calculations do bring estimates lower but still represent a stunning incidence over a short period of time.

13. The only direct reference I have found to the claim by Serwadda et al. is by Hooper (1990, 347), a journalist, although even he did not take it very seriously, based, it appears, in part on his personal experiences of living as a single, heterosexual man in East Africa for several years (Hooper, pers. comm.). Wilson Carswell believed that msm was taking place in boarding schools, seminaries, prisons, and perhaps among long-distance truckers, but "attempts to engage locally based social scientists (based in Makerere University) in [any kind of] AIDS research [let alone on msm] were largely unsuccessful at that time" (pers. comm., February 28, 2007). The so-called Kigozi report noted above (Carswell et al. 1986) makes no reference to any of these concerns.

14. Julie Dyer, medical officer of health for Pietermaritzburg/Msunduzi (South Africa, 1994–2005), interview by the author, Pietermaritzburg, June 19, 2006.

15. Maquet's bona fides have been questioned (e.g., Jefremovas 2002, 70), but on this issue the same finding could be adduced from J. M. M. van der Burgt's study of neighboring (ethnically and culturally similar) Burundi (1903; cited in Vangroenweghe 2000, 446), which documents no less than seven different terms for "homosexuality" or "hermaphrodite." The possibility of discreet bisexual relationships and "common" anal sex was also subsequently suggested in an almost equally overlooked survey from 1987 (Feldman, Friedman, and Des Jarlais 1987, 160).

16. Indeed, while it was likely not their intention, the Chirimuuta's thesis has been picked up by conspiracy theorists. See, for example, *Dissonance: A Journal of Things That Do Not Fit.* http://way.net/dissonance/index.html.

17. Julie Dyer, medical officer of health for Pietermaritzburg/Msunduzi (South Africa, 1994–2005), interview by author, Pietermaritzburg, June 19, 2006.

18. Zackie Achmat, pers. comm., August 3, 2006.

CHAPTER 5: ALTERNATIVES AND AMBIGUITIES: AFRICAN VOICES IN LITERATURE AND FILM

1. Over at least two hundred years, probably thousands of short stories, plays, and novels have been published in many different languages in and about Africa. There are poems and oral traditions going back much further, while films and alternate electronic media have proliferated in the last decade. In view of the enormity of the potential primary sources, I have had to rely more heavily on the secondary scholarship to support my argument here than in previous chapters. Among the

most helpful studies in that regard are Dathorne and Feuser (1969), Miller (1985), Brantlinger (1985), Stratton (1994), Msiska and Hyland (1997), Nfah-Abbenyi (1997b), Hay (2000), Carretta and Gould (2001), and Stobie (2007). Tcheuyap (2005) and Azodo and Eke (2007) provide an insightful overview of the treatment of sexuality in African cinema. Taiwo (1984) and Kolawole (1997) are important as examples of African literary critics' attempted assertions of heteronormative dogma upon sometimes recalcitrant African authors.

2. See also Golan (1994) and Blair (1976).

3. A rare exception to this tendency preceded colonial rule. The Marquis de Sade's "Histoire de Sainville et Léonore" (1990 [1795]) merits a footnote, if for no other reason than how it so strikingly highlights the disappearance of same-sex sexuality from the dominant discourse in the nineteenth century, even from satire. Not only was Sade's *Aline et Valcour* one of the very first European novels to be substantially set in Africa, it is also the first novel, and for more than a hundred years the only one, to feature African men having (or thinking about having) sex with men and boys. Particularly ironic is that Sade has a culturally Africanized character defend the principle of tolerance of sexual diversity against the character Sainville, a Christian, bourgeois prude. For more substantive discussion of this extraordinary work, see Beach (1980) and Epprecht (2007).

4. Marguerite Poland is well outside the time frame of reference but I include her here not only because her novel is set in the early 1900s with mine marriages (and tacit cover-up by mine managers) as an important part of the story. According to the biographical information provided in the book, she is also a direct descendent of Charles Taberer, the coauthor of the original enquiry that investigated these secrets. Family insider history?

5. See Armah (1974) for a notable example with sophisticated writing and brutal imagery. Antiracist literature by white authors sometimes shared the same sentiment. See, for example, Gordimer (1987), where sexual appetite binds a white woman to the revolutionary cause of the black antiapartheid leadership. A fascinating allusion to the shared, mutually reinforcing homophobia between whites and blacks in South Africa also appears in V. S. Naipaul's *In a Free State* (1973, 155). Here, a gay Englishman complains that white homosexuals when caught have their heads shaved, are dressed as women, are classified as natives, and then sent to their fate in the African townships by the white authorities.

6. For some of many more examples of this imagery, see Dunton (1989).

7. Gordimer (1980) offers a similar definition by contrast of a politically conscious, heterosexual, and admirable white South African woman against shallow, self-indulgent white European lesbians.

8. Among his critics: Wole Soyinka (1999). See also Dunton (1999).

9. For biographical background on Marechera, and an analysis of Marechera's uncertain relationship with hegemonic masculinity in his other writing, see Shaw (2005).

10. A voluminous novel set in prerevolutionary (fascist, homophobic) Lourenço Marques, for example, hints at a closeted gay scene in colonial Mozambique. The

author, Guilherme de Melo, subsequently became one of Portugal's leading gay authors (Melo 1981). Gayish milieux in Abidjan, Dakar, and Kampala are noted in some of the anthropology, but they did not, as far as I can discern, produce any fiction.

11. Interestingly, and pertinent to the present discussion, one of Beyala's (few) African interpreters underplays the lesbian potential by offering a literal translation from the French that erases the hint of sexual touching in the key love scene (rendered as maternal rather than sexual—Nfah-Abbenyi 1997a, 109).

12. For an anthology of lesbian writing, see Joint Working Group (2006); for some of the many gay-friendly Web sites out of South Africa, see the Linx link at www.mask.co.za.

13. For a comparative analysis of this film and the next, see Migraine-George (2003) and Eke (2007).

CHAPTER 6: CONCLUSION

1. For example, "Anti Gay Rights in Nigeria" discussions following Toyin Falola's *New York Times* op-ed piece denouncing the proposed bill. http://groups.google .com/group/USAAfricaDialogue/browse_thread/thread/cad72e987f4f457c?hl=en.

2. Makgoba's speech is cited in Cameron (2005, 83). See also Long, Brown, and Cooper (2003) on the word as claimed for seTswana.

3. www.africa-union.org/home/Welcome.htm; emphasis mine.

Works Cited

Aarmo, Margrete. 1999. "How Homosexuality Became 'Un-African': The Case of Zimbabwe." In Blackwood and Wieringa 1999, 255–80.

Abdool Karim, S. S., and Q. Abdool Karim, eds. 2005. *HIV/AIDS in South Africa.* Cambridge: Cambridge University Press.

Achebe, Nwando. 2003. "'And She Became a Man': King Ahebi Ugbabe in the History of Enugu-Ezike, Northern Igboland, 1880–1948." In Lindsay and Miescher, 2003, 52–68.

Achmat, Zackie. 1993. "'Apostles of Civilised Vice': 'Immoral Practices' and 'Unnatural Vice' in South African Prisons and Compounds, 1890–1920." *Social Dynamics* 19, 2:92–110.

———. n.d. "A Cape Coloured, a Botha, as well as a Lesbian: Carl Buckle, Louis Freed, and the Psychiatrization of Male Homosexuality." MA diss., University of Cape Town.

Achmat, Zackie, and Jack Lewis. 1999. *Apostles of Civilised Vice.* VHS. Muizenberg, South Africa: Idol Productions.

Adeokun, Lawrence, Jeremiah Twa-Twa, Agnes Ssekiboobo, and Rose Nalwadda. 1995. "Social Context of HIV Infection in Uganda." In Orubuloye et al., 1–26.

Afrika, Tatamkhulu. 1996. *Tightrope: Four Novellas.* Cape Town: Mayibuye Books.

Ahlberg, Beth Maina. 1994. "Is There a Distinct African Sexuality? A Critical Response to Caldwell." *Africa* 64, 2:220–24.

Ahmed, Samira Amin, and Al Haj Hamad M. Kheir. 2002. "Sudanese Sexual Behavior, Socio-Cultural Norms and the Transmission of HIV." In Dyson 2002, 303–14.

Aidoo, Ama Ata. 1977. *Our Sister Killjoy.* London: Heinemann.

Aina, Tade Akin. 1991. "Patterns of Bisexuality in Sub-Saharan Africa." In *Bisexuality and HIV/AIDS: A Global Perspective*, ed. Rob Tielman, Manuel Carballo, Aart Hendriks, 81–90. Buffalo: Prometheus.

Aken'ova, Cesnabmihilo Dorothy. 2002. "Reproductive Health Research in the North of Nigeria." Paper presented at the Women's Health Action Research Centre, University of Benin.

Akeroyd, Annie V. 2004. "Coercion, Constraints, and 'Cultural Entrapments': A Further Look at Gendered and Occupational Factors Pertinent to the Transmission of HIV in Africa." In Kalipeni et al. 2004, 89–103.

Alberton, Paulo, and Graeme Reid (dir.). 2000. *Dark and Lovely, Soft and Free.* VHS. Johannesburg: Gay and Lesbian Archives.

Aldrich, Robert. 2003. *Colonialism and Homosexuality.* London: Routledge.

Allman, Dan, Sylvia Adebajo, Ted Myers, Oludare Odumuye, and Sade Ogunsola. 2007. "Challenges for the Sexual Health and Social Acceptance of Men Who Have Sex with Men in Nigeria." *Culture, Health and Sexuality* 9, 2:153–68.

Allman, Jean, Susan Geiger, and Nyakanyike Musisi, eds. 2002. *Women in African Colonial Histories.* Bloomington: Indiana University Press.

Amadiume, Ifi. 1987. *Male Daughters, Female Husbands: Gender and Sex in an African Society.* London: Zed Books.

———. 1997. *Reinventing Africa: Matriarchy, Religion, and Culture.* London: Zed Books.

———. 2006. "Sexuality, African Religio-Cultural Traditions and Modernity: Expanding the Lens." *CODESRIA Bulletin,* 1–2:26–28.

Amory, Deborah P. 1997. "'Homosexuality' in Africa: Issues and Debates." *Issue* 25, 1:5–10.

———. 1998. "*Mashoga, Mabasha,* and *Magai:* 'Homosexuality' on the East African Coast." In Murray and Roscoe 1998, 67–87.

Anderson, R., O. W. Prozesky, H. A. Eftychis, et al. 1983. "Immunological Abnormalities in South African Homosexual Men." *South African Medical Journal* 64 (July 23): 119–22.

Andor, L. E., comp. 1983. *Psychological and Sociological Studies of the Black People of Africa, South of the Sahara: 1960–1975. An Annotated Select Bibliography.* Johannesburg: National Institute for Personnel Research.

Anele, Douglas. 2006. "Homosexuality and Its Enemies." *Vanguard* (Lagos), January 30.

Anon. 1982. "Immuniteitstekort en homoseksualiteit." Editorial. *South African Medical Journal* 61:298.

———. 1983a. "Acquired Immunodeficiency Syndrome (AIDS)." Editorial. *South African Medical Journal* 63 (January 22): 97–98.

———. 1987. "AIDS in South Africa—A Time for Action." Editorial. *South African Medical Journal* 71 (June 6): 677–78.

Anugworm, Edlyne E. 1999. "Perceptions of AIDS among University Students in Nigeria: Implications for AIDS Prevention Programmes." In Becker et al. 1999, 589–98.

Appiah, Kwame Anthony. 2006. *Cosmopolitanism: Ethics in a World of Strangers.* New York: Norton.

Arac de Nyeko, Monica. 2007. "Jambula Tree" In *African Love Stories,* ed. Ama Ata Aidoo. Banbury: Ayebia Clarke Publishing.

Armah, Ayi Kwei. 1974. *Why Are We So Blest?* London: Heinemann.

———. 1979. *Two Thousand Seasons.* London: Heinemann.

Arnfred, Signe, ed. 2004a. "'African Sexuality'/Sexuality in Africa" Tales and Silences." In *Re-thinking Sexualities in Africa,* ed. S. Arnfred, 59–76. Uppsala: Nordiska Afrikainstitutet.

———, ed. 2004b. *Re-thinking Sexualities in Africa*. Uppsala: Nordiska Afrikainstitutet.

ARSRC (Africa Regional Sexuality Resource Center). 2005a. *Sexuality in the Media*. Lagos: Africa Regional Sexuality Resource Center.

———, 2005b. *Socialisation and Sexuality Discourse in Nigeria*. Lagos: Africa Regional Sexuality Resource Center.

Ashe, Robert P. 1970 [1889]. *Two Kings of Uganda*. London: Frank Cass.

Ashforth, Adam. 2002. "An Epidemic of Witchcraft? The Implications of AIDS for the Post-apartheid State." *African Studies* 61, 1:121–43

———. 2005. *Witchcraft, Violence, and Democracy in South Africa*. Chicago: University of Chicago Press.

Asuni, Tolani, Friderun Schoenberg, and Charles Swift. 1994 [1975]. *Mental Health and Disease in Africa*. Ibadan: Spectrum Books.

Attah, Ayesha. 2007. "Chatting with Monica Arac de Nyeko, Caine Prize Winner." *African Magazine*. http://www.africanmag.com/viewer/magazines/article.asd/id/493/vts/design001, accessed October 31, 2007.

Attipoe, Dela. 2004. "MSM and HIV in Ghana." *Gully*. www.thegully.com/essays/gaymundo/0403_gay-men_hiv_ghana/msm_ghana_intro_summary .html, accessed August 28, 2006.

Azodo, Uzoamaka, and Maureen Ngozi Eke. 2007. "Survey of the Historical and Geographical Scope of Gender and Sexuality in African Film." In *Gender and Sexuality in African Literature and Film*, ed. U. Azodo and M. Eke, 229–38. Trenton, NJ, and Asmara: Africa World Press.

Azuah, Unoma N. 2005. "The Emerging Lesbian Voice in Nigerian Feminist Literature." In Veit-Wild and Naguschewski 2005, 129–41.

Bâ, Mariama, 1984. *Scarlet Song*. Trans. Dorothy S. Blair. London: Longman.

Barnard, Ian. 2004. *Queer Race: Cultural Interventions in the Racial Politics of Queer Theory*. New York: Peter Lang.

Baum, Robert M. 1995. "Homosexuality and the Traditional Religions of the Americas and Africa." In *Homosexuality and World Religions*, ed. Arlene Swidler, 1–46. Valley Forge, PA: Trinity Press International.

Bayer, Ronald. 1981. *Homosexuality and American Psychiatry: The Politics of Diagnosis*. New York: Basic Books.

Bayer, Ronald, and Gerald R. Oppenheimer. 2000. *AIDS Doctors: Voices from the Epidemic*. Oxford: Oxford University Press.

Beach, David. 1980. "The Marquis de Sade: First Zimbabwean Novelist." *Zambezia* 8, 1:53–61.

Becker, Charles, Jean-Pierre Dozon, Christine Obbo, and Moriba Touré, eds. 1999. *Vivre et Penser le Sida en Afrique. Experiencing and Understanding AIDS in Africa*. Dakar: CODESRIA; Paris: Karthala, IRD.

Becker, Charles, and René Collingnon. 1999. "Politiques démographiques et sanitaires face aux maladies sexuellement transmises en Afrique de l'ouest." In Becker et al. 1999, 133–49.

Bederman, Gail. 1995. *Manliness and Civilization: A Cultural History of Gender and Race in the United States, 1880–1917*. Chicago: University of Chicago Press.

Behr, Mark. 1997. *The Smell of Apples*. New York: Picador.

Beidelman, Thomas O. 1997. *The Cool Knife: Imagery of Gender, Sexuality, and Moral Education in Kaguru Initiation Ritual*. Washington, DC: Smithsonian Institute Press.

Beinart, William. 1987. "Worker Consciousness, Ethnic Particularism, and Nationalism: The Experiences of a South African Migrant, 1930–1960." In *The Politics of Race, Class, and Nationalism in Twentieth-Century South Africa*, ed. Shula Marks and Stanley Trapido, 286–309. Harlow: Longman.

Bell, Leland. 1991. *Mental and Social Disorder in Sub-Saharan Africa: the Case of Sierra Leone, 1787–1990*. Westport, CT: Greenwood.

Berglund, Axel-Ivar. 1970. "Transition from Traditional to a Westernized Outlook on Life." In *Migrant Labour and Church Involvement*, ed. Missiological Institute, 35–50. Umpumulo: Missiological Institute.

Beti, Mongo. 1971. *The Poor Christ of Bomba*. London: Heinemann.

Beyala, Calixthe. 1996. *Your Name Shall Be Tanga*. Trans. from the French by Marjolijn de Jager. Portsmouth, NH: Heinemann.

———. 2003. *Femme nue, femme noire: Roman*. Paris: Albin Michel.

Bibeau, Giles. 1991. "L'Afrique, terre imaginaire du Sida. La subversion du discours scientifique par le jeu des fantasmes." *Anthropologie et Sociétés* 15, 2–3:125–48.

Biggar, R. J. 1986. "The AIDS Problem in Africa." *Lancet* 327, 8472 (1986): 79–83.

Blacking, John. 1959. "Fictitious Kinship Idioms in Friendships among the Venda of Northern Transvaal." *Man* 59:255–58.

———. 1978. "Uses of Kinship Idiom in Friendships in Some Venda and Zulu Schools." In *Social System and Tradition in Southern Africa*, ed. John Argyle and Eleanor Preston-Whyte, 101–17. New York: Oxford University Press.

Blackwood, Evelyn, and Saskia Wieringa. 1999. *Female Desires: Same-Sex Relations and Transgender Practices across Cultures*. New York: Columbia University Press.

Blair, Dorothy S. 1976. *African Literature in French*. Cambridge: Cambridge University Press.

Bleys, Rudi C. 1995. *The Geography of Perversion: Male-to-Male Sexual Behaviour outside the West and the Ethnographic Imagination, 1750–1918*. Washington Square, New York: New York University Press.

Bloch, Joanne, and Karen Martin, comps. 2005. *Balancing Act: South African Gay and Lesbian Youth Speak Out*. Johannesbug: New Africa Education.

Boehmer, Elleke, 2005. "Versions of Yearning and Dissent: The Troping of Desire in Yvonne Vera and Tsitsi Dangarembga." In Veit-Wild and Naguschewski 2005, 113–28.

Boellstorf, Tom. 2007. *A Coincidence of Desires: Anthropology, Queer Studies, Indonesia*. Durham: Duke University Press.

Bokoum, Saido. 1974. *Chaine: Roman*. Paris: Denoel.

Bokwe, Dr. R. T., Rev. Y. Mbali, and Rev. James Jolobe. 1945. *Udaba Olusingiswe Kulutsha*. Lovedale College. English translation at South African Archives, Pretoria, 1460a/60/38.

Bonaparte, Marie. 1934. "Psychanalyse et ethnographie." In *Essays Presented to C. G. Seligman*, ed. Evans-Pritchard et al., 19–26. London: Kegan Paul.

Botha, M. C., F. A. Neetheling, I. Shai, et al. 1988. "Two Black South Africans with AIDS." Letter. *South African Medical Journal* 73 (January 23): 132–34.

Boykin, Keith. 2005. *Beyond the Down Low: Sex, Lies, and Denial in Black America*. New York: Carroll and Graf.

Bozongwana, Wallace. 1983. *Ndebele Religion and Customs*. Gweru: Mambo Press.

Brantlinger, Patrick. 1985. "Victorians and Africans: The Genealogy of the Myth of the Dark Continent." *Critical Enquiry* 12 (Autumn): 166–203.

Brooks, Philip, and Laurent Bocahut. 1998. *Woubi chéri*. VHS. Paris: ARTE France, 1998.

Browne, William George. 1806 [1799]. *Travels in Africa, Egypt, and Syria from the year 1792 to 1798*. London: T. Cadell and W. Davies.

Bryant, Alfred T. 1917. "Mental Development of the South African Native." *Eugenics Review* 9, 1:42–49.

———. 1929. *Olden Times in Zululand and Natal: Containing Earlier Political History of the Eastern-Nguni Clans*. Cape Town: C. Struik.

Bryk, Felix. 1964 [1925]. *Voodoo-Eros: Ethnological Studies in the Sex-Life of the African Aborigines*. New York: United Book Guild.

Burke, Timothy. 1996. *Lifebuoy Men, Lux Women: Commodification, Consumption, and Cleanliness in Modern Zimbabwe*. Durham: Duke University Press.

Burns, James. 2002. *Flickering Shadows: Cinema and Identity in Colonial Zimbabwe*. Athens: Ohio University Press.

Burton, Richard. 1885. *A Plain and Literal Translation of the Arabian Nights' Entertainments, Now Entitled: The Book of the Thousand Nights and a Night*, 10 vols. London: Burton Club.

Cage, Ken. 2003. *Gayle: The Language of Kinks and Queens*. Johannesburg: Jacana Press.

Caldwell, John C. 2000. "Rethinking the African AIDS Epidemic." *Population and Development Review* 26, 1:117–35.

Caldwell, John C., Pat Caldwell, and Pat Quiggin. 1989. "The Social Context of AIDS in Sub-Saharan Africa." *Population and Development Review* 15, 2:185–233.

Calixthe, Shana L. 2005. "Things Which Aren't to Be Given Names: Afro-Caribbean and Diasporic Negotiations of Same Gender Desire and Sexual Relations." *Canadian Woman Studies* 24, 2–3:128–37.

Camara, Mohamed, dir. 1997. *Dakan*. Conakry: ArtMattan.

———. 2005. "Visualizing Homosexualities in Africa-*Dakan*: An Interview with Filmmaker Mohamed Camara." Interview by Beti Ellerson. In Ouzgane and Morrell 2005, 61–73.

Cameron, Edwin. 2005. *Witness to AIDS*. Cape Town: Tafelberg.

Cape Colony. 1873. *Report and Evidence of the Commission on Native Laws and Customs of the Basutos*. Cape Town: Saul Solomon.

Caraël, Michel. 1987. "Le SIDA en Afrique." In *Le SIDA: Rumeurs et faits*, ed. Emmanuel Hirsch. Paris: Cerf.

Caraël, Michel, John Cleland, Jean-Claude Deheneffe, and Lawrence Adeokun. 1992. "Research on Sexual Behaviour That Transmits HIV: The GPA/WHO Collaborative Surveys." In Dyson 1992, 65–97.

Carothers, J. C. 1954. *The Psychology of Mau Mau*. Nairobi: Government Printers.

———. 1970 [1953]. *The African Mind in Health and Disease: A Study in Ethnopsychiatry*. New York: Negro Universities Press.

———. 1972. *The Mind of Man in Africa*. London: Tom Stacy.

Carretta, Vincent, and Philip Gould, eds. 2001. *Genius in Bondage: Literature of the Early Black Atlantic*. Lexington: University Press of Kentucky.

Carswell, Wilson, Roy Mugerwa, Nelson Sewankambo, Fred Kigozi, and Rick Goodgame. ca. 1986. "AIDS in Uganda." Mimeograph. Ministry of Health, Kampala.

Carter, Julian B. 2007. *The Heart of Whiteness: Normal Sexuality and Race in America, 1880–1940*. Durham: Duke University Press.

Carton, Benedict. 2006. "'We Are Made Quiet by This Annihilation': Historicizing Concepts of Bodily Pollution and Dangerous Sexuality in South Africa." *International Journal of African Historical Studies* 39, 1:85–106.

Castilhon, Jean-Louis. 1993 [1769]. *Zingha, reine d'Angola, histoire africaine*. Ed. Patrick Graille and Laurent Quilerie. Bourges: Ganymède.

Chanaiwa, David. 1980. "The Zulu Revolution: State Formation in a Pastoralist Society." *African Studies Review* 23, 3:1–20.

Chevrier, Odilon. n.d. "Croyances et coutumes chez les Basotho." Mimeograph. Morija Museum and Archives, Lesotho.

Chirimuuta, Richard C., and Rosalind J. Chirimuuta. 1989. *AIDS, Africa, and Racism*. London: Free Association Books.

Clowes, Lindsay. 2001. "A Modernized Man? Changing Constructions of Masculinity in *Drum* Magazine, 1951–1984." PhD diss., University of Cape Town.

———. 2005. "To Be a Man: Changing Constructions of Masculinity in *Drum* Magazine, 1951–1965." In Ouzgane and Morrell 2005, 89–108.

Clumeck, N., F. Mascart-Lemone, J. de Mauberge, et al. 1983. "Acquired Immunodeficiency Syndrome in Black Africans." *Lancet* 321, 8325:642.

Clumeck, N., J. Sonnet, H. Taelman, et al. 1984. "Acquired Immunodeficiency Syndrome in African Patients." *New England Journal of Medicine* 310, 8:492–97.

Cobham, Rhonda. 1993. "Misgendering the Nation: African Nationalist Fictions and Nuruddin Farah's *Maps*." In Parker et al. 1993, 42–59.

Cohen, Jonathan, and Tony Tate. 2005. *The Less They Know, the Better: Abstinence-Only HIV/AIDS Programs in Uganda*. http://hrw.org/reports/2005/uganda0305 /1.htm#_Toc98378357.

Colman, Robert, dir. 1998. "After Nines!" Unpublished play transcript and oral history research, Gay and Lesbian Archives of South Africa, AM 2894.

Comaroff, Jean. 1993. "The Diseased Heart of Africa: Medicine, Colonialism, and the Black Body." In *Knowledge, Power, and Practice: The Anthropology of Medicine and Everyday Life*, ed. ed. Shirley Lindenbaum and Margaret Lock. Berkeley: University of California Press.

Cooper, Frederick. 2005. *Colonialism in Question: Theory, Knowledge, History.* Berkeley: University of California Press.

Coplan, David B. 1994. *In the Time of Cannibals: The Word Music of South Africa's Basotho Migrants.* Chicago: University of Chicago Press.

Coquery-Vidrovitch, Catherine. 1997. *African Women: A Modern History.* Trans. Beth Raps. Boulder: Westview.

Cornwall, Andrea, ed. 2005. *Readings in Gender in Africa.* Bloomington: Indiana University Press.

Corre, Armand. 1894. *L'Ethnographie criminelle d'après les observations et les statistiques judiciaires recueilles dans les colonies françaises.* Paris: C. Reinwald.

Couzens, Tim. 1984. Introduction to *Wild Deer*, by Ethelreda Lewis. Cape Town: David Philip.

Cover, Rob. 2004. "Material Queer Theory: Performativity, Subjectivity, and Affinity-Based Struggles in the Culture of Late Capitalism." *Rethinking Marxism* 16, 3:293–310.

Crichlow, Wesley. 2004. *Buller Men and Batty Bwoys: Hidden Men in Toronto and Halifax Black Communities.* Toronto: University of Toronto Press.

Crowder, Michael. 1959. *Pagans and Politicians.* London: Hutchinson.

Crush, Jonathan, Brian Williams, Eleanor Gouws, and Mark Lurie. 2005. "Migration and HIV/AIDS in South Africa." *Development Southern Africa* 22, 3:293–318.

Cruz-Malavé, Arnaldo, and Martin F. Manalansan IV, eds. 2002. *Queer Globalizations: Citizenship and the Afterlife of Colonialism.* New York: New York University Press.

CSA (Conseil Scientifique pour l'Afrique au Sud du Sahara). 1959. *Report of the CSA Meeting of Specialists on the Basic Psychological Structures of African and Madagascan Populations.* Johannesburg: National Institute of Personnel Research.

Cureau, Adolphe Louis. 1904. "Essai sur la psychologie des races nègres de l'Afrique tropicale." *Revue générale des sciences pures et appliquées* 15:638–52.

———. 1915. *Savage Man in Central Africa: A Study of Primitive Races in the French Congo.* London: T. Fisher Unwin.

Curran, James, W. M. Morgan, A. M. Hardy, et al. 1985. "The Epidemiology of AIDS: Current and Future Prospects." *Science* 229:1352–57.

Dangarembga, Tsitsi. 1989. *Nervous Conditions: A Novel.* Seattle: Seal Press.

Dathorne, O. R., and Willfried Feuser, eds. 1969. *Africa in Prose.* Harmondsworth: Heinemann.

Davidson, Col. S. 1949. "Psychiatric Work among the Bemba." *Rhodes-Livingstone Institute Journal* 7:75–86.

Davidson, Michael. 1988 [1970]. *Some Boys*. Swaffham, UK: Gay Men's Press.

Davies, J. P. 1949. "Sex Hormone Upset in Africans." *British Medical Journal* 2:676–79

Davison, Jean. 1997. *Gender, Lineage, and Ethnicity in Southern Africa*. Boulder: Westview.

De Waul, Shawn. 1994. "A Thousand Forms of Love: Representations of Homosexuality in South African Literature." In Gevisser and Cameron 1994, 232–45.

Delafosse, Maurice. 1912. *Haut-Sénégal, Niger, Sudan Française, vol. 3*. Paris: Larose.

Delius, Peter, and Liz Walker, eds. 2002. *AIDS in Context*, special issue of *African Studies*, 61, 1.

Denis, Philippe, and Charles Becker, eds. 2006. *L'Épidémie du Sida en Afrique Subsaharienne: Regards historiens*. Paris: Karthala.

Dennett, Richard E. 1968 [1906]. *At the Back of the Black Man's Mind; or, Notes on the Kingly Office in West Africa*. London: Frank Cass.

Desai, Gaurav. 2001. "Out in Africa." In Hawley 2001, 139–64.

Dibia, Jude. 2005. *Walking with Shadows*. Lagos: BlackSands Books.

Diop, Samba. 2004. *African Francophone Cinema*. New Orleans: University Press of the South.

Dirsuweit, Teresa. 2006. "The Problem of Identities: The Lesbian, Gay, Bisexual, Transgender and Intersex Movement in South Africa." In *Voices of Protest: Social Movements in Post-apartheid South Africa*, ed. Richard Ballard, Adam Habib, and Imraan Valodia, 325–48. Scottsville: University of KwaZulu-Natal Press.

Ditsie, Beverly, and Nicky Newman. n.d. *Simon and I*. VHS. Cape Town/Johannesburg: See Thru Media/Steps for the Future.

Dlamini, Moses. 1984. *Hell Hole, Robben Island: Reminiscences of a Political Prisoner in South Africa*. Trenton, NJ: Africa World Press.

Dlamini, Busanogokwakhe. 2006. "Homosexuality in the African Context." *Agenda* (special issue on homosexuality) 67:128–36.

Dogliotti, M. 1971. "The Incidence of Syphilis in the Bantu: Survey of 587 Cases from Baragwanath Hospital." *South African Medical Journal* 45, pt. 1:8–10.

Doke, C. M., D. Malcolm, and J. M. A. Sikakana. 1958. *English-Zulu Dictionary*. Johannesburg: Witwatersrand University Press.

Don, Alexander M. 1963. "Transvestism and Transsexualism: A Report of 4 Cases and Problems Associated with Their Management." South African Medical Journal 37 (May 4): 479–85.

Donham, Donald L. 1990. *History, Power, Ideology: Central Issues in Marxism and Anthropology*. Cambridge: Cambridge University Press.

———. 1998. "Freeing South Africa: The 'Modernization' of Male-Male Sexuality in Soweto." *Cultural Anthropology* 13, 1:3–21.

Doukouré, Abdoul. 1978. *Le déboussolé: Roman*. Sherbrooke, Quebec: Naaman.

Dozon, Jean-Pierre, and Laurent Vidal. 1995. *Les Sciences sociales face au Sida: Cas africains autour de l'exemple ivoirien*. Paris: ORSTOM Éditions.

Driberg, Jack H. 1923. *The Lango: A Nilotic Tribe of Uganda.* London: T. Fisher Unwin.

Dubow, Saul. 1993. "Black Hamlet: A Case of 'Psychic Vivisection.'" *African Affairs* 92: 519–56.

———. 1995. *Scientific Racism in Modern South Africa.* Cambridge: Cambridge University Press.

Duiker, K. Sello. 2001. *The Quiet Violence of Dreams.* Cape Town: Kwela Books.

Dunton, Chris. 1989. "'Wheyting Be Dat?' The Treatment Of Homosexuality in African Literature." *Research In African Literatures* 20, 3:422–48.

———. 1990. "Mopeli-Paulus and *Blanket Boy's Moon.*" *Research in African Literatures* 21, 4:105–20.

———. 1999. "The Representation of Homosexuality in Ouologuem's *Le Devoir de violence.*" In C. Wise 1999, 47–53.

———. 2004. "Tatamkhula Afrika: The Testing of Masculinity." *Research in African Literatures* 35, 1:148–61.

———. 2007. "Face to Face." In GALZ 2008, 155–59.

Dynes, Wayne. 1983. "Homosexuality in Sub-Saharan Africa: An Unnecessary Controversy." *Gay Books Bulletin* 9:20–21.

Dyson, Tim, ed. 1992. *Sexual Behaviour and Networking: Anthropological and Socio-Cultural Studies on the Transmission of HIV.* Liège: DEROUAUX-ORDINA.

Eboussi Boulaga, Fabien, ed. 2007. *Dossier: L'homosexualité est Bonne à Penser* special issue of *Terroirs: Revue Africaine des Sciences Sociales et de Philosophie,* Nos. 1–2.

Echenberg, Myron. 2002. *Black Death, White Medicine: Bubonic Plague and the Politics of Public Health in Colonial Senegal, 1914–1945.* Portsmouth, NH: Heinemann.

Eke, Maureen Ngozi. 2007. "*Woubi Chéri:* Negotiating Subjectivity, Gender, and Power." In *Gender and Sexuality in African Literature and Film,* ed. Ada Uzoamaka Azodo and Maureen Ngozi Eke, 239–48. Trenton, NJ, and Asmara: Africa World Press.

El-Battahani, Atta. 1999. "AIDS and Politics in Sudan: Some Reflections." In Becker et al., 301–17.

Elbl, Ivana. 1996. "'Men without Wives': Sexual Arrangements in the Early Portuguese Expansion in West Africa." In *Desire and Discipline: Sex and Sexuality in Premodern West,* ed. Jacqueline Murray and Konrad Eisenbichler, 215–28. Toronto: University of Toronto Press.

Elder, Glen S. 2003. *Hostels, Sexuality, and the Apartheid Legacy: Malevolent Geographies.* Athens: Ohio University Press.

Ellis, A. B. 1890. *The Ewe-Speaking Peoples of the Slave Coast of West Africa.* London: Chapman and Hall.

Englund, Harri, and Francis B. Nyamnjoh, eds. 2004. *Rights and the Politics of Recognition in Africa.* London: Zed Books.

Epprecht, Marc. 2000. *"This Matter of Women Is Getting Very Bad": Gender, Development and Politics in Colonial Lesotho, 1870–1965.* Ed. Andrea Nattrass. Pietermaritzburg: University of Natal Press.

———. 2001. "'Unnatural Vice' in South Africa: The 1907 Commission of Enquiry." *International Journal of African Historical Studies* 34, 4:121–40.

———. 2002. "Male-Male Sexuality in Lesotho: Two Conversations." *Journal of Men's Studies* 10, 3 (special issue on African masculinities): 373–89

———. 2004. *Hungochani: The History of a Dissident Sexuality in Southern Africa.* Montreal: McGill-Queen's University Press.

———. 2007. "The Marquis de Sade's Zimbabwe Adventure: A Contribution to the Critique of African AIDS." *Sexualities* 10, 2:241–58.

Epstein, Helen. 2005. "God and the Fight against AIDS." *New York Review of Books* 52, 7 (April 28). http://www.nybooks.com/articles/17963.

Epstein, Steven. 1996. *Impure Science: AIDS, Activism, and the Politics of Knowledge.* Berkeley: University of California Press.

Equiano, Olaudah. 1987 [1969]. *The Interesting Narrative of the Life of Olaudah Equiano, or Gustavus Vasa, the African.* Ed. Paul Edwards. London: Dawsons.

Essex, Max, et al., eds. 2002. *AIDS in Africa.* 2d ed. New York: Kluwer Academic/ Plenum Publishers.

Estermann, Carlos. 1976. *The Ethnography of Southwestern Angola.* Ed. Gordon Gibson. New York: Africana.

Evans-Pritchard, E. E. 1970. "Sexual Inversion among the Azande." *American Anthropologist* 72:1428–34.

———. 1971. *The Azande: History and Political Institutions.* Oxford: Clarendon Press.

Evans-Pritchard, E. E., Raymond Firth, Bronislaw Malinowski, and Isaac Schapera, eds. 1934. *Essays Presented to C. G. Seligman.* London: Kegan Paul.

Falk, Kurt. 1998a [1923]. "Same-Sex Life among a Few Negro Tribes in Angola." Trans. Bradley Rose. In Murray and Roscoe, 167–70.

———. 1998b [1925–26]. "Homosexuality Among the Natives of Southwest Africa." Trans. Bradley Rose and Will Roscoe. In Murray and Roscoe, 187–96.

Fanon, Frantz. 1967 [1952]. *Black Skin, White Masks.* New York: Grove Press.

Faris, James. 1973. "Pax Britannica and the Sudan: S. F. Nadel." In *Anthropology and the Colonial Encounter*, ed. Talal Asad, 153–70. New York: Humanities Press.

Farmer, Paul. 2001. *Infections and Inequalities: The Modern Plagues.* Berkeley: University of California Press.

Fassin, Didier. 1999. "L'Anthropologie entre engagement et distanciation: Essai de sociologie des recherches en sciences sociales sur le Sida en Afrique." In Becker et al., 41–66.

———, ed. 2004. *Afflictions: L'afrique du sud, de l'apartheid au SIDA.* Paris: Karthala.

Faupel, J. F. 1962. *African Holocaust: The Story of the Uganda Martyrs.* New York: P. J. Kennedy.

Faure, William C. (dir.), and Joshua Sinclair (script). 1987. *Shaka Zulu.* VHS. Johannesburg: South African Broadcasting Corporation.

Fee, Elizabeth, and Daniel M. Fox, eds. 1988. *AIDS: The Burdens of History*. Berkeley: University of California Press.

Feierman, Steven, and John Janzen, eds. 1992. *The Social Basis of Health and Healing in Africa*. Berkeley: University of California Press.

Feldman, D. A., S. R. Friedman, and D. C. Des Jarlais. 1987. "Public Awareness of AIDS in Rwanda." *Social Science and Medicine* 24:97–100.

Ferguson, James. 1999. *Expectations of Modernity: The Meanings of Urban Life on the Zambian Copperbelt*. Berkeley: University of California Press.

Fischer, Arnold, et al. 1985. *English-Xhosa Dictionary*. Cape Town: Oxford.

Foucault, Michel. 1978. *The History of Sexuality*. Trans. Robert Hurley. New York: Random House.

Frankenberg, Ruth. 1993. *White Women, Race Matters: The Social Construction of Whiteness*. Minneapolis: University of Minnesota Press.

Frederiksen, Bodil Folke. 2008. "A 1930s Controversy over African and European Female Sexuality: Jomo Kenyatta, Marie Bonaparte, and Bronislaw Malinowski on Clitoridectomy." *History Workshop Journal* 65.

Freed, Louis F. 1941. "Homosexuality—As the Sexologist Sees It." *The Leech* 2, 2:12–16.

———. 1949. *The Problem of European Prostitution in Johannesburg: A Sociological Survey*. Cape Town: Juta.

———. 1954. "Medico-sociological Data in the Therapy of Homosexuality." *South African Medical Journal* 28, 48:1022–23.

———. 1968. "Homosexuality and the Bill." *South African Medical Journal* 42, 22:567.

———. n.d. "Light on the Sex Life of the Bantu People." Gay and Lesbian Archives of South Africa, AM 2909, undated newspaper article.

Freund, Bill. 1998. *The Making of Contemporary Africa: The Development of African Society Since 1800*. London: Macmillan.

Fuze, Magema M. 1979 [1922]. *The Black People and Whence They Came*. Trans. H. C. Lugg; ed. A. T. Cope. Pietermaritzburg: University of Natal Press.

Fynn, Henry Francis. 1950. *The Diary of Henry Francis Fynn*. Ed. James Stuart and D. Malcolm. Pietermaritzburg: Shuter and Shooter.

Galgut, Damon. 1982. *A Sinless Season*. Cape Town: Jonathan Ball.

———. 1991. *The Beautiful Screaming of Pigs*. London: Scribner.

GALZ. 1995. *Sahwira: Being Gay and Lesbian in Zimbabwe*. Harare: Gays and Lesbians of Zimbabwe.

———. 2005. *Understanding Human Sexuality and Gender*. Harare: Gays and Lesbians of Zimbabwe.

———, ed. 2008. *Unspoken Facts: A History of Homosexualities in Africa*. Harare: Gays and Lesbians of Zimbabwe.

Gaudio, Rudi. 1998. "Male Lesbians and Other Queer Notions in Hausa." In Murray and Roscoe 1998, 111–28.

Gay, Judith. 1985. "'Mummies and Babies' and Friends and Lovers in Lesotho." *Journal of Homosexuality* 11, 3–4:93–116.

Gear, Sasha. 2005. "Rules of Engagement: Structuring Sex and Damage in Men's Prisons and Beyond." *Culture, Health and Sexuality* 7, 3:195–208.

———. 2007. "Behind the Bars of Masculinity: Male Rape and Homophobia in and about South African Men's Prisons." *Sexualities* 10, 2:209–27.

Gear, Sasha, and Kindiza Ngubeni. 2002. *Daai Ding: Sex, Sexual Violence and Coercion in Men's Prisons.* Braamfontein: Centre for the Study of Violence and Reconciliation.

Gelfand, Michael. 1968. "The Shona Attitude to Sex." In *African Crucible: An Ethico-religious Study with Special Reference to the Shona-Speaking People.* Cape Town: Juta.

———. 1979. "The Infrequency of Homosexuality in Traditional Shona Society." *Central African Journal of Medicine* 25, 9:201–2.

———. 1985. "Apparent Absence of Homosexuality and Lesbianism in Traditional Zimbabweans." *Central African Journal of Medicine* 31, 7:137–38.

Gevisser, Mark. 1994. "A Different Fight for Freedom." In Gevisser and Cameron 1994, 14–86.

Gevisser, Mark, and Edwin Cameron, eds. 1994. *Defiant Desire: Gay and Lesbian Lives in South Africa.* Johannesburg: Ravan.

Gibbon, Edward. 1909 [1896, 1781]. *The History of the Decline and Fall of the Roman Empire,* vol. 4. Ed. J. B. Bury. London: Methuen.

Gisselquist, David, J. J. Potterat, Stuart Brody, and François Vachon. 2003. "Let It Be Sexual: How Health Care Transmission of AIDS in Africa Was Ignored." *International Journal of STD and AIDS* 14:148–61.

Gluckman, Max. 1960. "The Rise of the Zulu Empire." *Scientific American* 202 (April): 168.

———. 1974. "The Individual in a Social Framework: The Rise of King Shaka of Zululand." *Journal of African Studies* 1, 2:113–44.

Goddard, Keith. 2004. "A Fair Representation: The History of GALZ and the Gay Movement in Zimbabwe." *Journal of Gay and Lesbian Social Services* 16, 1:75–98.

Golan, Daphna. 1994. *Inventing Shaka: Using History in the Construction of Zulu Nationalism.* Boulder: Lynne Rienner.

Gordimer, Nadine. 1980. *Burger's Daughter.* Harmondsworth: Penguin.

———. 1987. *A Sport of Nature: A Novel.* London: Jonathan Cape.

Gordon, H. L. 1934. "The Mental Capacity of the African." *Journal of the Royal African Society* 33, 132:226–42.

Gorer, Geoffrey. 1962 [1935]. *African Dances: A Book about West African Negroes.* New York: Norton.

Gramsci, Antonio. 1971. *Selections from the Prison Notebooks.* Ed. and trans. Quintin Hoare and Geoffrey Nowell Smith. New York: International Publishers.

Gray, Robert W. 1999. "Black Mirrors and Young Boy Friends: Colonization, Sublimation, and Sadomasochism in Stephen Gray's *Time of Our Darkness.*" *ARIEL: A Review of International English Literature* 3012:77–98.

Gray, Stephen. 1988. *Time of Our Darkness*. London: Frederick Muller.

Greenslees, Thomas D. 1895. "Insanity among the Natives of South Africa." *Journal of Mental Science* 41:71–78.

Greenwood, B. M. 1984. "AIDS in Africa." *Immunology Today* 5, 10:293–94.

Grinker, Roy Richard. 2000. *In the Arms of Africa: The Life of Colin M. Turnbull*. New York: St. Martin's.

Grmek, M. D. 1990. *History of AIDS: Emergence and Origin of a Modern Pandemic*. Trans. Russell C. Maulitz and Jacalyn Duffin. Princeton: Princeton University Press.

Gueboguo, Charles. 2006a. "L'homosexualité en Afrique: Sens et variations d'hier à nos jours." *Socio-logos*. http://socio-logos.revues.org/document37.html.

———. 2006b. "Il était une fois . . . l'homosexualité contée aux journalistes camerounaises." Paper presented to the School of Journalism and Communication Sciences, Yaoundé. http://semgai.free.fr/doc_et_pdf/CG_il_etait_une_fois.pdf.

———. 2006c. *La question homosexuelle en Afrique: Le cas du Cameroun*. Paris: L'Harmattan.

Gurnah, Abdulrazak. 1994. *Paradise*. New York: New Press.

———. 1996. *Admiring Silence*. London: Hamish Hamilton.

Haberlandt, M. 1998 [1899]. "Occurrences of Contrary Sex among the Negro Population of Zanzibar." In Murray and Roscoe 1998, 63–66.

Hallpike, Christopher R. 1972. *The Konso of Ethiopia: A Study of the Values of a Cushitic People*. Oxford: Clarendon.

Hamilton, Carolyn, ed. 1995. *The Mfecane Aftermath: Reconstructive Debates in the History of Southern Africa*. Johannesburg: Witwatersrand University Press.

———. 1998. *Terrific Majesty: The Powers of Shaka Zulu and the Limits of Historical Invention*. Cambridge, MA: Harvard University Press.

Hannan, M., comp. 1984 [1959]. *Standard Shona Dictionary*. Harare: Literature Bureau.

Hanry, Pierre. 1970. *Érotisme africain: Le comportement sexuel des adolescents guinéens*. Paris: Payot.

Harries, Patrick. 1990. "La Symbolique du sexe: L'Identité culturelle au début d'exploitation des mines d'or du Witwatersrand." *Cahiers d'études africaines* 30, 120:451–74.

———. 1994. *Work, Culture, and Identity: Migrant Laborers in Mozambique and South Africa, c. 1860–1910*. Portsmouth, NH: Heinemann.

Harris, Karen L. 2004. "Private and Confidential: The Chinese Mine Labourers and 'Unnatural Crime.'" *South African Historical Journal* 50:115–33.

Hawkins, Sean. 2002. *Writing and Colonialism in Northern Ghana: The Encounter between the LoDagaa and "the World on Paper."* Toronto: University of Toronto Press.

Hawley, John C., ed. 2001. *Postcolonial, Queer: Theoretical Intersections*. Albany: SUNY Press.

Hay, Margaret Jean, ed. 2000. *African Novels in the Classroom*. Boulder: Lynne Rienner.

Hayes, Jarrod. 2000. *Queer Nations: Marginal Sexualities in the Maghreb*. Chicago: University of Chicago Press.

Hayes, M. M., P. J. Coghlan, H. King, and P. Close. 1984. "Kaposi's Sarcoma, Tuberculosis and Hodgkin's Lymphoma in a Lymph Mode—Possible Acquired Immunodeficiency Syndrome: A Case Report." *South African Medical Journal* 66, 6 (August 11): 226–29.

Head, Bessie. 1974. *A Question of Power*. London: Heinemann Educational.

Heald, Suzette. 1995. "The Power of Sex: Some Reflections on the Caldwells' 'African Sexuality' Thesis." *Africa* 65, 4:489–505.

Hennessy, Rosemary. 1995. "Incorporating Queer Theory on the Left." In *Marxism in the Postmodern Age: Confronting the New World Order*, ed. Antonio Callari, Stephen Cullenberg, and Carole Biewener, 266–75. New York: Guilford Press.

———. 2000. *Profit and Pleasure: Sexual Identities in Late Capitalism*. New York: Routledge.

———. 2005. "Returning to Reproduction Queerly: Sex, Labor, Need." *Rethinking Marxism* (special section on queer theory and Marxism) 18, 3:387–95.

Herdt, Gilbert. 1997. *Same Sex, Different Cultures: Exploring Gay and Lesbian Lives*. Boulder: Westview.

Herskovits, Melville J. 1932. "Some Aspects of Dahomean Ethnology." *Africa* 5, 3:266–96.

———. 1934. "Freudian Mechanisms in Primitive Negro Psychology." In Evans-Pritchard et al. 1934, 75–84.

———. 1967 [1938]. *Dahomey: An Ancient West African Kingdom*. Evanston: Northwestern University Press.

Herzfeld, Michael. 1997. *Cultural Intimacy: Social Poetics in the Nation-State*. New York: Routledge.

Herzog, Dagmar. 2005. *Sex after Fascism: Memory and Morality in Twentieth-Century Germany*. Princeton: Princeton University Press.

Heyns, Michiel. 1998. "A Man's World: White South African Gay Writing and the State of Emergency." In *Writing South Africa: Literature, Apartheid, and Democracy, 1970–1995*, ed. Derek Attridge and Rosemary Jolly, 108–22. New York: Cambridge University Press.

Hoad, Neville. 2004. "Homosexuality, Africa, Neoliberalism and the Anglican Church: The Lambeth Conference of Anglican Bishops, 1998." In *Producing African Futures: Ritual and Reproduction in a Neoliberal Age*, ed. Brad Weiss, 54–79. Leiden: Brill.

———. 2005. "Thabo Mbeki's AIDS Blues: The Intellectual, the Archive and the Pandemic." *Public Culture* 17, 1:101–27.

———. 2007. *African Intimacies: Race, Homosexuality, and Globalization*. Minneapolis: University of Minnesota Press.

Hoad, Neville, Karen Martin, and Graeme Reid, eds. 2005. *Sex and Politics in South Africa*. Cape Town: Double Storey.

Holmes, Rachel. 1994. "White Rapists Make Coloureds (and Homosexuals): The Winnie Mandela Trial and the Politics of Race and Sexuality." In Gevisser and Cameron 1994, 284–94.

Hooper, Edward. 1990. *Slim: A Reporter's Own Story of AIDS in East Africa*. London: Bodley Head.

———. 1999. *The River: A Journey to the Source of HIV and AIDS*. Boston: Little, Brown.

Hrdy, D. B. 1987. "Cultural Practices Contributing to the Transmission of Human Immunodeficiency Virus in Africa." *Review of Infectious Diseases* 9:1112–18.

Hulstaert, R. P. G. 1938. *Le mariage des Nkundó*. Brussells: L'Institute Royal Colonial Belge.

Hunt, Nancy R. 1999. "STD's, Suffering, and Their Derivatives in Congo-Zaire: Notes towards an Historical Ethnography of Disease." In Becker et al., 111–31.

Ibn Battuta. 1983 [1929]. *Ibn Battuta: Travels in Asia and Africa, 1325–1354*. Trans. and selected H. A. Gibb. London: Routledge.

ICAD (Interagency Coalition on AIDS and Development). n.d. "HIV/AIDS and Homophobia." www.icad-cisd.com/content/pub_details.cfm?ID=113&CAT=9&lang=e.

Igwe, Leo. 2006. "On the Proposed Bill to Ban Same Sex Marriages in Nigeria." *Sexuality in Africa Magazine* 3, 1:13–15.

Ijsselmuiden, C. B., et al. 1988a. "AIDS and South Africa: Part I—Towards a Comprehensive Strategy" *South African Medical Journal* 73 (16 April): 455–60.

———. 1988b. "AIDS and South Africa: Part III—the Role of Education." South African Medical Journal 73 (16 April): 465–67.

Iliffe, John. 2006. *The African AIDS Epidemic: A History*. Athens: Ohio University Press; London: James Currey; Cape Town: Double Storey.

Imasuen, Lancelot, dir. 2003. *Emotional Crack*. Emem Isong and Bob Emeka Eze (story). Emem Isong (screenplay). Lagos: RJP Productions.

Inhorn, Marcia C. 2005. "Sexuality, Masculinity, and Infertility in Egypt: Potent Troubles in Marital and Medical Encounters." In Ouzgane and Morrell 2005, 289–303.

Irwin, Alexander C., Joyce Millen, and Dorothy Fallows. 2003. *Global AIDS: Myths and Facts: Tools for Fighting the AIDS Pandemic*. Boston: South End Press.

Isaacs, Gordon, and D. Miller. 1985. "AIDS—Its Implications for South African Homosexuals and the Mediating Role of the Medical Practitioner." *South African Medical Journal* 68, 5 (August 31): 327–30.

Isaacs, Gordon, and Brian McKendrick. 1992. *Male Homosexuality in South Africa: Identity Formation, Culture and Crisis*. Cape Town: Oxford University Press.

Jackson, Frederick. 1930. *Early Days in East Africa*. London: Edward Arnold.
Jackson, Lynette. 1997. "Narratives of 'Madness' and Power: A History of Ingutsheni Mental Hospital and Social Order in Colonial Zimbabwe, 1908–1959." PhD diss., Columbia University.
———. 2002. "'When in the White Man's Town': Zimbabwean Women Remember Chibeura." In Allman, Geiger, and Musisi 2002, 191–215.
Jacob, Wilson Chacko. 2005. "The Masculine Subject of Colonialism: The Egyptian Loss of the Sudan." In Ouzgane and Morrell, 153–69.
Jacobs, Max. 1969. "The Treatment of Homosexuality." *South African Medical Journal* 43, pt. 2:1123–26.
Janzen, John. 1982. *Lemba, 1650–1930: A Drum of Affliction in Africa and the New World*. New York: Garland.
Jeater, Diana. 1993. *Marriage, Perversion, and Power: The Construction of Moral Discourse in Southern Rhodesia, 1894–1930*. Oxford: Clarendon.
———. 2007. *Law, Language, and Science: The Invention of the "Native Mind" in Southern Rhodesia, 1890–1930*. Portsmouth, NH: Heinmann.
Jeay, Anne-Marie. 1991. "Homosexualité et SIDA au Mali, variations sur l'étrange et l'étranger." In *Homosexualités et SIDA: Actes du colloque international*, ed. Michaël Pollak, Rommel Mendès-Leite, and Jacques Van Dem Borghe, 60–68. Lille: Cahiers Gai-Kitsch-Camp.
Jeeves, Alan. 2001. "Histories of Reproductive Health and the Control of Sexually Transmitted Disease in Southern Africa: A Century of Controversy. Introduction." *South African Historical Journal* 45:169–91.
Jefremovas, Villia. 2002. *Brickyards to Graveyards: From Production to Genocide in Rwanda*. Albany: SUNY Press.
Jewkes, Rachel, K. Dunkle, M. Nduna, et al. 2006. "Factors Associated with HIV Seropositivity in Young, Rural South African Men." *International Journal of Epidemiology* 35:1455–60.
Jochelson. Karen. 1999. "Sexually Transmitted Diseases in Nineteenth- and Twentieth-Century South Africa." In Setel, Lewis, and Lyons 1999, 217–43.
Johnson, Cary Alan. 2007. *Off the Map: How HIV/AIDS Programming is Failing Same-Sex Practicing People in Africa*. New York: International Gay and Lesbian Human Rights Commission.
Johnston, Harry H. 1897. *British Central Africa*. London: Methuen.
———. 1904. *The Uganda Protectorate*. 2 vols. London: Hutchinson.
Joint Working Group. 2006. *An Anthology of Lesbian Writing from South Africa*. Johannesburg: Triangle Project/Umzantsi Publishers.
Jolly, Rosemary. 1996. "'Intersecting Marginalities': The Problem of Homophobia in South African Women's Writing." In *Cross-Addressing: Resistance Literature and Cultural Borders*, ed. John C. Hawley, 107–20. Albany: SUNY Press.
Jolly, Susie. 2000. "'Queering' Development: Exploring the Links between Same-Sex Sexualities, Gender and Development." *Gender and Development* 8, 1:78–88.

Joubert, P. J., and K. J. Nkuzana. 1975. *Afrikaans-Engels-Tsonga*. Johannesburg: Suid-Afrikaanse Uitsaaikorporasie.

Joubert, P. J., and M. S. A. Khubheka. *Afrikaans-Engels-Zoeloe*, vol. 2. 1975. Johannesburg: Suid-Afrikaanse Uitsaaikorporasie.

Jung, Carl F. 1963. *Memories, Dreams, Reflections*. Ed. Aniela Jaffé. London: Collins and Routledge and Kegan Paul.

Junod, Henri Alexandre. 1911. *Zidji: Étude de moeurs sud-africaines*. St. Blaise: Foyer Solidariste.

———. 1962 [1916]. "Unnatural Vice in the Johannesburg Compounds." In *The Life of a South African Tribe*. 2 vols. New Hyde Park, NY: University Books.

Junod, Henri-Philippe. 1935. *The VaThonga*. Vol. 4 (sec. 1–2) of Alfred Duggan-Cronin, *The Bantu Tribes of South Africa: Reproductions of Photographic Studies*. 4 vols. Cambridge: Cambridge University Press.

Kagwa, B. H. 1965. "Observations on the Prevalence and Types of Mental Diseases in East Africa." *East African Medical Journal* 42:673–82.

Kaler, Amy. 2007. "Gender-as-Knowledge and AIDS in Africa: Shifting Concepts, Malawian Stories, Historic Contexts, and a Cautionary Tale." Paper presented to the Conference on Infectious Diseases in Poor Countries and the Social Sciences, Ithaca, NY.

Kalipeni, Ezekiel, Susan Craddock, Joseph R. Oppong, and Jayati Ghosh, eds. 2004. *HIV and AIDS in Africa: Beyond Epidemiology*. Oxford: Blackwell.

Kamradt, T., D. Niese, and F. Vogel. 1985. "Slim Disease (AIDS)." *Lancet* 326, 8469–70:1425.

Kaplan, Flora Edouwaye S., ed. 1997. *Queens, Queen Mothers, Priestesses, and Power: Case Studies in African Gender*. New York: New York Academy of Sciences.

Karsch-Haack, Ferdinand. 1911. *Das gleichgeschlechtliche Leben de Naturalvolker*. Munich: Ernst Reinhardt.

Kashamura, Anicet. 1973. *Famille, sexualité et culture: Essai sur les moeurs sexuelles et les cultures des peoples des Grands Lacs africains*. Paris: Payot.

Ken Bugul. 1984. *Le Baobab fou*. Dakar: Nouvelles Éditions Africains.

———. 1991. *The Abandoned Baobab*. Trans. Marjolijn de Jager. Chicago: Lawrence Hill Books.

Kendall. 1998. "'When a Woman Loves a Woman' in Lesotho: Love, Sex, and the (Western) Construction of Homophobia." In Murray and Roscoe, 223–41.

Kente, Gilbert. 1992 [1963]. *Too Late*. In *South African People's Plays: Ons phola hi*, ed. Robert Mshengu Kavanagh. Johannesburg: Heinemann Southern Africa.

Kenyatta, Jomo. 1961 [1938]. *Facing Mount Kenya: The Tribal Life of the Gikuyu*. London: Mercury Books.

Kets de Vries, Manfred F. R. 2004. *Lessons on Leadership by Terror: Finding Shaka Zulu in the Attic*. Cheltenham: Edward Elgar.

Khouthu, N. 1939. "La vie des travailleurs noirs." *Journal des missions évangéliques* 1:353.

Kidd, Dudley. 1904. *The Essential Kafir*. London: A. and C. Black.

———. 1908. *Kafir Socialism and the Dawn of Individualism: An Introduction to the Study of the Native Problem*. London: Black.

King, J. L. 2004. *On the Down Low: A Journey into the Lives of "Straight" Black Men Who Sleep with Men*. New York: Broadway Books.

Kirby, Percival R. 1942. "A Secret Musical Instrument: The *Ekola* of the Ovakuanyama of Ovamboland." *South African Journal of Science* 28:345–51.

Ki-Zerbo, Joseph. 2005. "African Intellectuals, Nationalism and Pan-Africanism." In Mkandawire 2005, 78–93.

Knobel, G. J. 1988. "An Urgent Warning—Contraction of HIV Infection during Mutual Masturbation." Letter. *South African Medical Journal* 73 (May 29): 617.

Kocheloff, Paul. 2006. "Le SIDA au Burundi et en Afrique du Sud: le vecu au quotidian." In Denis and Becker, 193–213.

Kolawole, Mary Modupe. 1997. *Womanism and African Consciousness*. Trenton, NJ: Africa World Press.

Koopman, Adrian. 1997. "Scratching Out One's Days: Graffiti in the Old Pietermaritzburg Prison," *Natalia* 27:69–91.

Krige, Eileen Jensen. 1956 [1937]. "Individual Development." In Schapera 1956, 95–118.

———. 1974. "Woman-Marriage, with Special Reference to the Lovedu." *Africa* 44:11–36.

Krouse, Matthew, ed. 1993. *The Invisible Ghetto: Lesbian and Gay Writing from South Africa*. Assisted by Kim Berman. Johannesburg: COSAW.

Kuria, David. 2005. *Understanding Homosexual People in Kenya*. Nairobi: gaykenya.

Labat, Jean-Baptiste. 1998 [1732]. "*Ganga-Ya-Chibanda*." Trans. W. Roscoe. In Murray and Roscoe, 163–64.

Lambo, T. Adeoye. 1955. "The Role of Cultural Factors in Paranoid Psychosis among the Yoruba Tribe." *Journal of Mental Science* 101:239–66.

Landes, Ruth. 1940. "A Cult Matriarchate and Male Homosexuality." *Journal of Abnormal and Social Psychology* 35:386–97.

Lanham, Peter, and A. S. Mopeli-Paulus. 1953. *Blanket Boy's Moon*. London: Collins.

Laubscher, B. J. F. 1937. *Sex, Custom, and Psychopathology: A Study of South African Pagan Natives*. London: George Routledge.

Leap, William L., and Tom Boellstorff, eds. 2004. *Speaking in Queer Tongues: Globalization and Gay Language*. Urbana: University of Illinois Press.

Leighton, Alexander H., T. Adeoye Lambo, Charles C. Hughes, Dorothea C. Leighton, Jane M. Murphy, and David B. Macklin. 1963. *Psychiatric Disorder among the Yoruba*. Ithaca, NY: Cornell University Press.

Lewis, Ethelreda. 1984 [1933]. *Wild Deer*. Cape Town: David Philip.

Lewis, Jack, and Thulane Phungula, dirs. 1998. *Sando to Samantha: A.k.a. The Art of Dikvel*. Cape Town: Idol Productions.

Lewis, Stephen. 2005. *Race against Time*. Toronto: House of Anansi Press.

Liddicoat, Renée. 1962. "Homosexuality." *South African Journal of Science* 58, 5:145–49.

Lindsay, Lisa A., and Stephan F. Miescher, eds. 2003. *Men and Masculinities in Modern Africa.* Portsmouth, NH: Heinemann.

Livie-Noble, F. S., and F. O Stohr. 1926. "Psychoanalysis: A Consideration of Its Value, and a Review of Some Common Misconceptions." *South African Journal of Science* 23:996–1005.

Livingstone, David and Charles. 1865. *Narrative of the Expedition to the Zambezi.* London: John Murray.

Lockhart, Chris 2002. "*Kunyenga*, 'Real Sex,' and Survival: Assessing the Risk of HIV Infection among Urban Street Boys in Tanzania." *Medical Anthropology Quarterly* 16, 3:294–311.

Long, Scott, A. Widney Brown, and Gail Cooper. 2003. *More Than a Name: State-Sponsored Homophobia and Its Consequences in Southern Africa.* New York: Human Rights Watch; San Francisco: International Gay and Lesbian Human Rights Commission.

Lwabaayi, R. Bangkok. 2004. "Sexual Minorities, Violence and AIDS in Africa." *HIV/AIDS Policy Law Review* 9, 3:103–5.

Lyons, Andrew P., and Harriet D. Lyons. 2004. *Irregular Connections: A History of Anthropology and Sexuality.* Lincoln: University of Nebraska Press.

Lyons, S. F., B. D. Schoub, G. M. McGillivary, and R. Scher. 1985. "Seroepidemiology of HTLV-III Antibody in southern Africa." *South African Medical Journal* 67:961–62.

MacDermot, Brian Hugh. 1972. *Cult of the Sacred Spear: The Story of the Nuer Tribe in Ethiopia.* London: Hale.

Machera, Mumbi. 2004. "Opening a Can of Worms: A Debate of Female Sexuality in the Lecture Theatre." In Arnfred 2004b, 157–72.

Maddy, Yulisa Amadu. 1973. *No Past, No Present, No Future.* London: Heinemann.

Madu, Sylvester Ntomchukwu, Peter Kakubeire Baguma, and Alfred Pritz, eds. 1996. *Psychotherapy in Africa: First Investigations.* Vienna: World Council for Psychotherapy.

Malinwa, D. N. 1969. "Everything under the Sun." In *Africa in Prose*, ed. O. R. Dathorne and Willfried Feuser. Harmondsworth: Heinemann.

Mama, Amina. 2005. "Gender Studies for Africa's Transformation." In Mkandawire 2005, 94–116.

Mann, Jonathan M. 1995. *The Impact of Homophobia and Other Social Biases on AIDS.* San Francisco: Public Media Center.

Mann, Kristen. 1985. *Marrying Well: Marriage, Status, and Social Change among the Educated Elite in Colonial Lagos.* Cambridge: Cambridge University Press.

Mannoni, Octave. 1984 [1950]. *Prospero et Caliban: Psychologie de la colonisation.* Paris: Éditions Universitaires.

Maquet, Jacques. 1961. *The Premise of Inequality in Ruanda.* London: Oxford University Press.

Marechera, Dambudzo. 1980. *Black Sunlight*. London: Heinemann.

———. 1984. *Mindblast, or, the Definitive Buddy*. Harare: College Press.

Martin, Maurice. 1913. *Au coeur de l'Afrique équatoriale*. Paris: Librairie Chapelot.

Matasha, E., T. Ntembelea, P. Mayaud, and W. Saidi. 1998. "Sexual and Reproductive Health among Primary and Secondary School Pupils in Mwanza, Tanzania: Need for Intervention." *AIDS Care* 10, 5:571–82.

Mathabane, Mark. 1986. *Kaffir Boy: The True Story of a Black Man's Coming of Age in Apartheid South Africa*. New York: Macmillan.

Matory, J. Lorand. 2004. "Gendered Agendas: The Secrets Scholars Keep about Yorùbá-Atlantic Religion." In *Dialogues of Dispersal: Gender, Sexuality and African Diasporas*, ed. Sandra Gunning, Tera W. Hunter, and Michele Mitchell, 13–43. Oxford: Blackwell.

———. 2005. *Black Atlantic Religion: Tradition, Transnationalism, and Matriarchy in the Afro-Brazilian Condomblé*. Princeton: Princeton University Press.

Mazrui, Ali. 1975. "The Resurrection of the Warrior Tradition in African Political Culture." *Journal of Modern African Studies* 13, 1:67–84.

Mbembe, Achille. 2001. *On the Postcolony*. Berkeley: University of California Press.

Mburu, John. 2000. "Awakenings: Dreams and Delusions of an Incipient Lesbian and Gay Movement in Kenya." In *Different Rainbows*, ed. Peter Drucker, 179–91. London: Gay Men's Press.

McCulloch, Jock. 1995. *Colonial Psychiatry and the African Mind*. Cambridge: Cambridge University Press.

———. 2000. *Black Peril, White Virtue: Sexual Crime in Southern Rhodesia, 1902–1935*. Bloomington: Indiana University Press.

McFadden, Patricia. 1992. "Sex, Sexuality, and the Problem of AIDS in Africa." In *Gender In Southern Africa*, ed. Ruth Meena, 157–95. Harare: SAPES Books.

McKenna, Neil. 1999. *The Silent Epidemic: Men Who Have Sex with Men in the Developing World*. London: PANOS.

McLean, Hugh, and Linda Ngcobo. 1994. "*Abangibhamayo bathi ngimnandi* (Those Who Fuck Me Say I'm Tasty): Gay Sexuality in Reef Township." In Gevisser and Cameron 1994, 158–85.

Mda, Zakes. 1990 [1980]. "The Hill." In *The Plays of Zakes Mda*, ed. Andrew Horn. Johannesburg: Ravan.

Meek, C. K. 1934. "Ibo Law." In Evans-Pritchard et al. 1934, 209–26.

Melo, Guilherme de. 1981. *A sombra dos dias*. Amadora: Livraria Bertrand.

Merriam, Alan. 1971. "Aspects of Sexual Behaviour among the Bala (Basongye)." In *Human Sexual Behavior: Variations in the Ethnographic Spectrum*, ed. Donald S. Marshall and Robert C. Suggs, 71–102. New York: Basic Books.

Mersham, Gary. 1989. "Political Discourse and Historical Television Drama: A Case Study of *Shaka Zulu*." PhD thesis, University of South Africa.

Migraine-George, Thérèse. 2003. "Beyond the 'Internalist' vs. 'Externalist' Debate: The Local-Global Identities of African Homosexuals in Two Films, *Woubi chéri* and *Dakan*." *Journal of African Cultural Studies* 16, 1:45–56.

Miller, Christopher. 1985. *Blank Darkness: Africanist Discourse in French*, Chicago: University of Chicago Press.

Mirde, M. 1975. "History of Mental Health Services in South Africa, Part I: Natal." *South African Medical Journal* 49:322–26.

Mkandawire, Thandika, ed. 2005. *African Intellectuals: Rethinking Politics, Language, Gender and Development*. Dakar: CODESRIA; London: Zed Books.

Mofolo, Thomas. 1981 [1931]. *Chaka*. London: Heinemann.

Molema, S. M. 1920. *The Bantu, Past and Present: An Ethnographical and Historical Study of the Native Races of South Africa*. Edinburgh: W. Green.

Moodie, T. Dunbar. 1988. "Migrancy and Male Sexuality on the South African Gold Mines." With Vivienne Ndatshe and British Sibuyi. *Journal of Southern African Studies* 14, 2:229–45.

———. 1994. *Going for Gold: Men, Mines, and Migration*. With Vivienne Ndatshe. Berkeley: University of California Press.

Moore, Henrietta, and Megan Vaughan. 1994. *Cutting Down Trees: Gender, Nutrition, and Agricultural Change in the Northern Province of Zambia, 1890–1990*. Portsmouth, NH: Heinemann.

Morgan, Ruth, and Saskia Wieringa, eds. 2005. *Tommy Boys, Lesbian Men, and Ancestral Wives: Female Same-Sex Practices in Africa*. Johannesburg: Jacana.

Morrell, Robert. 1998. "Of Boys and Men: Masculinity and Gender in Southern African Studies." *Journal of Southern African Studies* 24, 4:605–30.

———, ed. 2001. *Changing Men in Southern Africa*. Pietermaritzburg: University of Natal Press, and London: Zed Press.

Morris, Donald R. 1965. *The Washing of Spears: A History of the Rise of the Zulu Nation under Shaka and Its Fall in the Zulu War of 1879*. New York: Simon and Schuster.

Msiska, Mpalive-Hangson, and Paul Hyland, eds. 1997. *Writing and Africa*. London: Longman.

Mudimbe-Boyi, Elisabeth, ed. 2002a. *Beyond Dichotomies: Histories, Identities, Cultures, and the Challenge of Globalization*. Albany: SUNY Press.

———, ed. 2002b. *Remembering Africa*. Portsmouth NH: Heinemann.

Mullings, Leith. 1984. *Therapy, Ideology, and Social Change: Mental Healing in Urban Ghana*. Berkeley: University of California Press.

Mungoshi, Charles. 1996. "A Marriage of Convenience." *Horizon* (August): 37–40.

———. 1997. "Of Lovers and Wives." In *Walking Still*. Harare: Baobab Books.

Murray, Stephen O. 1995. *Latin American Male Homosexualities*. Albuquerque: University of New Mexico Press.

———. 1997. "Five Reasons I Don't Take 'Queer Theory' Seriously." *Independent Gay Forum*. http://www.indegayforum.org/authors/murray/murray4.html.

———. 1998. "'A Feeling within Me': Kamau, a Twenty-Five-Year-Old Kikuyu." In Murray and Roscoe 1998, 41–62.

———. 2000. *Homosexualities*. Chicago: University of Chicago Press.

Murray, Stephen O., and Will Roscoe. 1997. *Islamic Homosexualities: Culture, History, and Literature*. New York: New York University Press.

———, eds. 1998. *Boy-Wives and Female Husbands: Studies in African Homosexualities*. New York: St. Martin's.

Mutongi, Kenda. 2000. "Dear Dolly's Advice: Representations of Youth, Courtship, and Sexualities in Africa, 1960–1980." *International Journal of African Historical Studies* 33, 1:1–23.

Nadel, S. F. 1942. *A Black Byzantium: The Kingdom of Nupe in Nigeria*. London: Oxford University Press.

———. 1947. *The Nuba: An Anthropological Study of the Hill Tribes in Kordofan*. London: Oxford University Press.

Naipaul, V. S. 1973. *In a Free State*. Harmondsworth: Penguin.

Najmabadi, Afsaneh. 2005. *Women with Mustaches and Men without Beards: Gender and Sexual Anxieties of Iranian Modernity*. Berkeley: University of California Press.

Natal. 1951. *Annual Report of the Medical Officer of Health*. Pietermaritzburg: Local Heath Commission.

Nattrass, Nicoli. 2007. *Mortal Combat: AIDS Denialism and the Struggle for Antiretrovirals in South Africa*. Scottsville: University of KwaZulu-Natal Press.

Ndatshe, Vivienne. 1993. "Love on the Mines." In Krouse 1993, 45–51.

Newell, Stephanie. 2006. *The Forger's Tale: The Search for Odeziaku*. Athens: Ohio University Press.

Nfah-Abbenyi, Juliana. 1997a. "Calixthe Beyala's 'Femme fillette': Womanhood and the Politics of (M)Othering." In Nnaemeka 1997, 101–13.

———. 1997b. *Gender in African Women's Writing: Identity, Sexuality, and Difference*. Bloomington: Indiana University Press.

Ngubane, Harriet. 1977. *Body and Mind in Zulu Medicine*. London: Academic Press.

Niang, Cheikh Ibrahim, Moustapha Diagne, Youssoupha Niang, Amadou Mody Moreau, et al. 2002. *Meeting the Sexual Health Needs of Men Who Have Sex with Men in Senegal*. Washington, DC: USAID.

Niang, Cheikh Ibrahim, et al. 2003. "'It's Raining Stones': Stigma, Violence, and HIV Vulnerability among Men Who Have Sex with Men in Dakar, Senegal." *Culture, Health, and Sexuality* 5, 6:499–512.

Niehaus, Isak. 2002. "Renegotiating Masculinity in the South African Lowveld: Narratives of Male-Male Sex in Labour Compounds and in Prisons." *AIDS in Context*, special issue of *African Studies*, 61, 1:77–97.

Njau, Rebeka. 1978. *Ripples in the Pool*. London: Heinemann.

Njinge, Mpumi, and Paolo Alberton. 2002. *Everything Must Come to Light*. VHS. Johannesburg: Out of Africa Films.

Nkoli, Simon. 1994. "Wardrobes: Coming Out as a Black Gay Activist in South Africa." In Gevisser and Cameron 1994, 249–57.

Nkosi, Lewis. 1994. *The Black Psychiatrist: A One-Act Play. Weber Studies*, 11, 2 (Spring/Summer). http://weberstudies.weber.edu/archive/archive%20B%20Vol.%2011–16.1/Vol.%2011.2/11.2Nkoski.htm.

———. 2006. *Mandela's Ego*. Cape Town: Umuzi.

Nnaemeka, Obioma, ed. 1997. *The Politics of (M)Othering: Womanhood, Identity and Resistance in African Literature*. London: Routledge.

———. 2005. *Female Circumcisions and the Politics of Knowledge*. Westport, CT: Praeger.

Nolen, Stephanie. 2007. *28: Stories of AIDS in Africa*. Toronto: Alfred Knopf.

Nsamenang, A. Bame. 1995. "Factors Influencing the Development of Psychology in Sub-Saharan Africa." *International Journal of Psychology* 30:729–38.

Nussbaum, Felicity A. 2001. "Being a Man: Olaudah Equiano and Ignatius Sancho." In Carretta and Gould 2001, 54–73.

Nzekwu, Onuora. 1972. *Blade among the Boys*. London: Heinemann Educational.

Nzula, Alfred, I. I. Potekhin, and A. Z. Zusmanovich. 1979 [1933]. *Forced Labour in Colonial Africa*. Ed. Robin Cohen. Trans. Hugh Jenkins. London: Zed Press.

Obbo, Christine. 1980. *African Women: Their Struggle for Economic Independence*. London: Zed Books.

———. 1999. "Social Science Research: Understanding and Action." In Becker et al., 67–78.

O'Farrell, N. O. 1987. "South African AIDS." Letter. *South African Medical Journal* 72 (September 19): 436.

Offenstadt, G., D. Pinta, et al. 1983. "Multiple Opportunistic Infections Due to AIDS in a Previously Healthy Black Woman from Zaire." *New England Journal of Medicine* 308:775.

Oloruntoba-Oju, Taiwo. 2008. "A Lesbian Affair on Nigerian Video (A Film Review)." In GALZ 2008, 205–8.

Omotoso, Kole. 1971. *The Edifice*. London: Heinemann.

Oppong, J. R., and Ezekiel Kalipeni. 1996. "A Cross-Cultural Perspective on AIDS in Africa: A Response to Rushing." *African Rural and Urban Studies* 3, 2:91–112.

———. 2004. "Perceptions and Misconceptions of AIDS in Africa." In *HIV/AIDS in Africa: Beyond Epidemiology*, ed. E. Kalipeni, S. Craddock, J. R. Oppong, and J. Ghosh, 47–57. Oxford: Blackwell, 2004.

Orubuloye, I. O., John C. Caldwell, Pat Caldwell and Shail Jain, eds. 1995. *The Third World AIDS Epidemic: Health Transition Review Supplement*, 5, 2.

Orubuloye, I. O., O. P. Omoniyi, and W. A. Shonkunbi. 1995. "Sexual Networking, STD's and HIV/AIDS in Four Urban Gaols in Nigeria." In Orubuloye et al. 1995, 123–29.

Ouologuem, Yambo. 1971. *Bound to Violence*. Trans. Ralph Manheim. London: Heinemann.

Ouzgane, Lahoucine, and Robert Morrell, eds. 2005. *African Masculinities: Men in Africa from the Late Nineteenth Century to the Present*. London: Palgrave.

Owusu, Maxwell. 1978. "Ethnography of Africa: The Usefulness of the Useless." *American Anthropologist* 80, 2:310–34.

Oyéwùmí, Oyèrónké. 1997. *The Invention of Women: Making an African Sense of Western Gender Discourses.* Minneapolis: University of Minnesota Press.

Oyono, Ferdinand. 1966. *Houseboy.* London: Heinemann.

Packard, Randall M., and Paul Epstein. 1991. "Epidemiologists, Social Scientists, and the Structure of Medical Research on AIDS in Africa." *Social Science and Medicine* 33, 7:771–94.

Padian, Nancy, and J. Pickering. 1986. "Female-to-Male Transmission of AIDS: A Re-examination of the African Sex Ratio of Cases." *Journal of the American Medical Association* 256:590.

Panos Institute. 2005. "Homosexuality and the Trend of HIV in Kenya." http://www.mask.org.za/SECTIONS/AfricaPerCountry/ABC/kenya/Kenya_34.htm.

Pape, J. W., et al. 1986. "Risk Factors Associated with AIDS in Haiti." *American Journal of Medical Sciences* 291, 1:4–7.

Pape, Marc, and Claudine Vidal. 1984. "Libéralisme et vécus sexuels à Abidjan." *Cahiers internationaux de sociologie* 76:111–18.

Parin, Paul, Fritz Morgenthaler, and Goldy Parin-Matthèy. 1980. *Fear Thy Neighbor as Thyself: Psychoanalysis and Society among the Anyi of West Africa.* Trans. Patricia Klamerth. Chicago: University of Chicago Press.

Parker, Andrew, Mary Russo, Doris Summer, and Patricia Yaeger, eds. 1993. *Nationalisms and Sexualities.* New York: Routledge.

Parker, Richard, and Peter Aggleton, eds. 1999. *Culture, Society, and Sexuality: A Reader.* London: University College of London Press.

Parle, Julie. 2007. *States of Mind: Searching for Mental Health in Natal and Zululand, 1868–1918.* Scottsville: University of KwaZulu-Natal Press.

Patton, Cindy. 1999. "Inventing African AIDS." In Parker and Aggleton 1999, 387–404.

Pegge, John V. 1994. "Living with Loss in the Best Way We Know How: AIDS and Gay Men in Cape Town." In Gevisser and Cameron 1994, 301–10.

Phillips, Oliver. 1997. "Zimbabwean Law and the Production of a White Man's Disease." *Legal Perversions, Social and Legal Studies* 6, 4:471–92.

———. 2004. "The Invisible Presence of Homosexuality: Implications for HIV/AIDS and Rights in Southern Africa." In Kalipeni et al. 2004.

Phillips, Richard. 2006. *Sex, Politics, and Empire: A Postcolonial Geography.* Manchester: Manchester University Press.

Pincheon, Bill Stanford. 2000. "An Ethnography of Silences: Race (Homo)sexualities, and a Discourse of Africa." *African Studies Review* 43, 3:39–58.

Piot, P., T. C. Quinn, H. Taelman, et al. 1984. "Acquired Immunodeficiency Syndrome in a Heterosexual Population in Zaire." *Lancet* 324, 8394:65–69.

Poland, Marguerite. 1993. *Shades.* London and New York: Viking.

Posel, Deborah. 2005. "'Baby Rape': Unmaking Secrets of Sexual Violence in Post-apartheid South Africa." In *Men Behaving Differently: South African Men since 1994*, ed. Graeme Reid and Liz Walker, 21–64. Cape Town: Double Storey.

Potgeiter, Cheryl. 2005. "sexualities? hey this is what Black, South African Lesbians have to say about relationships with men, the family, heterosexual women and culture." In van Zyl and Steyn 2005, 177–92.

——. 2006. "The Imagined Future for Gays and Lesbians in South Africa: Is This It?" *Agenda* 67 (Special Issue on Homosexuality): 4–8.

Price, David H. 2004. *Threatening Anthropology: McCarthyism and the FBI's Surveillance of Activist Anthropologists*. Durham, NC: Duke University Press.

Prieur, Annick. 1998. *Mema's House, Mexico City: On Transvestites, Queens, and Machos*. Chicago: University of Chicago Press.

Pronyk, Paul M., James R Hargreaves, Julia C Kim, Linda A Morison, Godfrey Phetla, et al. 2006. "Effect of a Structural Intervention for the Prevention of Intimate-Partner Violence and HIV in Rural South Africa: A Cluster Randomised Trial." *Lancet* 368, 9551:1973–83.

Purchas, Samuel. 1905 [1613]. *Purchas, His Pilgrimes, vol. IV*. Glasgow: James MacLehose.

Putzel, James. 2004. "The Politics of Action: A Case Study from Uganda." *Public Administration and Development* 24:19–30.

Quinn, T. C., J. M. Mann, J. W. Curran, and P. Piot. 1986. "AIDS in Africa: An Epidemiologic Paradigm." *Science* 234:955–63.

Rachewiltz, Boris de. 1964. *Black Eros: Sexual Customs of Africa from Prehistory to the Present Day*. London: George Allen and Unwin.

Ramaka, Joseph Gaï, dir. 2001. VHS. *Karmen Gei*. Dakar: Les Ateliers de l'Arche.

Ranjani, Rakesh, and Mustafa Kudrati. 1996. "The Varieties of Sexual Experience of the Street Children of Mwanza, Tanzania." In *Learning about Sexuality: A Practical Beginning*, ed. Sondra Zeidenstein and Kirsten Moore, 301–23. New York: Population Council/International Women's Health Council.

Ras, G. J., I. W. Simson, R. Anderson, et al. 1983. "Acquired Immunodeficiency Syndrome: A Report of Two South African Cases." *South African Medical Journal* 64:140–42.

Red Cross Society. n.d. *Sex Hygiene and Venereal Disease*. Pretoria: South African Department of Public Health. Transvaal Archive Depot (Pretoria) GES 2268 60/38L.

Reddy, Vasu. 2001. "Institutionalizing Sexuality: Theorizing Queer in Post-apartheid South Africa." In *The Greatest Taboo: Homosexuality in Black Communities*, ed. Delroy Constantine-Simms, 163–84. Los Angeles: Alyson Press.

Reid, Graeme. 2002. "'The History of the Past is the Trust of the Future': Preservation and Excavation in the Gay and Lesbian Archives of South Africa." In *Refiguring the Archive*, ed. Carolyn Hamilton, Verne Harris, Jane Taylor, Michele Pickover, Graeme Reid, and Razia Saleh, 193–207. Cape Town: David Philip.

——. 2006. "How to Become a 'Real Gay': Identity and Terminology in Ermelo, Mpumulanga." *Agenda* 67, 2–3:137–45.

Reid, Graeme, and Theresa Dirsuweit. 2001. "Understanding Systemic Violence: Homophobic Attacks in Johannesburg and Its Surrounds." *Urban Forum* 13, 3:99–124.

Retief, Glen. 1994. "Keeping Sodom Out of the Laager." In Gevisser and Cameron 1994, 99–111.

Richardson, Peter. 1982. *Chinese Mine Labour in the Transvaal.* London: Macmillan.

Ritchie, John F. 1943. *The African as Suckling and as Adult: A Psychological Study.* Livingstone, Northern Rhodesia: Rhodes-Livingstone Institute.

———. 1944. "The African as Grown-up Nursling." *Rhodes-Livingstone Institute Journal* 1:57–63.

Ritter, E. A. 1955. *Shaka Zulu: The Rise of the Zulu Empire.* London: Longmans, Green.

Roazen, Paul. 1971. *Freud and His Followers.* New York: Meridian.

Robins, Steven. 2004. "Long Live Zackie, Long Live: AIDS Activism, Science, and Citizenship after Apartheid." *Journal of Southern African Studies* 30, 3:651–72.

Rödlach, Alexander. 2006. *Witches, Westerners, and HIV: AIDS and Cultures of Blame in Africa.* Walnut Creek, CA: Left Coast Press.

Rushing, William A. 1995. *The AIDS Epidemic: Social Dimensions of an Infectious Disease.* Boulder: Westview.

Rushton, J. Phillippe. 1997. *Race, Evolution and Behavior: A Life History Perspective.* New Brunswick, NJ: Transaction.

Sabatier, Renée. 1988. *Blaming Others: Prejudice, Race, and Worldwide AIDS.* London: Panos.

Sachs, Wulf. 1937. *Black Hamlet: The Mind of an African Negro Revealed by Psychoanalysis.* London: Geoffrey Bles.

———. 1947. *Black Anger.* Boston: Little, Brown.

Sade, Marquis de. 1990 [1795]. "Histoire de Sainville et de Léonore" (chapter 35 of *Aline et Valcour*). In *Sade: Oeuvres,* ed. Michel Delon, 1:550–608. Paris: Éditions Gallimard.

Sadowsky, Jonathan. 1997. "Psychiatry and Colonial Ideology in Nigeria." *Bulletin of the History of Medicine* 71, 1:94–111.

Said, Edward. 1978. *Orientalism.* New York: Pantheon.

Salamone, Frank. 2005. "Hausa Concepts of Masculinity and the 'Yan Daudu." In Ouzgane and Morrell 2005, 74–86.

Salo, Elaine, and Pumla Dineo Gqola. 2006. "Subaltern Sexualities." Editorial. *Feminist Africa 6: Subaltern Sexualities* (September): 1–7.

Sassine, Williams. 1976. *Wirriyamu.* Trans. John Reed and Clive Wake. London: Heinemann.

SAT. 2004. *Guidelines for Counselling Men Who Have Sex with Men.* Harare: Southern African AIDS Trust.

Schapera, Isaac. 1934. *Western Civilization and the Natives of South Africa.* London: George Routledge.

———, ed. 1956 [1937]. *The Bantu-Speaking Tribes of South Africa: An Ethnographical Survey.* London: Routledge and Kegan Paul.

———. 1963 [1930]. *The Khoisan Peoples of South Africa: Bushmen and Hottentots.* London: Routledge and Kegan Paul.

Schenkel, R. 1971. "Le vécu de la vie sexuelle chez les Africains acculturés du Sénégal." *Psychopathologie africaine* 7:313–58.

Schiller, Greta. 1998. *The Man Who Drove with Mandela.* VHS. London: Jezebel Productions.

Schumaker, Lyn. 2001. *Africanizing Anthropology: Fieldwork, Networks, and the Making of Cultural Knowledge in Central Africa.* Durham: Duke University Press.

Scully, William. 1912. *Daniel Vananda: The Life Story of a Human Being.* Cape Town: Juta.

———. 1923. *The Ridge of the White Waters.* Cape Town: Juta.

Sedgwick, Eve Kosofsky. 1990. *The Epistemology of the Closet.* Berkeley: University of California Press.

Segal, I., and L. O. Tim. 1979. "The Witchdoctor and the Bowel." *South African Medical Journal* 56, 8:308–10.

Seligman, Charles. 1924. "Anthropology and Psychology: A Study of Some Points of Contact." *Journal of the Royal Anthropological Institute of Great Britain and Ireland* 54:13–46.

Seligman, Charles, and Brenda Seligman. 1932. *Pagan Tribes of the Nilotic Sudan.* London: Routledge and Kegan Paul.

Sellers, William. 1941. "The Production of Films for Primitive People." *Oversea Education: A Journal of Educational Experiment and Research in Tropical and Subtropical Areas* (October): 221–26.

Senior, Kathryn. 2006. "AIDS Epidemic Still Not under Control." *Lancet Infectious Diseases* 6, (January 1): 10.

Serwadda, D., N. Sewankambo, J. Carswell, et al. 1985. "Slim Disease: A New Disease in Uganda and Its Association with HTLV-III Infection." *Lancet* 326, 8460:849–52.

Setel, Philip W. 1999. *A Plague of Paradoxes: AIDS, Culture, and Demography in Northern Tanzania.* Chicago: University of Chicago Press.

Setel, Philip W., Milton Lewis, and Maryinez Lyons, eds. 1999. *Histories of Sexually Transmitted Diseases and HIV/AIDS in Sub-Saharan Africa.* Westport, CT: Greenwood.

Sewankwambo, N. K., J. W. Carswell, R. D. Mugerwa, et al. 1987. "HIV Infection through Normal Heterosexual Contact in Uganda." *AIDS* 1, 2:113–16.

Shaw, Drew. 2004. "Transgression and Beyond: Dambudzo Marechera and Zimbabwean Literature." PhD diss., School of English and Drama, Queen Mary University of London.

———. 2005. "Queer Inclinations and Representations: Dambudzo Marechera and Zimbabwean Literature." In Veit-Wild and Naguschewski 2005, 89–112.

Shepherd, Gill. 1987. "Rank, Gender, and Homosexuality: Mombasa as a Key to Understanding Sexual Options." In *The Cultural Construction of Sexuality,* ed. Pat Caplan, 240–70. London: Tavistock.

Shilts, Randy. 1987. *And the Band Played On: Politics, People, and the AIDS Epidemic*. New York: St. Martin's.

Shuttleworth, Russell P. 2007. "Disability and Sexuality: Toward a Constructionist Focus on Access and the Inclusion of Disabled People in the Sexual Rights Movement." In Teunis and Herdt 2007, 174–207.

Sibuyi, Mpande wa. 1993. "*Tinconcana etimayinini*: The Wives of the Mine." In Krouse 1993, 52–64.

Sigal, Pete, ed. 2003. *Infamous Desire: Male Homosexuality in Colonial Latin America*. Chicago: University of Chicago Press.

Simooya, Oscar O., Nawa E. Sanjobo, Lovemore Kaetano, et al. 2001. "'Behind Walls': A Study of HIV Risk Behaviours and Seroprevalence in Prisons in Zambia." *AIDS* 15, 13:1741–44.

Singlton-Gates, Peter, and Maurice Girodias. 1959. *The Black Diaries: An Account of Roger Casement's Life and Times with a Collection of his Diaries and Public Writings*. Paris: Olympia Press.

Sivadon, P. 1958. "Problèmes de santé mentale en Afrique noire." *World Mental Health* 10:106–20.

Smartt, Cyril G. F. 1956. "Mental Maladjustment in the East African." *Journal of Mental Science* 102:441–66.

Sonnet, J., and H. Taelman. 1986. "Clinical and Biological Profile of African AIDS: A Study of Forty-two Patients." In *Clinical Aspects of AIDS and AIDS-Related Complex*, ed. M. Staquet, R. Hemmer, and A. Baert, 78–89. Oxford: Oxford University Press.

South Africa. 1913. *Director of Prisons Report for 1912*. Pretoria.

———. 1987. "AIDS: The 1979 Epidemic with Special Reference to South Africa." *Epidemiological Comments* 14, 4:1–63.

Sow, A. Ibrahim. 1980. *Anthropological Structures of Madness in Black Africa*. New York: International Universities Press.

Soyinka, Wole. 1973. *Season of Anomy*. London: Rex Collings.

———. 1976 [1965]. *The Interpreters*. London: Heinemann.

———. 1999. "Remarks on Yambo Ouologeum's *Le devoir de violence*." In *Yambo Ouologuem: Postcolonial Writer, Islamic Militant*, ed. Christopher Wise, 17–22. Boulder: Lynne Rienner.

Sprackle, F. H. N., R. G. Whittaker, W. B. Becker, et al. 1985. "The Acquired Immune Deficiency Syndrome and Related Complex." *South African Medical Journal* 68, 3:139–43.

Sprengnether, Madelon. 1990. *The Spectral Mother: Freud, Feminism, and Psychoanalysis*. Ithaca, NY: Cornell University Press.

Spurlin, William J. 2006. *Imperialism within the Margins: Queer Representation and the Politics of Culture in Southern Africa*. New York: Palgrave Macmillan.

Stillwaggon, Eileen. 2003. "Racial Metaphors: Interpreting Sex and AIDS in Africa." *Development and Change* 34, 5:809–32.

Stobie, Cheryl. 2007. *Somewhere in the Double Rainbow: Representations of Bisexuality in Post-apartheid Novels*. Scottsville: University of KwaZulu-Natal Press.

Stoler, Ann. 2002. *Carnal Knowledge and Imperial Power: Race and the Intimate in Colonial Rule*. Berkeley: University of California Press.

Stratton, Florence. 1994. *Contemporary African Literature and the Politics of Gender*. London: Routledge.

Stychin, Carl Franklin. 1998. *A Nation by Rights: National Cultures, Sexual Identity Politics, and the Discourse of Rights*. Philadelphia: Temple University Press.

Summers, Carol. 1991. "Intimate Colonialism: The Imperial Production of Reproduction in Uganda, 1907–1925." *Signs* 16, 4:787–807.

Swarr, Amanda Lock. 2004. "Moffies, Artists, and Queens: Race and the Production of South African Gay Male Drag." *Journal of Homosexuality* 46, 3–4:73–89.

———. Forthcoming. "'I Just Wonder What They Are Doing in the Bed': Secrecy, Sexuality, and Stabane in Soweto." *Feminist Studies*.

Swarr, Amanda Lock, and Richa Nagar. 2004. "Dismantling Assumptions: Interrogating 'Lesbian' Struggles for Identity and Survival in India and South Africa." *SIGNS: Journal of Women in Culture and Society* 29, 2:491–516.

Sweet, James. 1996. "Male Homosexuality and Spiritism in the African Diaspora: The Legacies of a Link." *Journal of the History of Sexuality* 7, 2:184–202.

———. 2003. *Recreating Africa: Culture, Kinship and Religion in the Afro-Portuguese World*. Chapel Hill: University of North Carolina Press.

Swift, Charles, and Tolani Asuni. 1975. *Mental Health and Disease in Africa*. Edinburgh: Churchill Livingston.

Symington, P. B. 1972. "Sexual Behaviour of Rhodesian Africans." *Journal of Biosocial Science* 4:263–75.

Taiwo, Oladele. 1984. *Female Novelists of Modern Africa*. London: Macmillan.

Tamale, Sylvia. 2003. "Out of the Closet: Unveiling Sexuality Discourses in Uganda." *Feminist Africa* 2 (October–November): 42–49.

Tanner, Ralph E. S. 1969. "The East African Experience of Imprisonment." In *African Penal Systems*, ed. Alan Milner, 293–315. New York: Praeger.

Tatchell, Peter. 2005. "The Moment the ANC Embraced Gay Rights." In Hoad, Martin, and Reid 2005, 140–47.

Tauxier, Louis. 1912. *Les noirs du Soudan: Pays Mossi et Gourounni*. Paris: Émile LaRose.

Tcheuyap, Alexie. 2005. "African Cinema and Representations of (Homo)Sexuality." In Veit-Wild and Naguschewski 2005, 143–54.

Terry, Jennifer. 1999. *An American Obsession: Science, Medicine, and Homosexuality in Modern Society*. Chicago: University of Chicago Press.

Tessmann, Günther. 1998 [1921]. "Homosexuality among the Negroes of Cameroon and a Pangwe Tale." Trans. B. Rose. In Murray and Roscoe 1998,159–61.

Teunis, Niels. 1996. "Homosexuality in Dakar: Is the Bed the Heart of a Sexual Subculture?" *Journal of Gay, Lesbian, and Bisexual Identity* 1, 2:153–69.

———. 2001. "Same-Sex Sexuality in Africa: A Case Study from Senegal." *AIDS and Behavior* 5, 2:173–82.

Teunis, Niels, and Gilbert Herdt, ed. 2007. *Sexual Inequalities and Social Justice.* Berkeley: University of California Press.

Theal, G. M. 1896. *The Portuguese in South Africa: With a Description of the Native Races between the River Zambezi and the Cape of Good Hope during the Sixteenth Century.* London: T. F. Unwin.

Thornton, John. "Legitimacy and Political Power: Queen Nzinga, 1624–1663." *Journal of African History* 32:25–40.

Tilley, Brian (dir.). 2001. *It's My Life.* Cape Town: Steps for the Future, New York: First Run/Icarus Films.

Tooth, Geoffrey. 1950. *Studies in Mental Illness in the Gold Coast.* London: HMSO.

Treichler, Paula A. 1988. "AIDS, Gender, and Biomedical Discourse." In Fee and Fox 1988, 190–267.

Turnbull, Colin M. 1972. *The Mountain People.* New York: Touchstone.

United Kingdom (Home Office). 2004. *World Prison Population List.* www.homeoffice.gove.uk, accessed February 6, 2006.

Vance, Carole S. 1991. "Anthropology Rediscovers Sexuality: A Theoretical Comment." *Social Science and Medicine* 33, 8:875–84.

Van den Berg, Adrian. 1993. "Wild Trade." In Krouse 1993, 9–16.

Van de Perre, P., N. Clumeck, R. Gallo, et al. 1985. "Female Prostitutes: A Risk Group for Infection with Human T-Cell Lymphotropic Virus Type III." *Lancet* 326, 8454:524–26.

Van de Perre, P., D. Rouvroy, P. Lepage, et al. 1984. "Acquired Immune Deficiency in Rwanda." *Lancet* 324, 8394:62–65.

van der Burgt, J. M. M. 1903. *Un grand peuple de l'Afrique équatoriale.* Bois-le-Duc, Netherlands : Société L'Illustration Catholique.

Vangroenweghe, Daniel. 2000. *SIDA et sexualité en Afrique.* Trans. Jean-Marie Flémal. Brussels: Editions EPO.

Vanita, Ruth, ed. 2002. *Queering India: Same-Sex Love and Eroticism in Indian Culture and Society.* New York: Routledge.

Van Onselen, Charles. 1976. *Chibaro: African Mine Labour in Southern Rhodesia, 1900–1933.* London: Pluto Press.

———. 1982. *Studies in the Social and Economic History of the Witwatersrand, 1886–1914.* Burnt Hill, UK: Longman.

———. 1984. *The Small Matter of a Horse: The Life of "Nongoloza" Mathebula, 1867–1948.* Johannesburg: Ravan.

Van Zyl, Mikki. 1993. "Pathway to the Moon." In Krouse 1993, 31–34.

Van Zyl, Mikki, and Melissa Steyn, eds. 2005. *Performing Queer, Shaping Sexuality—Ten Years of Democracy in South Africa.* Cape Town: Kwela Books.

Vaughan, Megan. 1991. *Curing Their Ills: Colonial Power and African Illness.* Cambridge: Polity Press.

Veit-Wild, Flora, and Dirk Naguschewski, eds. 2005. *Versions and Subversions in African Literatures I: Body, Sexuality and Gender*, ed. 129–41. Amsterdam: Rodopi.

Vignal, Daniel. 1983. "L'homophilie dans le roman négro-africain d'expression anglaise et française." *Peuples noirs, peuples africains* 33:63–81.

Ward, Kevin. 2002. "Same-Sex Relations in Africa and the Debate on Homosexuality in East African Anglicanism." *Anglican Theological Review* 83, 1 (Winter): 81–112.

Webb, C. de B., and J. B. Wright, eds. and trans. 1975–2001. *The James Stuart Archives.* 5 vols. Pietermaritzburg: University of Natal Press.

Webb, Douglas. 1997. *HIV and AIDS in Africa.* London: Pluto Press.

Weeks, Rev. John H. 1909. "Anthropological Notes on the Bangala of the Upper Congo River (part 2)." *Journal of the Royal Anthropological Society* 39:416–59.

Weinstock, Carolyn B. 1996. "An Exploration of Meanings Ascribed to Homophobic Statements in the Printed Media by Gays and Lesbians in Harare." Photocopy, GALZ centre, Harare.

West, Michael. 2002. *The Rise of an African Middle Class: Colonial Zimbabwe, 1898-1965.* Bloomington: Indiana University Press.

Westley, David. 1993. *Mental Health and Psychiatry in Africa: An Annotated Bibliography.* London: Hans Zell.

Weston, Kath. 1998. *Long Slow Burn: Sexuality and Social Science.* New York: Routledge.

White, Luise. 1990. *The Comforts of Home: Prostitution in Colonial Nairobi.* Chicago: University of Chicago Press.

Whithead, Ann. 2001. "Continuities and Discontinuities in Political Constructions of the Working Man in Rural Sub-Saharan Africa: The 'Lazy Man' in African Agriculture." In *Men at Work: Labour, Masculinities, Development*, ed. Cecile Jackson, 23–52. London: Frank Cass.

Wieringa, Saskia. 2001. "Tradition, Sexual Diversity and AIDS in Post-colonial Southern Africa." Unpublished paper., The Hague: Institute of Social Studies.

———. 2002. "Gender, Tradition, Sexual Diversity and AIDS in Postcolonial Southern Africa: Some Suggestions for Research." In *Challenges for Anthropology in the "African Renaissance": A Southern African Contribution*, ed. Debie LeBeau and Robert J. Gordon, 124–37. Windhoek: University of Namibia Press.

Wilson, Monica. 1951. *Good Company: A Study of Nyakyusa Age-Villages.* Oxford: Oxford University Press.

Wilkinson. Jane. 1992. "Tsitsi Dangarembga." In *Talking with African Writers: Interviews with African Poets, Playwrights and Novelists*, ed. Wilkinson, 189–98. London: James Currey.

Williams, A. Olufemi. 1992. *AIDS: An African Perspective.* Boca Raton: CRC Press.

Wober, Mallory. 1975. *Psychology in Africa.* London: International Africa Institute.

Wylie, Dan. 2000. *Savage Delight: White Myths of Shaka.* Pietermaritzburg: University of Natal Press.

———. 2006. *Myth of Iron: Shaka in History.* Pietermaritzburg: University of KwaZulu-Natal Press.

X, Dr. Jacobus. 1937. *Untrodden Fields of Anthropology.* Ed. Charles Carrington. New York: Falstaff.

Yamba, C. Bawa. 1997. "Cosmologies in Turmoil: Witchfinding and AIDS in Chiawa, Zambia." *Africa* 67, 2:200–223.

Yavoucko, Cyriaque. 1979. *Crépuscule et défi.* Paris: L'Harmattan.

Young, Robert. 1995. *Colonial Desire: Hybridity in Theory, Culture, and Race.* London: Routledge.

Zachernuk, Philip S. 2000. *Colonial Subjects: An African Intelligentsia and Atlantic Ideas.* Charlottesville: University Press of Virginia.

Zeleza, Paul Tiyambe. 1993. *A Modern Economic History of Africa.* Dakar: CODESRIA.

———. 2005. "The Academic Diaspora and Knowledge Production in and on Africa: What Role for CODESRIA?" In Mkandawire 2005, 209–34.

———. 2006–7. *The Study of Africa,* 2 vols. Dakar: CODESRIA; Ann Arbor: University of Michigan Press.

Zinanga, Evelyn. 1996. "Sexuality and the Heterosexual Form: The Case of Zimbabwe." *Southern African Feminist Review* 2, 1:3–6.

Zwelonke, D. M. 1973. *Robben Island.* London: Heinemann.

Index

apartheid, 2, 54–55, 84–86, 96–98, 106, 124–25, 137–39, 143–45, 160, 164
Appiah, K. A., 166, 176n32, 178n13
Arabian Nights, 43
Arabs and Arabic, 40–44, 56, 137–40, 142, 147, 160, 177n12
Arac de Nyeko, M., 12, 157, 174n13
Armah, Ayi Kwei, 137–38, 185n5
Arnfred, S., 13, 19, 177n5
Asante, 166
Ashe, R., 43
Ashforth, A., 11, 21, 181n18, 183n2
ashtime, 61–62
Asuni, T., 82–83, 90, 181n5, 181n7
Attah, A., 174n13
Attipoe, D., 128–29, 177n12
aversion therapy, 84–85, 182n7
Azande, 47, 56–57, 61
Azodo, U., and M. Eke, 175n17
Azuah, Unoma N., 8

Bâ, M., 138, 178n19
Bambara, 116
Banana, Canaan, 20
Bantu, Past and Present, The (Molema), 52
Barnard, I., 174n14
Basongye, 57
Basotho. *See* Lesotho
"Bat d'Af," 48, 178n18
Battell, A., 37
Baum, R., 176n3
Bayer, R., 116, 180n4, 183n9
Beach, D., 36, 185n3
Beautiful Screaming of Pigs, The (Galgut), 146
Becker, C., 10, 19–20, 183n9
Bederman, G., 177n8
Behind the Mask, 7, 13, 15, 22, 26, 175n18, 175n25, 176n31, 186n12
Behr, Mark, 146, 182n15
Beidelman, T., 51
Beinart, W., 183,5
Belgium and Belgians, 50, 55, 114, 119, 122. *See also* Congo; Rwanda
Bell, L., 49
Bemba, 80
berdache, 57
Berger, J., 126
Berglund, A., 58
bestiality, 16, 41, 47, 50, 58, 59, 108
Beti, M., 136
Beyala, Calixthe, 148, 152, 154–55, 157–58,

165, 186n11
Bibeau, G., 19, 35, 173n2
Biesheuvel, Simon, 81
Biggar, R., 109
biphobia, 53
bisexuality, 2, 18–21, 35, 43, 47, 51, 60–62, 68, 89, 101, 108 *passim*, 130, 132, 147, 150–51, 158, 162. *See also* msm; wsw
Black Hamlet (Sachs), 75–76, 81
Blacking, John, 57
Black Peril, 18, 49. 76–77, 80–81, 104, 160
Black Skin, White Masks (Fanon), 87
Black Sunlight (Marechera), 144
Blade among the Boys (Nzekwu), 142
Blair, D., 92, 185n2
Blanket Boy's Moon (Lanham/Mopeli-Paulus), 134–35
Bleys, Rudi C., 7, 44, 61, 177n4, 8
Bloch, J., and K. Martin, 179n27
Blyden, E. W., 52
Bocahut, L. *See* Brooks, P.
Boehmer, E., 145, 159
Boellstorff, T., 8, 174n15
Boers. *See* Afrikaners and Afrikaans
Boesak, A., 167
Bokoum, S., 136–37
Bokwe, R. T., 178n20
Bonaparte, M., 66, 74–75, 78, 88, 180n3
Botswana and Tswana language, 11, 45, 52, 67, 149, 167, 174n12, 186n2. *See also* Falk, K.; Schapera, I.
Botha, M., 110, 112
Bound to Violence (Ouologuem), 140
Boykin, K., 21
Bozongwana, W., 61
Brantlinger, P., 185n1
Brazil, 25, 54, 59–60, 177n11
Britain and British, 50. *See* names of individual British colonies; Ireland; Scotland
Brooks, P., 62, 126, 149, 157, 165
Browne, W., 40
Bryant, A. T., 74, 94–97
Bryk, Felix, 46, 50
bukhontxana, 54–55. *See also* ngochani
Burke, T., 178n20
Burns, J., 91
Burton, Sir Richard, 37, 42–44, 46, 52, 55, 73, 136, 161, 163, 164, 178n13, 178n20
Burundi, 116, 122–23, 173n1, 184n15
Bushmen. *See* Khoi and Khoisan
Butler, J., 12

Cage, K., 8
Caldwell, J., 1, 3, 11, 18, 110, 161
Calvinism, 146
Camara, M., 149, 157
Cameron, E., 7, 12, 165, 183n2, 186n2
Cameroun, 38, 44–45, 116, 148, 171. *See
also* Beti, M.; Beyala, C.; Eboussi
Boulaga, F.; Guebogou, C.; Oyono, F.
Canada and Canadians, 175n21, 176n35.
See also North America
candomblé, 25, 54
Cape Town, 86, 125, 142, 152
Caraël, M., 110, 183n9
Caribbean, 117. *See also* African Ameri-
can; Haiti; Martinique
Carothers, J. C., 82, 181n12
Carretta, V., and P. Gould, 133, 185n1
Carswell, W., 113, 122, 184n13
Carter, J., 163, 174n10, 177n8
Carton, B., 184n10
Casement, R., 177n11
Castilhon, J. L., 37
Catholics and Roman Catholic
Church, 116, 123, 142, 177n11
Cele, H., 97–98
celibacy, 37, 76–77, 142, 158. *See also*
abstinence
censorship, 10, 68, 94, 97. *See also* self-
censorship
Central African Republic, 136
Chanaiwa, D., 92
chastity, 37
Chavafambira, J., 75–76, 81
Chevrier, O., 47, 166
chibado, chibanda, 37, 57, 177n6
chibeura, 103
childhood socialization, 79–82. *See also*
initiation, sexual; circumcision,
male; female genital cutting
Chimurenga (magazine), 14
China and Chinese, 43, 49
Chirimuuta, R. C. and Rosalind, 122,
173n2, 184n16
Christianity: African converts, 51–55,
132–34, 142, 178n20; missionaries, 30,
41–41, 34, 49–51, 71, 93–94, 96, 101–2,
144. *See also* Anglican Church;
Calvinism; Catholics and Roman
Catholic Church; homophobia:
Christian
circumcision, female. *See* female genital cutting

circumcision, male, 77. *See also* initia-
tion
clitoridectomy. *See* female genital cutting
Clumeck, N., 108, 122, 184n11
Cobham, R., 24
Cohen, J., and T. Tate, 32
Cold War, 53, 131, 179n21
Colman, R., 150, 165
colonial gynaecology, 10
colonialism, 10, 19–20, 29–31, 34, 40–43,
46, 48–53, 57–60, 65–66, 71–76, 83,
86–87, 90, 101–7, 119, 121, 131, 133–37,
160, 176n1, 177n8, 180n1. *See also in-
dividual colonies or countries*
Comintern, 102
Comaroff, J., 182n1
Conakry. *See* Guinea
Congo, 37, 106, 177n11. *See also* Zaire
Conseil Scientifique de l'Afrique, 81–82,
85
conspiracy theories, 28, 184n16. *See also*
AIDS denialism
Cooper, F., 24
Coplan, D., 55–56, 134, 166
Coquery-Vidrovitch, C., 176n1
Cornwall, A., 176n1, 183n3
Corre, A., 178n19
Côte d'Ivoire, 60, 64, 89, 149–50, 157
Couzens, T., 91
Cover, R., 174n14
Craddock, S., 20
Crichlow, W., 152, 175n15
cross-dressing. *See* transvestism
Crowder, M., 178n9
Crush, J., 3
"cultural intimacy," 25–26, 60, 87, 130,
132
cunnilingus, 6. *See also* oral sex
Cureau, A., 43, 44, 72–73, 104, 164,
178n16, 181n8
Curran, A., 110, 118

Dahomey, 43, 47, 54, 178n13
Dakan (film), 149
Dakar, 64, 128, 186n13. *See also* Senegal
Damara, 10
Dangarembga, Tsitsi, 144–45, 165
Dar es Salaam, 140. *See also* Tanzania
Dark and Lovely, Soft and Free (Alber-
ton and Reid), 150
Dathorne, O.R., 133

Malawi and Malawians, 21, 26, 42, 50, 59, 73, 92, 112, 167
male bias. *See* androcentrism
Mali, 36, 88, 92, 116, 137
Malinowski, B., 52–53, 78
Malinwa, D. N., 140, 165
Mama, A., 176n33
Mandela, N., 123, 139
Mandela, W., 124
Mandela's Ego, 139
Mann, J., 110, 118, 174n12
Mann, K., 178n20
Mannoni, O., 181n11
Mapantsula, 63
Maquet, J., 55, 120, 184n15
Marechera, D., 144, 157
marriage: as a cover for homosexual desire, 148, 155, 158; heterosexual, 7, 9–10, 37–38, 41, 46, 49, 61, 89, 94, 142, 149, 155; female-female (woman-woman), 6, 47, 58–59, 62–63; male-male, 48–50, 58, 104, 106, 140, 143, 183n6, 185n4. *See also* polygyny
Martin, M., 47
Martinique, 86–87
Marxism, 12, 87, 171. *See also* Cold War; Gramsci, A.; Hennessy, R.; Nzula, A.; Reich, W.; Van Onselen, C.
masturbation, 18, 42, 55, 58, 63, 72, 77, 88–89, 104–5, 107, 115–16, 128, 136–37. *See also* dildos
matanyola, 23, 167
Matasha, E., 127
Mathabane, M., 4–5, 112, 120
Mathari Mental Hospital, 82
Matory, J. L., 25, 59–60, 177n6, 7, 179n21
Mazrui, A., 92, 96–97, 132, 182n20
Mbaye, M., 147
Mbeki, T., 2, 145, 173n2
Mbembe, A., 13
Mburu, J., 53, 62
Mbuti, 58
McCulloch, J., 18, 49, 180nn2–3, 181n11
McFadden, P., 175n19
McKenna, N., 174n12
McLean, H., 63
Mda, Z., 142–43
medicine, 38, 177n7. *See also* orisa; traditional healers
Meek, I., 48
Melo, G. de, 182n15, 186n19

mental illness, 69–71. *See also* psychological theories; traditional healers
Merriam, A., 57
Mersham, G., 182n21
methodology, 15–33, 59–63, 73–75, 77, 87–88, 90, 112–20, 130, 163–64
mfecane, 67, 97. *See also* Shaka
Miescher, S., 13
migrant labor. *See* mines and migrant labor
military, 48, 84, 150, 178n18
Miller, C., 185n1
Mindblast (Marechera),144
mines and migrant labor, 4–5, 9, 34, 43, 44, 48–51, 58–59, 72, 102–4, 112, 123, 133–35, 143, 150, 162, 167, 178n18, 183n6
Mirde, M., 181n9
misogyny and sexism, 12, 54, 93, 128, 150, 153, 168, 170, 182nn1–2. *See also* gender-based violence; rape
Mkandawire, T., 24–25
moffies, 139
Mofolo, T., 94, 133
Moi, Daniel arap, 123
Molema, S. M., 52, 161
Moodie, T. D., 7, 49, 165, 178n18, 183nn5–6
Moore, H., 176n1
Mopeli-Paulus, A. S., 134–35, 157, 165
Morgan, R., 7, 10, 14, 62, 174n7, 176n2
Morgenthanler, F., 88–89
Morocco, 139
Morrell, R., 13, 176n32, 176n1 (ch. 2)
Morris, D., 92, 96
Mossi, 47, 81
Mozambique and Mozambicans, 49–50, 136, 182n15, 185–86n10
Msiska, M., 185n1
msm: definition, 17–18, 36; as an identity, 23, 64. *See also* HIV/AIDS; mines and migrant labor; prisons
Mudimbe-Boyi, E., 24
Mugabe, R., 5, 148
Mullings, L., 180n3
mummy-baby relationship. *See* Gay, J.; Kendall, K. L.
Mungoshi, C., 148, 157
Murray, S. O., 7, 35–36, 45, 53, 165, 174n11, 175n17, 176n2, 178n12
Museveni, Yoweri and Janet, 124
Muslims. *See* Islam

Tanner, R., 56, 120
Tanzania, 14, 51, 63, 74, 92, 107, 116–17, 127–28, 140, 147, 170
Tatchell, P., 22, 145, 175n24
Tauxier, L., 44, 47
Tcheuyap, A., 185n1
television, 10, 97–98
Tembu, 77
terminology, 6–8, 23–24, 38, 54–55, 63–64, 115–16, 163–64, 174n9, 175n29. *See also* dictionaries; translation
Terry, J., 180n4
Tessman, G., 38, 44–45, 47, 164
Teunis, N., 126, 174n9, 176n32
Theal, G. M., 177n4
theater, 27, 137, 142–43, 150
thigh sex, 37, 42, 94, 104, 178n20
Thonga. *See* Shangaans
Thornton, J., 177n6
tikoloshi, 77
Tilley, B., 150
Time of Our Darkness (Gray), 146
Tirailleurs Sénégalaise (Lawler), 178n18
Tooth, G., 74, 81
Towles, J., 58, 179n25
traditional healers, 37–38, 46, 60, 62, 70–71, 75–76, 89, 142, 157, 165
transference, 79, 94–95
transgender, 149–50, 177n6, 180n2
translation, 36, 41–42, 51, 54–55, 60–61, 113–14, 163, 177n10, 186n11
transvestism, 41, 45, 48, 51, 61, 76, 84, 87
Treatment Action Campaign. *See* TAC
Treichler, P., 183n1
tsarance. See thigh sex
Tsonga. *See* Mozambique and Mozambicans; Shangaans
Turks, 40, 43, 73
Turnbull, C., 58, 179n25, 181n8
Tutsi, 55
Tutu, D., 167
Two Thousand Seasons (Armah), 137–38

Uganda, 4, 12, 14, 16, 31–32, 41, 42–43, 55, 58, 63, 82, 97, 107, 109, 111, 113, 117–20, 122–24 147, 149, 157, 171, 173n1, 174n13, 179n25, 180n3, 181n8, 182n2, 182n9, 184n13, 186n10
ukumetsha. See thigh sex
UNAIDS, 18, 173n6
UNICEF, 174n12
United Democratic Front, 123–24

United States and Americans, 4, 5, 16, 32, 53, 97–98, 111, 120, 137–38, 163, 174n10, 180n4, 183n9. *See also* African Americans; North America
urbanization, 9, 45, 48–52, 65–66, 72–73, 85, 100–103, 106, 133, 160, 162, 181n8
USAID, 32, 175n21
Uzoata, U. M., 158

Vance, C., 179n2
Van de Perre, P., 109, 113–14, 118–20
Van den Berg, A., 145
Van der Burgt, J.M.M., 184n15
Vangroenweghe, D., 61, 166, 173n1, 177n6, 179n28, 184n15
Van Onselen, C., 49, 58–59, 62, 120, 183n15
Van Zyl, M., 24, 145
VaThonga. *See* Shangaans
Vaughan, M., 105, 176n1, 180n3, 182n11
Venda, 57
videos. *See* film and videos; television
Vignal, D., 132, 139, 158

Walking with Shadows (Dibia), 155–56, 158
Ward, K., 173n2
weaning, 79–82, 98
Weeks, J. H., 44, 178n16
Weinstock, C., 55
West, M., 178n20
Westley, D., 88, 189on3
Westocentrism, 12. *See also* Eurocentrism; gay imperialism
Weston, K., 179n21
White, L., 13
whiteness (racial identity), 9, 30, 38–39, 74–75, 160–63, 174n10, 182n15, 185n5
Whithead, A., 180n2
widows, 41, 47
Wieringa, S., 7, 14, 62, 174n7, 178n15
Wild Deer (Lewis), 91
Williams, A. O., 11, 18–19
Wilson, M., 51, 164
witchcraft, 11, 21, 69–71, 77, 180n2, 181n8, 183n2
Wober, M., 85–86, 180n3
Wolof, 50, 147
woman-woman marriage. *See* marriage: female-female
World Bank, 175n21

World Health Organization, 5, 82, 108, 110, 116–17, 174n12
Woubi Chérie (film), 149–50, 157
wsw, definition, 17, 36. *See also* lesbians and lesbianlike behavior
Wylie, D., 91–92, 94, 182n17

X, Dr. Jacobus, 46, 161
xenophobia, 17, 19, 21, 44, 117, 136, 152, 157, 165, 170
Xhosa (including Mpondo, Tembu), 77, 153, 178n20, 179n23, 183n6

Yamba, C. B., 183n2
yan daudu, 10
Yavoucko, C., 136
yaws, 102
yoos, 64
Yoruba, 54, 59–60, 89. *See also* Nigeria
Young, R., 180n4

Your Name Shall be Tanga (Beyala), 148, 154

Zachernuk, P., 178n20
Zaire, 108, 112, 116, 118, 123. *See also* Congo
Zambia and Zambians, 11, 78–79, 92, 106, 174n12. *See also* Yamba, C.
Zeleza, P. T., 24, 180n1
zero grazing, 111
Zidji (Junod), 133
Zimbabwe and Zimbabweans, 3, 5, 9, 15–16, 20, 26–29, 36–37, 55–60, 70, 75, 91–92, 103, 107, 120, 126, 141, 144–45, 147–49, 155, 165, 167, 175n21, 178n20, 179n24, 26, 182n14, 185n13, 185n19
Zimbabwe International Book Fair, 148
Zulu, 54, 60, 67, 91–99, 123, 179n22
Zuma, J., 101
Zwelonke, D. M., 137

Technique
self

- une ch. 2 - H. - p
  read for class
    - p. Annotation heterometria

Karol
Saussé   Inequalities

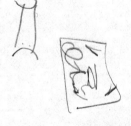